DEATH IN ANCIENT ROME

Death in Ancient Rome: A Sourcebook is an expertly selected compilation of ancient texts in translation on the subject of death in ancient Rome.

Mortality rates were high in ancient Rome and how a person died was no less important than how they lived. Despite the brutality of the assassinations that feature in accounts of Roman political life, laudable figures faced their deaths with dignity and stoicism, their last words set down for posterity. Whether a Roman's end was met in war, gladiatorial combat, execution, murder, suicide, or simply ill health, it was almost certain to have been a visible part of Roman life; even a spectacle. To understand life in Rome, we need to understand death in Rome.

This book will enable you to do just that by providing the essential primary sources on death, dying and the dead in Roman society and investigating their value and significance.

The sources include literary evidence such as poetry, letters and philosophy, as well as epitaphs and other inscriptions, along with visual material of, in particular, funerary monuments and cemeteries.

This varied evidence collectively builds a vivid picture of how people died, were buried, commemorated and remembered, and what the living believed happened to the dead after they were gone.

Topics covered include the deathbed, making a will, memory promotion, the funeral, the cemetery, funerary monuments, mourning rituals, expressions of grief and afterlife beliefs.

Valerie M. Hope is Lecturer in the Department of Classical Studies at the Open University. Her main research interest is Roman social history, focusing on Roman funerary customs and funerary monuments. Her previous publications include *Constructing Identity: The Roman Funerary Monuments of Aquileia, Mainz and Nimes* (2001) and *Death and Disease in the Ancient City* (2000).

DEATH IN ANCIENT ROME

A sourcebook

Valerie M. Hope

Routledge
Taylor & Francis Group

LONDON AND NEW YORK

First published 2007
by Routledge
2 Park Square, Milton Park, Abingdon, Oxon OX14 4RN

Simultaneously published in the USA and Canada
by Routledge
711 Third Avenue, New York, NY 10017

Routledge is an imprint of the Taylor & Francis Group, an informa business

© 2007 Valerie M. Hope

Typeset in Sabon by Bookcraft Ltd, Stroud, Gloucestershire

British Library Cataloguing in Publication Data
A catalogue record for this book is available from the British Library

Library of Congress Cataloging in Publication Data
Hope, Valerie M., 1968–
Death in ancient Rome: a source book / Valerie M. Hope. — 1st ed.
p. cm.
Includes bibliographical references and index.
1. Death—Social aspects—Rome. 2. Funeral rites and ceremonies—
Rome. 3. Rome—Religious life and customs. I. Title.
HQ1073.5.R66H67 2007
306.90937'6—dc22
2007020941

ISBN10: 0-415-33157-9 (hbk)
ISBN10: 0-415-33158-7 (pbk)
ISBN10: 0-203-39248-5 (ebk)

ISBN13: 978-0-415-33157-9 (hbk)
ISBN13: 978-0-415-33158-6 (pbk)
ISBN13: 978-0-203-39248-5 (ebk)

In memory of
Valentine Lewis Stephens
14 February 1914 to 26 November 2003
and
Rona Mary Stephens
7 July 1915 to 19 February 2007
May the earth lie lightly upon you

CONTENTS

FIGURES

ACKNOWLEDGEMENTS

I am grateful to Emma-Jayne Graham, Janet Huskinson, Paula James and David Noy for reading parts, or all, of this book while it was in preparation. I appreciate their time and help. I would also like to thank the staff at Routledge for their assistance and patience. I owe a debt of thanks to my colleagues in the Department of Classical Studies at the Open University for creating a stimulating, but above all, friendly and supportive working environment. Most of all I thank my family: my parents for their encouragement; and my husband, Art, for his toleration of 'Roman death'. Our children, Oliver, Matthew and Jacob, have often been a welcome distraction from the sombre nature of this project. I would defy anyone to read the words of Quintilian (5.25) and not to give thanks for their family. Finally I acknowledge my maternal grandparents who died while this book was being written; it is dedicated to their memory.

ABBREVIATIONS

AE   *Année Epigraphique*
CIG   *Corpus Inscriptionum Graecorum*
CIL   *Corpus Inscriptionum Latinarum*
CLE *Carmina Latina Epigraphica*
IA   *Inscriptiones Aquileiae*
IG   *Inscriptiones Graecae*
ILS   *Inscriptiones Latinae Selectae*
SB   *Sammelbuch Griechisher Urkunden aus Aegypten*

INTRODUCTION

Writing and compiling a sourcebook can be a challenging and, at times, a thankless task. I have often agonized over what to include and what to omit, and the best ways to select, shape and organize the material. And still I am haunted by the prospect that I have overlooked some gems or, perhaps even worse, other people's favourite quotations and images! Producing this book, nevertheless, has been an enjoyable task. It was a stimulating process to confront, explore and piece together such a vast array of evidence, and engage with scholarly interpretations of it.

I was motivated initially by the need for an overview of Roman death; for an access point into both the rituals of death and the diverse available evidence. My own interest in Roman death began as a social historian who, in exploring varied social groups, heavily plundered the evidence of death, but often found that evidence removed from the actual context and meaning of death itself. Roman death, everything from deathbed to afterlife, has rarely been addressed as an overall subject by modern scholars (see below). Not since Toynbee's book (1971) has death in the Roman world properly taken centre stage, and this work was heavily biased toward monumental evidence. Therefore in the breadth of its coverage this volume represents something new. The book is designed to appeal to those interested in Roman death in all its guises, archaeological, epigraphic, literary and art historical, who often want or need to see their own specialist topics in a wider context. It will also be of value to those interested in death during other historical periods, death specialists from other disciplines (for example sociology and anthropology), students of Classical Studies and the general reader who simply wants to know more about how the Romans disposed of, commemorated and remembered their dead.

Studying Roman death

Death is very much a part of life, and where mortality rates are high the presence of death was, and is, a constant reality. How death shapes life and how life is reflected in the customs and rituals of death are areas of interest to researchers in many fields. But Roman death has in general not been well

1

explored as a subject. This is not to say that the evidence, the remains of death and its rituals, has been ignored. Far from it: the evidence of Roman death is rich and varied, and a valuable resource for a range of studies. The evidence, however, is often divided and studied by its nature, be it archaeological, monumental, visual, epigraphic or literary, and only rarely are the different fields united.

Archaeological evidence such as graves, grave goods and whole cemeteries, provides essential insights into how the dead were disposed of, the use of cremation and inhumation, and other aspects of the ritual processes. This evidence has often been exploited as a window on society, to detect cultural expression and social structure. Archaeological evidence for burial practices has been particularly influential in illuminating 'transition periods' such as population movements, cultural change and conversion to Christianity (Pearce 2000: 1). For the provinces, how people were treated at death can been viewed as indicative of the extent of the Romanization (or not) of the population at large (for example Curchin 1997; Fontana 2001). Do the rites reflect 'Roman' customs? Do the graves include Roman items? However, there is an increasing realization of the complexity of cultural dialogue, especially across time; influence did not just flow in one direction, from Rome to the indigenous population (Hitchner 1995; Struck 1995). Burial evidence may also provide insights into social differentiation; rites might differ according to wealth, status, gender or age, reflecting the relative values attached to individuals (Jones 1984, 1993). But there are not always simple correlations between, for example, the presence and absence of grave goods and the status of those buried. In death some people become what they had not been in life (Hodder 1982: 146). In addition, these approaches to burial evidence can at times remove death from the dead and overlook the familial, emotional, spiritual or religious content of the rituals involved. In short, death is a process and, in general, archaeological evidence represents only some parts of that process.

Some Roman graves, probably only the minority, were marked by permanent stone structures. These have long captured the attention of scholars. Corpora of monument types (for example, altars, stelae, urns, sarcophagi), and the themes of sculpture with which they were decorated, abound. Many of the monuments were inscribed with epitaphs; often simple, but occasionally lengthy texts, which provide verbal insights into the Roman world and can give voice to groups such as slaves, women and children who are often poorly represented in other sources. Thousands upon thousands of these epitaphs have survived (or were recorded by previous generations) and have thus lent themselves to statistical analysis. Data can be extracted from them on names, legal status, origins, age at death, careers and family relationships. The analysis of epitaphs has led to fundamental insights into Roman society on subjects such as demography, legal status, family structure, social mobility and employment (see for example Joshel 1992; Noy 2000c). The suggestion, for example, that the

Roman family was largely 'nuclear' in structure springs from statistical evaluation of thousands of epitaphs (Saller and Shaw 1984; Shaw 1984). Yet these analyses are not without difficulties of interpretation. In the 1960s Hopkins noted the drawbacks of using epigraphic age statements to reconstruct Roman life expectancy; certain ages were over-represented, some groups were more likely to supply ages than others and many people were imprecise about their exact age (Hopkins 1966, 1987; see also Duncan-Jones 1977). When looked at collectively, age statements do not provide an accurate picture of the age structure of Roman society, yet they do reflect what was important to certain people within that society and the image that they wished to create at death.

Recent decades have seen a more integrated approach to the art historical and epigraphic aspects of monuments; in particular in studies of how certain social groups were commemorated and used the funerary sphere to construct, rather than simply reflect, their social identity (Carroll 2006; Hackworth Petersen 2006; Hope 2001; Kockel 1993; Koortbojian 1996; Sigismund Nielsen 1996). A funerary monument used words, images, scale and design to communicate to the living and commemorate the dead, and these elements need to be viewed together not separately. In addition, where a funerary monument was located, its visibility and accessibility were also crucial. Ideally, monuments need to be studied in the context of the cemetery, surrounded by other memorials, and protecting the human bones and ashes that were their root purpose. A few Roman cemeteries survive in good condition and have been researched sympathetically to show the inter-relationships between monuments, change across time and the relationship between the living and the dead (Kockel 1983; von Hesberg 1992; von Hesberg and Zanker 1987). Ian Morris in particular has stressed the importance of taking an overall view of the burial record; context is the key to manipulating the evidence (Morris 1992: 203). Full context may often be an unobtainable ideal; witness the thousands of epitaphs that now survive as only a few letters and words in epigraphic volumes, bereft of any further context. But the goal remains: to understand epitaphs, monuments, cemeteries, and the rituals they represent, we must try to integrate the evidence and access the overall picture.

Simultaneously, but very much separately, to research on graves, monuments and cemeteries, there has been a recent increased interest in what can be termed, loosely, the literature of Roman death. In many ways this represents a more rarefied and limited source, largely reflecting the perspective of élite men based at the centre of the empire. Much of what we read in Latin and Greek literature of the Roman period may not be representative of the population at large. Philosophical discussions of the afterlife are a good illustration of this (see Chapter 6); would ordinary people from across the empire have shared, understood or related to the views of great writers such as Seneca or Cicero? Much remains unanswered, but we can sometimes add depth to our understanding by placing literary evidence alongside epitaphs and ritual remains, providing the former is not automatically seen as a simple explanation for the latter.

Roman writers of all genres wrote about death. Unfortunately, for us at least, authors rarely wrote systematic descriptions of death rituals and funerals, but they did write a lot (if often indirectly) about how people died, how they were mourned and how they were remembered. There were also literary genres that were inspired by grief, such as poetic laments and poetic and philosophical consolations, and these genres are an area of specific study (for example, Kierdorf 1980; Markus 2004; Wilcox 2005). Death, and its representation, often remains a genre-based subject and it does not tend to be viewed as a cohesive literary theme. Yet in studying death, dying, grief and mourning it is necessary to cut across genres while gauging the specific conventions of those genres. The representation of grief and grieving Romans, for example, provides an interesting case study. From poetic laments we might imagine a Roman mourner as inconsolable, howling at the graveside and doing himself or herself personal injury, whereas in prose philosophical consolations a Roman mourner is defined as calm, restrained and distanced from emotion. However, neither genre should be read at face value; each type of literature was written for specific purposes and audiences. It is only when we evaluate the roles and conventions of different literary genres that we can begin to get past the veil that obscures our view of mourning Romans. So Seneca's harsh words to Marullus on the death of his son (5.16) are sometimes taken as evidence that Romans were not expected to grieve for their children; but these words were written to be provocative, and there is much other evidence – literary, epigraphic and archaeological – which suggests that children were mourned for, buried with care and remembered (see Chapter 5). Literature can provide valuable, and sometimes unique, insights into funerary customs, mourning for and remembrance of the dead, but should not automatically be prioritized over other forms of evidence.

Roman death, from deathbed to afterlife, is a huge subject which cross-cuts literary genres and encompasses all types of evidence. It is perhaps inevitable that this evidence has been broken down into its constituent elements for purposes of research. Sometimes, however, it is possible and essential to reinstate the overall perspective. For the Romans, death was integrated with life. This may be an obvious statement to make, but from a western twenty-first century perspective perhaps it is not. For us, death of the self, and of others, can often be isolated to, and an isolating part of, old age; in contrast, the death of the young is perceived as tragic, shocking and removed from everyday life, while death overall is managed by medical specialists, hospitals and professional undertakers. In studying Roman death we need to see it not as something separate from, but rather as part of the Roman experience; something that impacted upon individuals and the society as a whole. How people died, how they were disposed of, commemorated and remembered, and what was thought to happen in the hereafter were important social factors. The customs and beliefs that surrounded death can help us to better understand Roman society, and an integrated approach to the evidence more readily allows us to access that society. We can note for example recent work on funerals (Bodel 1999b; Noy 2000a), monuments (Hope 2001), funerary masks (Flower 1996) and ghosts (Felton 1999; Ogden 2002) that integrate different sources (not necessarily sources of every type) to provide important insights not just into death but into Roman society. All these illustrate that Roman death can be an exciting and worthwhile area of study and research.

What this book is and isn't

This book does not, nor could not, include everything written or connected with Roman death. This would represent an impossible task. The evidence available is vast; hundreds of thousands of epitaphs; thousands of excavated graves and hundreds of excavated cemeteries. Some aspects have been well surveyed or sampled in other volumes: for example, types of monuments (Toynbee 1971; von Hesberg 1992); verse epitaphs (Courtney 1995); themes in epitaphs (Lattimore 1962) and it is not my intention to replicate this work. But nor is it the purpose of this book to centre on one type of evidence or on one feature of death rituals and customs. So this is not a book exclusively about funerary monuments, or epitaphs, or consolation literature or ghost stories. Instead, the purpose of the book is to provide a taster of the available evidence and to illustrate the central rituals and beliefs associated with Roman death.

My intention has been to take death as a subject and to think about the processes, rituals, beliefs and emotions involved; to evaluate the relevant evidence and to organize it to tell a story of Roman death. The rationale was to integrate different types of evidence. However, the range of evidence represented is dependent upon the subject of each chapter and more textual evidence (including varied literary genres, epitaphs and other types of inscriptions) is included than visual. Where the latter is relevant I have endeavoured to select representative examples and have sought to integrate these as evidence rather than using them as illustrative asides.

For some subjects explored in the book the bulk of the evidence for a particular practice or custom is included; for example, on aspects of the funeral (Chapter 3). On other topics it is only possible to provide examples of what is available; this is well illustrated by the chapter on grief (Chapter 5) since long laments and many poems and letters expressing loss survive, and thus it is possible only to provide short extracts to give a flavour of these. Excerpting and isolating chunks of texts from their fuller context presents its own problems and debates (see below). It would be possible to compile a 'reader' on Roman death, focusing on major authors such as Cicero, Seneca and Pliny, and there is undoubtedly more work to be done on specific authors and how they represent death, bereavement and commemoration, but this is not the purpose of this book.

Parameters

The following parameters of the book should also be noted. In short these parameters serve to remind that there was no such thing as an 'average Roman', and that the limits and biases of every source should always be evaluated.

1 *Geography*. At its height the Roman empire was vast. Relevant evidence stretches across the empire and some of that breadth is represented here, with evidence drawn from the modern countries of Algeria, Austria, Britain, Croatia, Egypt, France, Germany, Greece, Spain, Tunisia and Turkey. However, the central focus of this study remains the city of Rome and Italy. This reflects the bias of the written sources, most of which were composed by an élite living at the heart of the empire (even if they did not always originate from there). Archaeological and epigraphic evidence provides wider insights, and the cultural diversity present in funerary customs is often illustrated by this, but cannot always be explored in detail here.

2 *Chronology*. Rome, and its empire, existed for centuries. Much of the evidence presented here dates from the 1st c. BC and the 1st and 2nd c. AD. The chosen period covers both the Republic and the rule of the emperors; this change in political structures is not the focus of this book, but it should be noted that it did impact on the nature of some of the sources included. The chosen era reflects the height of Rome's power and geographic empire, and the flourishing of literature and other types of evidence. Epitaphs and funerary monuments, for example, were set up only rarely before the late 1st c. BC. and in many areas had declined in use by the early 3rd c. AD. Such chronological patterns are of interest and have been a discussion point for modern scholars, including their relationship to political structures and the display of power and status (von Hesberg 1992; MacMullen 1982; Meyer 1990; Woolf 1996). Where relevant, such chronological changes are explored here. However, when looking at any piece of evidence it is always essential to note the date; things may not have been the same a few years before or after.

3 *Culture*. Roman literature, as already noted, often represented a Rome-focused view of the world. It also provides us with a largely male, élite and educated perspective. Thus what is represented and recorded can advocate a view, or mindset, that may not have been shared by the majority of inhabitants of Rome, let alone the empire. We simply don't have the voices of women, children, slaves, the poor and (most) provincials in these texts. For this reason, other non-literary evidence is of great importance. Epitaphs in particular provide an access point to non-élite groups, and archaeological evidence provides insights into the variety inherent in broader Roman culture. There would have been cultural differences across the provinces and between urban and rural

areas that may have found expression at death. Here the focus falls on what can largely be termed as central Roman reactions to death, while acknowledging the cultural diversity of the empire.

4   *Religion and philosophy*. Much of the evidence represented here can be described as 'pagan'; how belief systems impacted upon death is explored in Chapters 2 and 6. In general, due to fundamental changes in belief concerning the soul and the body, this book stops short of the Christian period. A few extracts from Christian authors are included where these illuminate 'pagan' practices or more general customs. Evaluating people's beliefs is problematic (see Chapter 6); for the aristocratic élite philosophy was often of great importance and thus it can be relevant to note which philosophical school, especially Stoic or Epicurean, an individual chose to follow.

Using this book

Any sourcebook, by its very nature, is open to criticism, especially for excerpting and removing evidence from context. In the previous section I have set out some of the parameters employed, but it must be stressed that the book still represents only a small selection of material; it is a collection of short extracts, texts and images. To a large extent this reflects the nature of what is available. If one wants to learn about the Roman funeral procession, for example, there are only a few relevant images and texts, many of which are indirect; a few lines that form part of something else often on an unrelated subject. This reflects the reality of the work for many a historian, especially the social historian. Gaining insights into Roman society can be a process of gathering together bits and pieces to assemble the whole. The danger is that we will build a composite picture that, by drawing together evidence of different types, from different places, periods and social groups, may never have been a reality for anyone! For this reason the evaluation of the context and purpose of individual sources remains crucial.

To remind the reader of the importance of looking at evidence in context, each source is provided with some basic pointers: the type of source and its date, or at least approximate date. For some sources references are provided to other material of interest, and for inscriptions references to other places of publication. Where necessary, sources have been provided with some explanatory notes but it is not my intention to provide detailed commentary on texts. Numbers in bold type refer to the numbered sources. Within the sources points of clarification and summaries of omissions are placed in square brackets. The user should also refer to the Appendix which lists the sources, provides brief biographies on authors and some comments on the nature of their writings. Before basing an argument on a source the interested reader would do well to find out further details (for example, on the author, the nature of the work and, where necessary, refer to commentaries).

The book is divided into six chapters but these often interlink and overlap. I have attempted to cross-reference wherever possible. My intention has been to produce an introduction to Roman death, providing access not just to the primary materials but also to recent scholarship. Secondary sources are listed in the bibliography. The latter is not comprehensive and largely represents publications in English, but will provide a valuable starting point for anyone wishing to find out more about Roman death and other aspects of Roman life that the evidence illuminates.

1

DYING

Introduction

In the modern western world we have become accustomed to quantifying the risk of mortality; percentages and figures per thousand define life and death. We know how long we can expect to live for, what is likely to kill us and our relative risk of morbidity in relation to our age, gender and socio-economic group. It comes as no surprise that there are no such comparable figures and statistics for ancient Rome, or at least none that can be guaranteed as reliable. Some numbers are available to conjure with, since the recording of ages was fairly commonplace. Inscribed ages of death, literary anecdotes, census data and Ulpian's life table (used for calculating tax to be paid on bequests) all provide valuable data. In addition, skeletal analysis of human remains can age individuals and thus potentially whole cemetery populations. However, it has often been noted that all these sources have shortcomings in providing reliable figures for the demography of the Roman population (Frier 2000; Parkin 1992). Skeletons, for example, can be difficult to age precisely and rarely do we have access to a cemetery that preserves sufficient numbers from a full range (age and gender) of the population. Equally, epitaphs may record thousands of ages at death, but these tend to reflect certain commemorative habits rather than mirroring standard life expectancy. In short, those commemorated in epitaphs may not be representative of the population at large, and epigraphic age statements, when given, often characterize certain groups and relationships (Hopkins 1966, 1987). Besides which, age statements, found on epitaphs and elsewhere, were often inaccurate; ages were frequently rounded up or down to numbers that included the numerals V and X (Duncan-Jones 1977, 1990). Census data is defined by similar inaccuracies and age exaggeration. Pliny the Elder records some figures from a census carried out in AD 72–4. In one region of Italy many people had claimed to be over 100 years old and several over 140 years (Pliny the Elder, *Natural History* 7.49). Despite Pliny's claims to accuracy the quoted numbers, as so often in ancient writing, make for an interesting and entertaining rather than a strictly accurate read. This is not to say that Pliny or those who participated in the census were deliberately dishonest. Old age

9

warrants respect and the older members of a community may have claimed to be older than they were. We also need to remember that in a world where only the minority of the population was literate, and where few records were kept, many may have had only an imprecise notion of their actual age.

Is it possible to move from such anecdotal evidence to some real numbers? One possible avenue is the simulation of life expectancy through comparisons between Rome and other more recent societies. Thus the study of Roman demography has been influenced by so called 'Model Life Tables'; the closest fit for the Roman empire has been taken to be that of a developing country in the mid to late twentieth century (Parkin 1992: 67–90). This suggests that at birth the chances of an individual surviving into adulthood were low and that the average life expectancy of the population as a whole was around 25 to 30 years. If childhood was survived, however, a life expectancy of 40 or 50 years was more realistic. In short: in Rome and its empire many children died, but those who survived childhood stood a reasonable chance of seeing old age. These simulations and figures may always remain speculative, but model life tables help us to recreate the impact of death upon daily life (Harlow and Laurence 2002; Saller 1994; compare Scheidel 2001a, 2001b).

The following sections in this chapter consider how death affected, and thus helped to characterize, the extremes of life (infancy and old age), and also some of the myriad ways in which people died. Latin literature is inevitably filled with stories about people's final moments; death was very much a part of life, and thus the material selected for this chapter (and more so here than elsewhere in the book) reflects some personal choices. Roman death was not monopolized by medical practitioners and the dying were not routinely secluded from the rest of society. Death was visible, talked about and idealized in ways that at times can seem alien to a modern reader. For the élite classes the ideal death could even entail an element of spectacle, which could turn such a death into an uplifting literary tale or anecdote. To have a good death, one that was positively met with suitably dramatic or virtuous content, would be a lasting legacy for posterity. A central theme emerges; how you died mattered more than what killed you. There was a literary interest, and a prevalent ideal, that death should be met well, whatever the circumstance.

Infant mortality

For babies and children the risk of death was particularly acute. Many infants would not have survived childbirth, and the weeks thereafter were critical (Garnsey 1991: 56–8; Shaw 2001: 96–9). Parents frequently saw their children predecease them. Cornelia, the mother of Tiberius and Gaius Gracchus (politicians of the 2nd c. BC), is reputed to have borne 12 children, only three of whom survived to adulthood (Plutarch, *Tiberius Gracchus* 1). Others were more fortunate (**1.1**). For families to survive into the next generation, and for them to see their offspring reach adulthood, could entail the production of many infants. We can envisage the potential physical and psychological impact that repeated pregnancies and deaths may have had on parents, surviving siblings and other family members (**1.2**).

1.1 Suetonius, Gaius 7

Biography: early 2nd c. AD

Gaius Caesar (Caligula) was born in AD 12. His father, Germanicus, was the son of Nero Claudius Drusus. The latter was the son of Livia, the stepson of Augustus, and the brother of Tiberius. Gaius' mother, Agrippina the Elder, was the daughter of Augustus' daughter Julia.

For reactions to the death of Germanicus see **2.60** and **5.6**; for Gaius' recovery of the remains of his mother and brother see **2.63**.

> Germanicus married Agrippina the Elder, daughter of Marcus Agrippa and Julia, who bore him nine children. Two died in infancy, and a third, a charming child, just as he was reaching the age of boyhood. Livia dedicated a statue of him, dressed as Cupid, in the temple of Capitoline Venus; Augustus had another statue in his bedroom and used to kiss it fondly whenever he entered. The other children – three girls, Agrippina the Younger, Drusilla, and Livilla, born in successive years; and three boys, Nero, Drusus, and Gaius Caesar, survived their father. But Nero and Drusus were executed as public enemies on the accusations of Tiberius.

1.2 Fronto, To Antoninus Augustus ii. 1–2

Letter (to the emperor Marcus Aurelius): AD 165. The subject is the loss of Fronto's 3-year-old grandson.

Victorinus was Fronto's son-in-law.

For a further extract from this letter see **5.18**.

> With many sorrows of this kind has Fortune troubled me all through my life. For, not to mention my other pains, I have lost five children under the most miserable conditions for myself. For all five I lost separately, in every case an only child, enduring this series of bereavements in such a way that I never had a child born to me while not bereaved of another. So I always lost children without one remaining to console me and with my grief still fresh I produced others. But I tolerated with greater strength these sorrows by which I alone was tormented. For my mind, consumed with my own grief, opposed as in a single contest, man to man, equal with equal, made a vigorous resistance. But no more do I struggle with a single or solitary opponent, for grief upon bitter grief is multiplied and I can no

longer endure the increasing of my sorrows, but as my Victorinus weeps, I waste away, I melt away with him. Often I even make complaint to the immortal Gods and censure the Fates with reproaches.

For the children of the poor the risks of infant mortality, compounded by poor diet, poor sanitation and inadequate medical knowledge, must have been so much the greater. Accessing non-élite voices is challenging, but epitaphs do reflect a wider social range than literature, although the inscribing of these simple texts still implies a level of disposable income. Statistical analysis of epitaphs suggests that infants were under-represented (Hopkins 1966; King 2000; McWilliam 2001); that is to say that many, many more than those recorded would have died. This under-representation may reflect that young children were not excessively mourned due to the frequency of their deaths (see Chapter 5). Epitaphs were also constrained by convention and couched in expected language. Nevertheless these simple texts often powerfully capture the frequency and poignancy of early death.

1.3 CIL IX 3184

Epitaph: 1st c. AD. Corfinium (Corfinio, Italy).
   = *CLE* 1313; Courtney 1995: n.178.
   Compare **5.19**.

> Quintus Caecilius Optatus, son of Quintus, of the Palatina voting tribe. He lived 2 years and 6 months. Quintus Caecilius Hermes, a freed imperial slave, and Licinia Repentina, his most dutiful parents, set this up; and his brother Quintus Caecilius Paelinus, son of Quintus, of the Palatina voting tribe.
>   Here lies Optatus, an infant known to all for his devotion; I pray that his ashes be violets and roses, and that the earth, which is now his mother, be light on him, for the boy's life was oppressive to no one. Therefore his unhappy parents have set up this epitaph to their son, all that they can do.

1.4 CIL VI 7308

Epitaph: 1st c. AD. Rome (the columbarium of the Volusii, via Appia).
   For threats in epitaphs see **4.53** and **4.54**.

> To the spirits of the departed Felix. He lived 8 months. Cheone, slave of Cornelia Volusia, set this up to her very dear son. If anyone moves him may they feel the same grief as I have felt.

1.5 CIL XII 7113

Epitaph: 2nd c. AD. Mogontiacum (Mainz, Germany). Funerary altar. Carved above the epitaph is the seated figure of a child with hands outstretched toward a basket.

= Boppert 1992b: n.88; Selzer 1988: n.127.

Telesphoris and her husband, the parents, to their very sweet daughter. One must lament for this sweet girl. Oh that you had never been born, when you were to become so loved! And yet it was determined at your birth that you would shortly be taken from us, much to your parent's pain. She lived half a year and 8 days. The rose bloomed and soon wilted.

1.6 CIL III 4471

Epitaph: 3rd c. AD. Carnuntum (Petronel, Austria). The tombstone is now lost.

= Vorbeck 1980a: n.315.

It is unclear whether the children died together in an epidemic or on separate occasions. Their father was a member of the emperor's mounted bodyguard.

To Lucius Genucius Honoratianus aged 8 years and 10 months, Lucius Genucius Lucianus aged 2 years and 30 days, Lucius Genucius Kapito aged 4 months, and Lucius Genucius Lucius aged 4 years, 4 months and 15 days. Their parents Lucius Genucius Exsoratus, a *curator* of the *equites singulares*, and Cantabria Exsorata, from Siscia [Siscia, Croatia], made this.

Cherished children died, unwanted children could be disposed of. Babies could be abandoned and exposed. A father could choose not to rear a child on the basis of poverty, disability, gender or presumed illegitimacy, although understanding exact motivation remains elusive (Scott 2001). For the poor, exposure may have sometimes been an economic necessity, but not an easy decision to make (1.7). For other social groups exposure may have been an extreme rarely employed, a severe reaction to testing circumstances (1.8). Overall it remains difficult to establish the extent to which exposure of infants was actually practised (Corbier 2001; Harris 1994), but in general exposure was not infanticide: there was a reasonable chance that the infant would be recovered and reared by someone else, even if as a slave.

1.7 Oxyrhynchus Papyri 744

Letter: 1st c. BC. Oxyrhynchus (Egypt). Hilarion is writing to his wife Alis, while working more than 200 miles away in Alexandria.
= Hunt and Edgar 1970: n.105.
Compare Ovid, *Metamorphoses* 9, 669–84.

> I send you many greetings. I want you to know that we are still in Alexandria. And please do not worry if all the others return but I stay in Alexandria. I beg you and call upon you to take care of the child and, if I receive my money soon, I will send it up to you. If you give birth before I return, if it is a boy, let it live; if it is a girl, expose it. You sent a message with Aphrodisias, 'Don't forget me'. How can I forget you? I beg you, then not to worry.

1.8 *Suetonius,* Claudius 27. 1–3

Biography: early 2nd c. AD. Events of *c.* AD 24.
Sejanus was captain of the Praetorian Guard under Tiberius, and was thought to have undue influence over the emperor and designs on imperial power.
For the execution of Messalina, see **1.56**; for the death of Claudius see **1.59**; and for the hasty burial of Britannicus see **3.24**.

> Claudius had children by three of his wives. Urgulanilla bore him Drusus and Claudia; Paetina a daughter, Antonia; and Messalina bore Octavia and a son, first named Germanicus and later Britannicus. He lost Drusus just before he came to manhood, choked by a pear which he had playfully thrown up and caught in his open mouth; since he had been betrothed, only a few days before, to Sejanus' daughter, I find it hard to believe the rumour that Sejanus murdered him. Claudia's real father was Claudius' freedman Boter and although she was born within five months of the divorce, and Claudius had begun to rear her, he disowned her and ordered her to be cast out naked at her mother's door.

Death in old age

At the other extreme was death in old age. Defining or setting a numerical boundary for Roman old age is problematic since the impact of age and the use of age terms such as *senex* (old man) was often subjective and impressionistic (Parkin 2003: 25). There were, nevertheless, many distinctions drawn between the young and not so young (see below), and people did regularly live into their sixties and seventies, and some for much longer. Not all could claim the advanced years of the census data (see above), but there could be a sense of achievement in surviving to a great age provided good health was maintained and the mind remained active. In epitaphs age statements were more characteristic of children than adults (Hopkins 1966), but some epitaphs do claim and celebrate advanced ages.

1.9 CIL VIII 1558

Epitaph: 2nd c. AD. Agbia (Tunisia).
Age statements to the elderly were particularly common in some parts of Roman Africa, see Shaw 1991: 78–9.

> To the spirits of the departed Quintus Arsacius Quadratus who lived 99 years. He lies here.

1.10 CIL VIII 2985

Epitaph: 2nd or 3rd c. AD. Lambaesis (Tazoult, Algeria).
A *librarius* was a clerk. Age statements were often supplied for soldiers (see **4.37– 4.40**).

> To the spirits of the departed Lucius Tonneius Martialis a veteran who lived 93 years. His son Tonneius Martialis a *librarius* in *legio III Augusta* and his grandson Martialis made this.

1.11 CIL XIII 7101

Epitaph: 1st c. AD. Mogontiacum (Mainz, Germany). The stele has a simple gable decorated with floral motifs.
= Boppert 1992b: n. 48; Selzer 1988: n.123.
Note the single names of those commemorated, indicating that they were non-citizen, but Romanized, members of the indigenous population. The emphasis on neatly rounded age statements, including that of someone not yet deceased, may suggest prestige attached to age, but may also indicate a military influence on the identity created at death since Mainz was a legionary base.

> Pusa, son of Trougillius, aged 120 years lies here. Prisca, daughter of Pusa, aged 30 years lies here. Vinda, daughter of Ategniomarus, aged 80 years, will lie here in the future.

There was a traditional ideal of the old and wise *paterfamilias* (father of the family) who, surrounded by his descendants, continued to manage the family affairs and estate (for example, see Valerius Maximus 8.13). Demographic patterns would suggest, however, that many fathers died while their children were still relatively young, and few would have lived long enough to see the birth of their grandchildren (Saller 1987, 1994). Old age was not always admired and aspired to. Instead it was a source of ambivalent attitudes (Parkin 2003: 76), since it was perceived as bringing risks, discomforts and dangers. The fears associated with living too long were articulated by the literate élite: to be plagued by infirmity and senility could make life little better than death. For those who lived in poverty the reality must have been much harsher. In literary descriptions we need to be conscious of potential stereotyping; the elderly might be respected, but just as readily they were targets for ridicule and pity (Cokayne 2003: 4).

1.12 Juvenal, Satire 10, 198–204 and 241–5

Satirical poetry: early 2nd c. AD.

Compare Pliny the Younger's description of the bedridden Domitius Tullius who couldn't even clean his own teeth; 'every day he licked the fingers of his slaves' (*Letters* 8.18).

For legacy-hunters see **2.27–2.32**.

> But old men all look alike. Their voices are as shaky as their limbs, their heads without hair, their noses drip like an infant's, and their bread, poor wretches, has to be chewed by toothless gums. They become so offensive to their wives, their children and themselves that even the legacy-hunter, Cossus, turns from them in disgust. Their numbed palate no longer takes pleasure in wine or food, and sex has long been forgotten.

> And even if the powers of his mind remain strong, he [an old man] must carry his sons to burial and he must see the funeral pyres of his dear wife and his brothers and urns filled with the ashes of his sisters. Such are the penalties of the one who lives for long: he sees renewed disasters hit his house, he lives in a world of sorrow, growing old among constant grief and mourning clothes.

The loss of mental faculties was a particular concern for the aged. For the intellectual élite the decline of the mind was a frightening prospect and might entail the death of the self. From the philosophical perspective old age could serve as a warning to live life well, since not only was the time of death unknown (see Chapter 2), but also when and if the mind might be affected by senility (see for example, Marcus Aurelius, *Meditations* 3.1). Physical strength and vitality, and a lively mental capacity were the characteristics of youth. The cliché that 'the good die young' is of ancient origin. This idea could be a consolation to the bereaved relatives and friends of young people, but could entail dwelling, once more, upon the negative aspects of advanced age. The young became the antithesis of the elderly. The death of the young could be viewed as bitter, disappointing and devastating (*mors acerba*), while the death of the elderly was natural and expected.

1.13 Plautus, The Two Bacchises 816–17

Comic play: late 3rd or early 2nd c. BC.
   The words are spoken by the slave Chrysalus about his aged master, whom he implies the gods do not love! Compare Menander (*Fragment* 125) 'Those whom the gods love die young'.

> He whom the gods love dies young while he still has his strength, senses and mind.

1.14 Ovid, Amores 2.6, 39–40

Elegiac poetry: late 1st c. BC.
   These lines come from Ovid's lament to a parrot, see **5.63**.

> The best things are snatched away by the greedy hands of fate; while the worst complete their full number of years.

1.15 Cicero, On Old Age 19.71

Philosophical dialogue: 44 BC.

> Now the fruit of old age, as I have often said, is the memory of plentiful things attained earlier in life. But above all what happens according to nature should be seen as good; and what is more in accordance with nature than that the elderly die? But when the same fate befalls the young, Nature resists. So when the young die it seems to me as if a strong flame has been extinguished by a flood of water, but when old men die it is as if a fire has extinguished itself, without the use of force, after all the fuel has been consumed. And just as apples, when they are unripe can only be picked with difficulty from the tree, when they are ripe they fall by themselves, so with the young death comes by force while for the old it comes with maturity. To me it is agreeable, the closer I get to death, to feel like someone who is in sight of land at last and is about to arrive in port after a long voyage.

   The contrasting of youth and age also raised the issue as to whether it was better to die with one's beauty, power and strength intact or to live long enough to enjoy these things, but also see them pass away. This question was never resolved by Roman society, no more than it has been by any other society, as the simultaneous respect and loathing for the elderly so well illustrate. To die at the zenith, at the height of individual glory, may have been an élite male aspiration, but who was to say when exactly that zenith had been reached?

1.16 Cicero, Tusculan Disputations 1.35.86

Philosophical dialogue: 45 BC.

Pompey (106–48 BC), the great Roman general and statesman, formed the first triumvirate with Crassus and Caesar, and married Caesar's daughter Julia. In 50 BC he had been dangerously ill, but recovered. A rift developed between Caesar and Pompey, made worse by Julia's death, and eventually Caesar marched on Rome in 48 BC. Pompey left Rome for Greece and was defeated at the Battle of Pharsalus. Pompey then fled to Egypt where he was murdered on arrival.

For Pompey see also **3.42**.

> Had his [Pompey's] life come to an end then [in 50 BC], would he have departed from the good things or the bad? Certainly he would have escaped wretchedness. He would not have gone to war with his father-in-law, he would not have taken up arms when inadequately prepared, he would not have left home, he would not have fled from Italy, he would not have lost his army and fallen defenceless into the hands of armed slaves; his poor children and his wealth would not have passed into the powers of his conquerors. Had he died at Naples, he would have fallen at the zenith of his good fortune, instead in continuing his life he felt the full force of many unbelievable disasters.

Disease and disaster

Many deaths, whether of children, adults or the elderly, would have been protracted and painful. Doctors tended the sick and were often present at the bedside of the dying (**2.31**, **3.11**, **5.3** and **5.27**). Pain relief was probably rudimentary and many deaths would have been frightening and shocking. In his final moments the emperor Valentinian (died AD 375) was speechless, sweating, and breathless; he ground his teeth, flailed his limbs and was covered in a hideous rash; doctors were called but there was nothing to be done (Ammianus Marcellinus 30.6.3–6). Few deaths, through illness, are described as graphically as this. The emphasis fell on idealizing the 'good death' (see below) rather than dwelling on the real pain involved. Pliny the Elder does at least note that life's supreme happiness was a sudden death (*Natural History* 7.52.180); to be taken quickly, by a heart attack for example, was the best end. The alternative was suffering that could be so great that it could lead to suicide (**1.17**), and weighing one's pain against reasons for living might become part of the process of an illness (**1.18**).

1.17 Pliny the Elder, Natural History 25. 7. 23

Natural history: 1st c. AD. This forms part of Pliny's discussion of medicinal uses for plants.

> Indeed to consider this makes one pity the lot of man; besides chance occurrences and changes and the new events that every hour brings, there are thousands of diseases that every man has to fear. To distinguish which are the most serious of them might be considered a foolish act, since every man believes that the particular disease from which he is suffering at the moment is the most atrocious. However, on this point the experience of time has indicated that the disease causing the severest torment is caused by bladder stones; next come stomach diseases, and third pains brought by diseases of the head; these are the only diseases known to cause suicide.

1.18 Pliny the Younger, Letters 1.22. 8–10

Letter (to Catilius Severus): late 1st c. AD.
Pliny is expressing his admiration and concern for Titius Aristo, a Roman lawyer of high reputation.
For ill health that did result in suicide see Pliny, Letters 1.12 and 6.24.

> A few days ago he sent for me and some of his close friends, and told us to ask the doctors what the result of his illness would be. If it was to be fatal he would put an end to his life, although he would carry on resisting if it was only to be long and difficult. He owed it to his wife's prayers and his daughter's tears, and to us his friends, not to disappoint our hopes by a voluntary death providing these hopes were not in vain. This I think was a very difficult decision to make, which deserves the highest praise. Many people have his instinct and intention to procure death, but the ability to examine critically the reasons for dying, and to accept or reject the idea of living or not, shows true greatness of mind.

Inadequate medical knowledge coupled with poor hygiene, diet and sanitation often hastened death (Scobie 1986). Disease was no respecter of age and status (1.19) and in crowded urban areas epidemics could spread quickly, especially in the extremes of seasonal weather (Shaw 1996). Major epidemics in Rome, and other cities of the empire, may have been so commonplace as to be rarely commented upon, except in the year by year accounts of authors such as Livy and Tacitus (Duncan-Jones 1996: 110–1). The number of deaths recorded in such accounts may be included for impact rather than historical accuracy, but at the very least they suggest the devastation that diseases could bring. Cassius Dio noted that 2,000 people a day died in a plague that hit Rome in AD 189 (Cassius Dio, *Histories* 73. 14.4). Suetonius suggested that 30,000 people similarly died of plague in Rome during the reign of the emperor Nero (Suetonius, *Nero* 39.1). Under Nero this devastation was indicative of the moral wasteland created by the emperor; even if the plague was a natural disaster it still reflected badly on the emperor (**1.19**).

1.19 *Tacitus,* Annals 16.13

History: early 2nd c. AD. Events of AD 66.
  For the impact of other plagues see **3.3** and **4.5**.

> Heaven also marked with storms and disease this year, disgraced by so many shameful deeds. Campania was devastated by a hurricane which far and wide destroyed farms, orchards, and crops and extended its fury to the neighbourhood of the capital. At Rome a deadly plague was affecting all the population. No outward sign of disease was visible in the air. Yet the houses were full of lifeless bodies, and the streets with funerals. Neither sex nor age gave immunity from danger. Slaves and the free-born alike were cut down, amid the laments of their wives and children, who them-selves, infected while nursing or mourning, were often cremated on the same pyre. Senators and knights, although they died as well were less mourned, as if by dying like common men they were cheating the emperor's savagery.

Natural disasters such as earthquakes, famines, fires and floods could also lead to large numbers of fatalities. Once more the numbers of dead may not be accurately recorded in the sources, but literary accounts still capture a sense of the scale of the tragedies.

1.20 *Cassius Dio, 68. 24.4–25.3*

History: late 2nd or early 3rd c. AD. The earthquake occurred in December AD 115, while the emperor Trajan was wintering in Antioch (Syria) during his campaigns against Parthia.

> Many people, even those who were outside the houses, were hurt; they were lifted up, thrown about violently and then dropped to the ground as if falling from a cliff; some were injured and others were killed. Even some trees were thrown into the air, roots and all. The number of people who were trapped and died in the houses was innumerable; for large numbers were killed by the weight of the falling débris, and others were suffocated in the ruins. Those who lay with a part of their body buried beneath the stones or

timbers suffered terribly since they could neither live any longer nor find an immediate death. Nevertheless, many even of these were saved, as was to be expected among such a large number of casualties, although not all escaped unscathed. Many people lost legs or arms, some had their skulls fractured, and others vomited blood; Pedo the consul was one of these, and he died at once. In short at this time there was no kind of violence that those people did not experience.

The built-up urban environment also brought dangers of its own; fire and shoddy building construction could leave the poor particularly vulnerable. On several occasions stands built for various kinds of shows collapsed, leading to substantial loss of life (**1.21**). Even walking the streets was not without its hazards, although these are undoubtedly exaggerated in Juvenal's account (**1.22**).

1.21 *Tacitus*, Annals 4.62

History: early 2nd c. AD. Events of AD 27 at Fidenae (Castel Giubileo, Italy). Tacitus claims that 50,000 people were killed.

The unstable structure [an amphitheatre] was packed when it collapsed, it broke inwards and also fell outwards crushing and burying a huge crowd of people who were watching the spectacle or standing around. Indeed those killed in the first moment of the disaster at least escaped torture, as far as their fate allowed. More to be pitied were those whose mutilated bodies life had not yet deserted, who by day recognized their wives or children by sight, and at night by their screams and moans. The news attracted crowds of people, one lamenting a brother, another a relative and someone else his parents. Even those whose friends and relations had gone away for a different reason still felt alarmed, for uncertainty about whom the disaster had killed gave wide range to fears.

1.22 *Juvenal*, Satire 3, 257–78

Satirical poetry: early 2nd c. AD.

For if that axle with its load of Ligurnian marble snaps, and empties an overturned mountain on to the crowd, what is left of their bodies? Who can identify the limbs and bones? The poor man's crushed corpse vanishes just like his soul. Meanwhile the folk at home, all unwitting, are cleaning the dishes, blowing the fire with puffed-up cheeks, clattering over greasy flesh-scrapers, filling the oil-flasks, and laying out the towels. And while each of the slave-boys is busy with his tasks, the master sits, a new arrival on the bank, shuddering at the hideous ferryman; he has no coin in his mouth to offer for his fare and no hope of crossing the muddy stream, poor man. And now consider the different and diverse dangers of the night. How far it is to that towering roof from which a potsherd comes crack upon your head every time that some broken or leaky vessel is thrown from the window. Note with what a crash it strikes and dents the pavement! You will be judged a fool, improvident of such an accident, if you go out to dinner without making your will. There is death in each open window as you pass along at night. Therefore hope and pray that they will be content to pour down on you a bucket full of slops!

Juvenal pokes fun at the perils of Rome's streets, but the humour may be grounded in an element of truth. Large-scale tragedies may have been rare, but more mundane mishaps, which were nevertheless tragic for the victims and the bereaved, must have claimed lives, even if such deaths are rarely commented upon in our sources. Note, for example, the brief comment that the son of the emperor Claudius choked to death on a pear (**1.7**). In general, epitaphs did not supply information on how the deceased person had died. When supplied, causes of death are either unusual or add to the sense of pathos created by the epitaph.

1.23 CIL VI 16740

Epitaph: 1st or 2nd c. AD. Rome.
  = *ILS* 8518.
  The Baths of Mars (*Balneum Martis*) is otherwise unknown.

> Daphnus and Chryseis, freed slaves of Laco, to their Fortunatus. He lived 8 years. He died in a pool at the Baths of Mars.

1.24 CIL VI 29436

Epitaph: 1st or 2nd c. AD. Rome.
  = *CLE* 1159; *ILS* 8524; Courtney 1995: n.196.
  The festival at which the deceased met their fate may have been the *agon Capitolinus*.

> This tomb protects the spirit of Ummidia, and also the spirit of the home-born slave Primigenius, who were taken away on the same day. For together they attained the final day of destiny crushed in the mass of the Capitoline crowd. Publius Ummidius Anoptes, freedman, made this for Ummidia Agathe and Publius Ummidius Primigenius, who lived 13 years.

Murder and mayhem

Horrific deaths inflicted not by nature but by man were also part of people's lives and even daily experience. Warfare, the amphitheatre, public executions, political assassinations, pirates, brigands, thieves and muggers all contributed to violent death (see for example, Grünewald 2004; Rauh 2003: 187–201). Anecdotes abounded: for example, the emperor Nero was said to have roamed Rome attacking and mugging people just for fun (Suetonius, *Nero* 26). Such descriptions and vignettes were included to shock and also to entertain the reader. Attacks and murders perpetrated on the élite were particularly scandalous and thus all the more worthy of note.

1.25 Pliny the Younger, Letters 3.14. 1–5

Letter (to Publius Acilius): early 2nd c. AD.
  Compare Pliny, *Letters* 8.14; Tacitus, *Annals* 14. 42–5.

> The terrible treatment that Larcius Macedo, a senator and an ex-praetor, lately received at the hands of his own slaves deserves more publicity than a private letter. It must be acknowledged that he was a cruel and haughty master, he little remembered that his father had been a slave, or perhaps he remembered it too well. He was taking a bath at his villa at Formiae [Formia, Italy] when suddenly he found himself surrounded by his slaves; one seized him by the throat, another struck his face and others hit him in the chest, stomach and even in his private parts. When they thought life had left him they threw him onto the hot pavement, to see if he was still alive. He lay there motionless, whether unconscious or pretending to be so, thus they concluded that he was quite dead. Then they carried him out, as if he had fainted with the heat of the bath, and he was received by some of his faithful slaves, while his concubines ran up, screaming and lamenting. The noise of their cries and the fresh air revived him a little; he opened his eyes and moved his body to show them, as he now safely could, that he was still alive. The guilty slaves fled, but most of them have been caught and a search is being made for the others. Macedo was kept alive with difficulty for a few days; at last he died with the satisfaction of having revenged himself as well in his lifetime as he would have done after his death. There you see the dangers, indignities and insults to which we are exposed. Kindness and consideration are no protection; for it is malice, not reason, which leads slaves to murder masters.

The scandal was all the greater when the élite committed the crimes (**1.26**). Many other people of lower status no doubt both met and perpetrated violent deaths, but these did not grab the popular imagination in quite the same fashion as the sex lives, infidelities and superstitions of the élite, which could provide telling insights into morality of life in the imperial court.

1.26 Tacitus, Annals 13.44

History: early 2nd c. AD. Events of AD 58.
  Octavius Sagitta was tribune of the plebs.
  See also Tacitus, *Annals* 4.21.

> As he [Octavius Sagitta] had been spurned, he asked as a consolation for one night, to allay his passion and to help him control himself in future. The night was fixed and Pontia had a maid, who was in their confidence, watch the bedroom. Octavius arrived with a freed slave and a dagger hidden in his clothes. Love and anger ran their course. They quarrelled, pleaded, insulted each other, and made it up. For part of the night they made love and as if incensed by passion he ran her through with the dagger, while she suspected nothing. The maid running to help was frightened away wounded and he escaped from the room. Next day the murder was discovered and the murderer was not in doubt for it was proved that he had been there. The freed slave, however, claimed that the crime was his, that he had avenged the insults done to his patron. Some were moved by this example of great devotion, but when the maid recovered from her wound she revealed the truth.

A political career could come with a lethal price tag. The pursuit of power in both the Republic and the Empire was ruthless. To oppose the leading members of the Senate, and later the emperor, was to take your life in your hands. Civil conflict, proscriptions and reigns of terror marked the power struggles. Those in power, or the victors of factional struggles, could rarely afford to show their opponents any mercy. The dictator Sulla, for example, was presented as cruelly suppressing those who had crossed him (**1.27**). However, it needs to be remembered that accounts such as these were composed to characterize the perpetrators of these 'crimes' in a certain way and to emphasize the cruelty and frequent absence of morality in public life. These powerful figures disrupted the laws of nature through their inhumanity; they divided families and denied people the right to mourn and bury their dead (see **2.59–2.64** and **4.49–4.51**). For many leading figures the atrocities of which they stood accused became a by-word for the corruption of power.

1.27 Plutarch, Sulla 31

Biography: 2nd c. AD. Events of 83 BC.

Sulla (138–78 BC) was a leading senator of the Republic who became dictator in Rome. At this time opposition was ruthlessly suppressed as Sulla attempted extensive governmental reform.

Compare **4.50**; and for Sulla's funeral see **3.61**.

> Sulla immediately, and without consulting any magistrate, published a list of 80 men to be condemned; and in spite of the public shock, after an interval of a single day, he published another list containing 220 more names; and the next day a third list with the same number of names on it. In a public speech which he made on the matter he said he was proscribing as many as he could remember: those who currently escaped his memory would be listed later. He also condemned anyone who sheltered or tried to save a proscribed person, making death the penalty for such humanity, and there were to be no exceptions in the cases of brothers, sons or parents. Anyone who killed a proscribed person was rewarded with two talents for the murderous act, even if a slave killed his master or a son his father.

Battle and siege

Ancient warfare was by nature harsh and defeat could entail awful consequences. Rome could inflict severe reprisals on her opponents, but the city and its inhabitants also suffered at the hands of enemies. Some of the black or inauspicious days (*dies nefasti*) of the Roman calendar were anniversaries of military calamities. One of the most damaging and humiliating moments came with the sack of Rome by the Gauls in the 4th c. BC. Defeat, and the fear of the invasion of Italy, subsequently played heavily on the Roman mind (Williams 2001). In triumph, however, Rome was ruthless and in her turn sacked and destroyed cities. Some literary descriptions may evoke pity for the defeated, and clemency towards enemies could be characterized as a virtue (Konstan 2001: 95–104), but in general the fate of the defeated served as a powerful example to any who wished to oppose Rome.

1.28 Polybius, Histories 10.15. 4–7

History: 2nd c. BC. Events of 209 BC, when Scipio Africanus stormed New Carthage.

Note the advice of Quintilian (8.3.67–70) to orators and writers on how to describe the storming of a city with maximum impact; sieges were the stuff of high literary drama.

> Scipio, when he judged that a sufficient number of troops had entered the town, directed the majority of them, according to the Roman custom, against the inhabitants. He told them to kill

everyone and to spare no one, and not to start looting until the order was given to do so. The purpose of this custom is to inspire terror, and so when cities are captured by the Romans often you will see not only human beings massacred, but even dogs cut in two and the severed limbs of other animals.

1.29 Josephus, Jewish War 4.83

History: 1st c. AD. Events of AD 67 in Gamala (near the Sea of Galilee), during the first Jewish revolt.

For a summary of the devastating impact of the second Jewish rebellion (AD 132–5) see Cassius Dio 69.14.

> A great number of those who were surrounded on all sides, despairing of escape, threw their wives and children and themselves as well from the cliffs into the very deep valley which had been dug around the citadel. In fact the anger of the Romans was less excessive than the madness of the captured; 4,000 fell by Roman hands, whereas those who jumped to their death were more than 5,000.

Numbers of battle casualties supplied by ancient authors can be horrifying, but are often inaccurate; excessive estimates for the enemy dead, and under-estimates for Roman casualties, could strengthen Rome's claims to power and might. Nevertheless, we cannot doubt that military activity must have caused enormous loss of life. The ancient battlefield was a gruesome place. Any accounts of military engagements could not avoid the horrific nature of hand-to-hand combat (**1.30–1.32**). The awful death suffered by many soldiers, both Roman and non-Roman, was compounded by the mutilated state of their bodies, the stripping and looting of the dead and no, or at best, very basic burial (see Chapter 4). The aftermath of a battle served as a recurrent literary theme, the bloody scene emphasizing the destructive forces of war in contrast to the benefits of peace (Pagán 2000: 446).

1.30 Livy, 22.51.5–8

History: late 1st c. BC or early 1st c. AD. Events of 216 BC, after the Battle of Cannae (Italy), when Rome was defeated by Carthage.

> The day after, as soon as it was light, they began to collect the spoils and to view the carnage that was a ghastly sight even to enemies. There lay all these thousands of Romans, infantry and cavalry indiscriminately mixed, as chance had brought them together in the battle or the flight. Among the dead there rose up some figures covered in blood whose wounds had begun to smart with the cold of

dawn, and these were cut down by the enemy. Some were found lying there alive, with thighs and knees slashed; these bared their necks and throats and begged them drain the last of their blood. Others were discovered with their heads buried in the ground. They had apparently made these holes for themselves, and heaping the earth over their faces had suffocated.

1.31 Polybius, Histories 15.14

History: 2nd c. BC. The Battle of Zama (in Tunisia) saw the defeat of Hannibal by the Roman army led by Scipio Africanus in 202 BC.

The space which still separated the two forces on the field was by now covered with blood, bodies and the injured, and this physical obstacle created a difficult problem for the Roman general in completing the rout of the enemy. It would be hard for him to press forward without breaking his ranks since the ground was slippery with blood, and corpses soaked with blood were lying in heaps, and any spaces between were filled with arms that had been dropped at random.

1.32 Ammianus Marcellinus, Histories 31.13.6

History: late 4th c. AD. The battle of Adrianople took place in AD 378 between the Goths and Rome, and saw the death of the emperor Valens.

The ground, covered with streams of blood, made the soldiers slip and fall, but they still struggled to sell their lives as dearly as possible; and with such determination did they resist the enemies who rushed at them, that some were killed by the weapons of their own comrades. Finally when the whole field was one dark pool of blood, and wherever the eye turned, it could see nothing but heaps of bodies, the soldiers trampled on the corpses without mercy.

The rhetoric of the battlefield descriptions provided political messages about the might of Rome and sometimes about her potential vulnerability. The greatest poignancy in literary descriptions is reserved for civil war and the psychological consequences of Romans spilling Roman blood (1.33). Literary scenes set on civil war battlefields were designed to pull on patriotic heartstrings and emphasize the destructive nature of civil conflict.

1.33 Tacitus, Histories 3.25

History: early 2nd c. AD. Cremona (Italy), was sacked by Vespasian during the civil war of AD 69.

DEATH IN ANCIENT ROME

For a poetic perspective on civil war see Propertius, *Elegies* 1.21.

> A son chanced to encounter his father and brought him to the
> ground wounded. As he searched the dying enemy, father and son
> recognized each other. Clasping the dying man in his arms, in
> piteous tone the son implored the spirit of his father to forgive him,
> and not to turn from him with hatred as from a parricide. 'The guilt'
> he said 'is shared by all; one soldier is only a small part of civil war.'
> With these words he took the body, dug a grave and discharged the
> last duties to his father. This was noticed by those nearby and then
> by many others; astonishment and indignation affected the whole
> army and they cursed this cruellest of all wars. However as eagerly
> as ever they stripped the bodies of slaughtered relatives, kinsmen
> and brothers. They spoke of the impious act that had been done and
> then did it themselves.

Death as entertainment

The battlefield was also brought into the heart of the city of Rome, and
many Italian and provincial cities, through the amphitheatre. Gladiators,
trained fighters generally recruited from criminals and slaves, fought to the
death. The gladiatorial career was an ignominious one. To become a gladiator was shameful. Yet simultaneously, successful gladiators could be
treated like stars and heroes and could command respect for their dedica-
tion and training (**1.34**). The gladiator was admired for his bravery and
fighting prowess, but despised for his lowly status and bloodstained hands
(Wiedemann 1992).

1.34 Cicero, Tusculan Disputations 2.17.41

Philosophical dialogue: 45 BC.

> Look at gladiators, who are either ruined men or foreigners, and
> consider what blows they endure! See how they, who have been well
> disciplined, prefer to receive a blow rather than avoid it like a
> coward! How often it is made clear that they consider nothing other
> than the satisfaction of their master or the people! Even when they
> are weakened with wounds they send word to their masters to find
> out their will; if they have given satisfaction to their masters they are
> pleased to fall. What gladiator of ordinary merit has ever groaned or
> changed expression? Which one of them has disgraced himself upon
> his feet or in his fall? And which of them after defeat has drawn in
> his neck when ordered to suffer the final blow? Such is the force of
> training, practice and habit.

Gladiatorial contests had their origin in funeral rituals (see Chapter 3), but by the late Republic all sorts of shows and entertainments were funded by leading politicians and were a powerful way of winning popularity with the people of Rome. Under the principate, providing such displays increasingly became the prerogative of the emperor in Rome, although in the cities of the empire members of the local élite still played their part. A benefactor was judged by the splendour of his shows and the novelties he provided. These shows generally are viewed, in the surviving sources, from the perspective of the audience (or for the intended impact on the audience); only through a few epitaphs do we catch a glimpse of what it may have been like for the gladiator, standing in the arena and facing death (Hope 2000b). It is difficult to know the rate of mortality for active combatant gladiators; defeat did not automatically lead to death and some gladiators retired from the arena after successful careers. But the epitaphs make it clear that not all gladiators cheated death, even if the emphasis often falls on glory, the victories won and a successful career (see also Chapter 4).

1.35 CIG 2942

Epitaph (Greek): undated. Tralles (Aydin, Turkey). Funerary altar. Beneath the epitaph is a sculpted panel depicting an armed gladiator surrounded by symbols of victory.
    = Robert 1971: n.148.

I, Victor, who conquered all, died according to Fate in the stadium where fame is won. Strong Fate took me and led me to Hades, and now I lie in the grave. I got my death at the bloody hands of Amarantus.

1.36 CIL V 5933

Epitaph: 2nd or 3rd c. AD. Mediolanum (Milan, Italy). Stele. Above the epitaph is an image of a gladiator holding a sword and shield, with a dog at his feet.
    = ILS 5115; Gregori 1989: n.50.

To the spirits of the departed. To Urbicus from Florence, a first class *secutor*, who fought 13 times and who lived 22 years. Also to his daughters, Olympia, who lived 5 months, and Fortuna. Laurica his wife set this up to her well-deserving husband. I warn you to kill those whom you have defeated.

1.37 CIL VI 10197

Epitaph: 2nd c. AD. Rome.
= *ILS* 5089; Sabbatini Tumolesi 1988: n.97.

> To the spirits of the departed. To the well-deserving Macedo, from
> Alexandria, a Thracian gladiator who died in his first fight. His
> fellow Thracian gladiators set this up. He lived 20 years, 8 months
> and 12 days.

The gladiator's life was a precarious one, but he was given a chance,
through the amphitheatre, to redeem himself (Kyle 1998). The fact that
epitaphs and tombstones, even if few in number, do commemorate gladiators suggests that they were a recognized if marginalized part of society
(see Chapter 4). This final recognition was not available for others who
met their death in public arenas. Criminals could experience the complete
destruction of both their personal identity and physical bodies. They were
executed publicly, sometimes in the amphitheatre, in humiliating and
excruciating ways. Death by crucifixion, burning (**1.39**), wild beasts
(**1.38**) or through spectacular re-enactments of battles and myths (**1.38**
and **1.39**) awaited those who transgressed the law or challenged Rome's
authority. Death of the guilty could become entertainment for the 'inno-
cent' spectators. Humanitarian concerns about quick and painless executions are very much a modern concern (Coleman 1990: 461) and in Rome
a terrible fate engendered little pity. The philosopher Seneca's complaints
about the midday executions, that happened in between shows at the
amphitheatre, are about the behaviour of the crowd rather than the fate
of the criminals (**1.40**). The extract from Tertullian (**1.39**) is mainly
included here for the light it sheds on mythical re-enactments and elaborate punishments, but it is worth noting that early Christian criticisms of
the arena also tended to focus on the immoral impact of the spectacles on
the audience rather than on the suffering of the participants. Such experiences were a diversion to the Christian, who should be listening to the
word of God, not enjoying the spectacle of the Games (Wiedemann 1992:
147–60).

1.38 Strabo 6.2.273

Geography: early 1st c. AD.

> And recently in my time, a certain Selurus, called 'son of Etna', was
> sent to Rome because he had put himself at the lead of an army and
> for a long time had overrun the area of Etna with frequent raids: I
> saw him torn to pieces by wild beasts at an organized gladiatorial
> fight in the Forum: he was put onto a tall structure, as though on

Etna, and this structure suddenly broke up and collapsed, and he went down with it into fragile cages of wild-beasts that had been set up underneath the structure for that purpose.

1.39 *Tertullian,* Apology 15.4–5

Christian defence against paganism: late 2nd c. AD.

Attis was beloved by Cybele and was castrated to stop him loving anyone else; he was worshipped at Pessinus (Balihisar). The hero Hercules opted to be burnt to death to end his suffering; Mercury was a guide to those entering Hades; Jupiter's brother was Pluto, the king of Hades.

> But you [pagans] are, I suppose, more religious in the amphi-theatre, where in the same fashion your gods dance over human blood, over the polluting stain of capital punishment; supplying the stories and themes for criminals, except that the criminals often impersonate your very gods. We have seen at one time or another Attis, that god from Pessinus, being castrated, and a man being burnt alive as Hercules. We have enjoyed amid the mid-day combats Mercury examining the dead with a branding iron. We have seen the brother of Jupiter, hammer in hand, dragging out the corpses of the gladiators.

1.40 *Seneca,* Letters 7.3–4

Philosophical letter: mid 1st c. AD.

> By chance I went to one of the mid-day shows, expecting some fun, wit and relaxation, an entertainment at which men's eyes have a break from the slaughter of their fellow men. It was the reverse. The earlier contests were compassionate in comparison. Now the trifling is set aside and it is pure murder. The men have no armour and their entire bodies are exposed to blows, so no one strikes in vain. Many spectators prefer this to the ordinary pairings and even the contests given by popular request. Of course they prefer it! There is no helmet and no shield to stop the weapons. What is the need for armour or for skill? These things just delay death. In the morning men are thrown to the lions and bears: but it is to the spectators they are thrown at noon.

Suicide

Gladiators, criminals and traitors were cast out from the community in life, by means of their death and also in the treatment their bodies received (see above and **4.48–4.51**). In this context we can also consider those who took

31

their own lives. Voluntary death (*mors voluntaria*; the word suicide is not derived from Classical Latin) was a cause of ambivalent attitudes in the ancient world. In popular belief the souls of suicides achieved no rest; they were among the discontented dead.

1.41 Virgil, Aeneid 6, 434–40

Epic poetry: late 1st c. BC.

In Book 6 of the *Aeneid* the hero Aeneas visits the underworld in search of his father.

> Next to them were those unhappy people who had killed themselves, not through guilt, but because they loathed life. But now how they would wish to be in the world above, enduring poverty and work, how ever hard! This is forbidden, for they are bound and entwined by the horrible swamp with its waters of death, trapped in the nine bends of the river Styx.

Those who hanged themselves were particularly despised and could be equated to criminals and denied burial. For élite males at least, hanging was seen as a cowardly rather than a manly exit (Van Hoof 1990: 67). For others, with less or no social reputation to lose, it may have represented a relatively painless exit, while for the authorities a hanged body of a slave or pauper was yet another nameless corpse to be removed (**3.10**).

1.42 Digest (Ulpian) 3.2.11.3

Legal text: 6th c. AD (3rd c. AD).

> People do not go into mourning for enemies of the state, those convicted of treason, those who have hanged themselves and those who have killed themselves, not because they were weary of life but from consciousness of guilt.

By means other than hanging and in certain contexts, suicide was respected as a positive choice and not as something that contravened the laws of nature. Suicide was often viewed as a conscious intentional act and not one caused by mental imbalance or illness. For members of the élite in particular, especially during the late Republic and early Empire, suicide was not the negative act of the desperate but a reasoned and rational choice to destroy the self, the ultimate means of self definition (Hill 2004: 21).

1.43 Cicero, Tusculan Disputations 1.30.74

Philosophical dialogue: 45 BC.

Socrates, the great Greek philosopher, died by poison in 399 BC, and his suicide was the ultimate model. Cato fell upon his sword rather than surrender to Julius Caesar at Utica in 46 BC.

For Cato and his suicide see also Cicero, *On Duties* 3.60–1; 1.112 and Seneca, *On Providence* 2.10–11. Note Cicero made various pronouncements on suicide which can seem contradictory, see Hill 2004: 31–71.

> Cato left life with a feeling of joy in having found a reason for death; for the god who is the master within us forbids our departure without his agreement; but when the god himself gives a just reason, as he did in the past to Socrates and more recently to Cato, and often to many others, then surely your true wise man will happily pass from the darkness here into the light beyond. All the same he will not break the chains of his prison-house, the laws forbid it, but as if in obedience to a magistrate or some lawful power he will pass out at the call and release of the god.

For Seneca the Younger suicide was a matter of free will and could provide a path to liberty allowing the individual to escape a life that had ceased to have virtue (**1.44**). Seneca's rhetorical reflections were not meant to encourage the reader to commit suicide, but to contemplate mortality, morality, virtue and the choices an individual could make. Seneca sought to live up to these ideals in his own death (**1.45**). It is worth noting that Seneca had earlier contemplated suicide on the grounds of ill health, but had stopped himself for the sake of his father (*Letters* 78, 2–3). The suicide of Seneca was faced with Stoic bravery and resignation, but proved to be a long and painful affair. Nevertheless Seneca maintained his composure, conforming to the ideal of a noble suicide and achieving a memorable and dramatic death.

1.44 Seneca, Letters 70.14–16

Philosophical letter: mid 1st c. AD.

Elsewhere Seneca lists different ways of committing suicide when considering ways of escaping tyranny and torment (*On Anger* 3.15.4).

> You will find some men, who profess to be wise, who argue that you should not take your own life, and state that suicide is wicked. They say that we should wait for the end set by nature. Those who say this do not see that they are closing off the path to freedom. The best thing ordained by eternal law is that it gives us one entrance into life but many exits from it. Must I wait for the cruelty of disease or man,

when I can leave in the middle of torture and set aside my troubles? This is the one reason why we cannot complain about life: it keeps no one against their will. It is a good thing about human affairs that no one is unhappy except by his own fault. Live, if it pleases you; if not, you can return to the place you came from.

1.45 *Tacitus*, Annals 15.63–4

History: early 2nd c. AD. Seneca committed suicide in AD 65 at the orders of Nero.
See also Cassius Dio 62.25.

> Then Seneca embraced his wife [Paulina] and, softening momen-
> tarily on account of the terrors threatening her, he begged and
> implored her to moderate her grief, not to mourn forever, but to find
> legitimate solace for the loss of her husband by contemplating the
> life he had spent in virtue. She replied that she had also chosen to die
> and demanded the executioner's blow. Seneca did not oppose her
> wish for glory and from affection he was reluctant to leave behind
> the woman whom he loved so wholeheartedly to be insulted. He
> said 'I have shown you how to remember my life, but you prefer the
> distinction of death. I will not begrudge you that example. Let the
> courage of this brave death be divided equally between us, but may
> more fame be attached to your end.' After this they cut their arms
> with a single stroke. But Seneca lost blood slowly, since his body was
> old and made thin by frugal living, so he also severed the arteries in
> his legs and knees. Exhausted by extreme pain and afraid that his
> suffering might break the spirit of his wife and that the sight of her
> agony might weaken his resolve, he persuaded her to go into
> another room ... [Tacitus tells how the suicide of Paulina was
> stopped at Nero's orders and how she outlived her husband by
> several years. Seneca tried to hasten his own end by taking poison,
> to little effect.] ... He was then lifted into a bath, where he suffo-
> cated from the steam. He was cremated without ceremony. He had
> ordered this in his will when at the height of his wealth and power,
> he was already thinking about his end.

A good suicide was one that had sound motives and was bravely met. A considered decision to take one's life was esteemed whereas an impulsive decision to do so was not. Suicide could be a matter of aristocratic honour and even privilege. If death was all but inevitable, by choosing the time, place and means of death himself the individual avoided further destruction of his reputation, distress to his family and possible abuse of the corpse. For some members of the élite suicide served as a means to make a statement about or criticism of the political regime and we can note that these suicides had a semi-public dimension; to make an impact the death needed to be suitably witnessed and recorded. An élite suicide was rarely simply a gesture of freedom, however, since if allowed or enforced by the emperor the suicide could become a symbol of the emperor's power (Plass 1995). A rationally chosen suicide could be greatly admired and described in detail. The suicide of Cato was to become a well-quoted example (**1.43**) and it is notable that Virgil, who places suicides in after-world misery (**1.41**), spares Cato from this fate (Virgil, *Aeneid* 8.670). Lucretia's suicide after her rape was also portrayed as a paradigm of self-sacrifice to save family honour.

1.46 Livy, 1.59

History: late 1st c. BC or early 1st c. AD. Events of *c.* 510 BC.

The rape of Lucretia by Sextus, the son of Tarquinius Superbus, was the catalyst for the expulsion of the Tarquins from Rome.

> They all tried to console the devastated woman, by turning the guilt from the victim to the criminal. They said that it was the mind that sinned, not the body and where there was no consent there was no guilt. 'It is for you' Lucretia said, 'to see that he gets his due. Although I acquit myself of the sin I do not escape punishment; no unchaste woman shall live and plead Lucretia's example.' She had a knife hidden in her dress which she plunged into her heart, and fell dying to the floor.

Suicide was not always seen as justified. The view of the Jews, a minority group within Roman society to be sure, suggests that there was a range of attitudes towards suicide (**1.47**). This is also hinted at by Seneca (**1.44**); other philosophical schools (Pythagorean and Epicurean) could be less positive about self-inflicted death, and as noted above suicide was not without stigma.

1.47 Josephus, Jewish War 3.8.5

History: 1st c. AD. Josephus speaks against suicide following the fall of Jotapata (AD 67) during the Jewish War.

Contrast Josephus' account of the mass suicide at Masada, *Jewish War* 7.315–415.

> Again suicide is against that nature that all living creatures share, and an act of impiety towards the God who created us. Among the animals there is none that dies on purpose or kills itself; for nature's law is strong for all, the will to live.

Many factors did lead people to kill themselves: ill health (see above), old age, despair, knowledge of guilt, family honour or avoidance of public shame. Options for ending life were varied: self starvation, poison, weapons, opening the veins, jumping from great heights, as well as hanging (Van Hoof 1990). The use of weapons or opening the veins was often chosen by those wishing for a rapid, but honourable exit, while self starvation was employed by those in ill health (**1.17** and **1.18**). For those who had been defeated in battle or who faced captivity or public trial and execution, suicide, most frequently by the sword or dagger, was the only honourable exit (**1.54**). Petronius sees the funnier side of the desperation and avid intent of the suicidal man who seeks to die not for a great political cause but for love (**1.48**). Suicide for a broken heart, or other emotional reasons, was far removed from the noble ideal, and seen as trivial and irrational (see below). But high-minded suicide was the preserve of the élite, and for many others taking one's life may have been an exit from a life of misery, toil and suffering (see **1.41**) or an escape from guilt (**1.49**).

1.48 Petronius, Satyricon 94

Satirical novel: 1st c. AD. The narrator, Encolpius, has been locked in a room by his travelling companion Eumolpus, while the latter tries to seduce the slave boy Giton.

Finding myself locked in, I decided to hang myself and die. I had already tied my belt to the bed frame, which stood against the wall, and was just putting my neck in the noose, when the door was unlocked, and Eumolpus came in with Giton and brought me back from the moment of death to the light of life. Giton, turned from grief to rage, raised a shout, and pushed me onto the bed with both hands and said, 'Encolpius, you're wrong if you think you can possibly die before me. I thought to die first. I looked for a sword in Ascyltos' lodgings. If I had not found you, I would have thrown myself over a cliff. I will show you that death is not far away from those who seek him. You will look at the sight that you wished me to see.' With these words he snatched a razor from Eumolpus' hired servant, and drew it once and then once again across his throat, and fell down at our feet. I gave a cry of horror and rushed to him as he fell and sought the road of death with the same weapon. But Giton did not show the smallest trace of a wound, and I did not feel any pain. The razor had no edge and was specially blunted to give pupils the courage of a barber and so had its own sheath. This was why the servant had not been alarmed when the razor had been snatched from him, and why Eumolpus did not interrupt our fake deaths.

1.49 CIL XIII 7070

Epitaph: 1st c. AD. Mogontiacum (Mainz, Germany). The stele is decorated, beneath the epitaph, with a small sculpted scene of a man tending cattle.
= Boppert 1992b: n.52; Courtney 1995: n.193; Selzer 1988: n.116.

> For Iucundus, the freedman of Marcus Terentius, a herdsman. Passer-by, you who read this, stop, traveller and see how undeservedly I was snatched away. I could not live longer than 30 years, for a slave robbed me of my life. He threw himself into the river afterwards. The river took from him what he took from his master, his life. The patron set this up at his own expense.

Love and death

In Latin literature the intensity of love could be compared to death. The idea of people who felt that love was killing them or would kill them was a literary cliché. Love could lead to despair and a longing for death, even if suicide was rarely the end result. Self-killing for love, and thus a failure to control emotion, would not be a good and rational suicide for a man (see above). In comedy heroes may claim to be in a state of love-sick suicidal despair, but are soon talked out of self-harm (see Plautus, *Asinaria* 617–43; *Cistellaria* 644; *Pseudolus* 95–106). A love poet such as Propertius may imagine death for love, and its shameful side, but this is dramatic imagery that plays upon Propertius' overwhelming, and potentially destructive (as much to a serious career as a poet, as to his life) passion for Cynthia. Propertius is deliberately stretching the boundaries of acceptable ways to live and die.

1.50 Propertius 2.1, 71–8 and 2.8a, 17–28

Elegiac poetry: late 1st c. BC.

In Elegy 2.1 Propertius is excusing his lack of mighty war-like subjects; he will not die in battle but from love.

Antigone was the daughter of the legendary Oedipus and was condemned to death for burying her brother against the command of the Theban king, the father of Haemon.

> Therefore when at last the Fates claim back my life, and I shall be no more than a brief name on a little marble slab, then, Maecenas, the hope and envy of our youth, and, whether I live or die, my own true glory; if by chance your road leads you near my tomb, stop your British chariot with its carved yoke, and weeping say these words to the silent ashes: 'This poor man's end was an unrelenting girl'.

So then, Propertius, must you die in your early years? So die! Let her rejoice in your destruction! Let her disturb my ghost, and annoy my shade, let her trample on my pyre and insult my bones! Did not Boeotian Haemon die by Antigone's tomb, his side wounded by his own sword, and mingle his bones with those of the unhappy girl, without whom he did not wish to return to his Theban home? But you will not escape; you must die with me; on this same steel will drip the blood of both! For me such a death will be a cause of shame; although it will be shameful we must die.

For lovers and couples to die together or to refuse to live without each other was a romanticized ideal. It was often women who apparently showed the greater resolve to die and who exhibited legendary fortitude and self-sacrifice. Porcia, the wife of Brutus, was much admired for killing herself when she heard of her husband's death (**1.54**; note she had in fact most probably pre-deceased Brutus some months before). Seneca's wife wished to die with him and opened her veins, although she survived (**1.45**). Pliny tells of Arria who put the well-being of her husband before her own emotional needs and ultimately showed him how to die.

1.51 Pliny the Younger, Letters 3.16. 3–7

Letter (to Maecilius Nepos): late 1st c. AD.

Pliny is recording the famous deeds of Arria, the wife of Aulus Caecina Paetus who was condemned by the emperor Claudius for his part in the conspiracy of Scribonianus (AD 42).

See also Martial, *Epigram* 1.13. For Arria's daughter, who was dissuaded from committing suicide beside her condemned husband in AD 66, see Pliny, *Letters* 7.19.

> Caecina Paetus, Arria's husband, and her son were both suffering from a life-threatening illness. The son died. He was a young man of great beauty and modesty, and was very dear to his parents as much for his virtues as for being their son. Arria took care of the funeral so privately that Paetus did not know of the death. Whenever she entered his room, she pretended that their son was alive and getting better. If he asked about the son's health, she would answer, 'He has had a good rest and eaten with a good appetite'. Then, when the tears she was holding back were about to overflow, she would leave the room. When she had wept, she would dry her eyes and with a calm expression on her face, act as though she had left her mourning outside the door of her husband's room. It was brave indeed when she took the dagger, plunged it into her breast, withdrew it, and presented it to her husband with those famous words, 'Paetus, it

doesn't hurt'. But when she did that, immortality and glory were before her eyes. How much greater it was, without the prospect of such motives, to hide her tears, to conceal her grief and act like a mother when she was a mother no more.

Arria's suicide exemplified a good death, well and resolutely met. But such female-initiated suicide pacts often had as much to do with politics as love. The husband must die and the wife does not wish to survive him; life without his love may have been a daunting prospect, but so too would be the prospect of living in probable disgrace with life under continuing threat. Death gave women such as Arria (**1.51**), Lucretia (**1.46**), Paulina (**1.45**) and even Dido (**5.33**) a chance to salvage honour and win fame. There are very few comparable examples of husbands who were prepared to do the same for their wives. To be sure women were less often forced to suicide in political manoeuvrings, but nor were men inclined to kill themselves because they could not carry on without a dead or dying wife. Exceptions were worthy of special comment and commemoration (**1.52**), but what was admirable behaviour in a woman may have been less so in a man. A wife was replaceable and it was not manly to be overcome by grief (see Chapter 5).

1.52 *Valerius Maximus 4.6.3*

Memorable deeds and sayings: 1st c. AD.
   Marcus Plautius may have served under Sulla in the 1st c. BC.

> Marcus Plautius' wife became ill and died. At the funeral when she was placed on the pyre and was being anointed and kissed, he fell on his drawn sword. His friends put his body next to his wife's, just as he was in toga and sandals, and then put torches under the pyre and cremated them together. Their tomb was made there and can still be seen in Tarentum [Taranto, Italy], and it is called 'The tomb of the two lovers'. I do not doubt that if the dead have any sense of existence Plautius and Orestilla went to the shades in happiness at their shared fate. For where love is at its greatest and most honourable it is far better to be united by death than separated by life.

Good deaths and bad deaths

Death by violence or suicide may not have been a pleasant or pain-free demise, but if met well it could be seen as a good death. Tacitus' description of Seneca's suicide captures this well (**1.45**). How people met their end, both physically and emotionally, could be one of the defining characteristics of their posthumous memory. Ancient literature frequently contained descriptions and comments upon the deaths of famous people. Books existed which were simply collections of famous deaths. Pliny the Younger refers to two authors who were compiling works on the deaths of illustrious men (*Letters* 5.5 and 8.12). Such commemorations of aristocratic deaths, especially death by suicide, no doubt had a political dimension (Hill 2004: 187). Death scenes were also particularly relevant in biography where the subject's final moments provided the climax to the work, summing up the person's character. But in all types of literature the death scene, with its heightened emotions, was popular. The cause of death, the manner in which the person died, whether they struggled or were accepting, any last words, how those who survived reacted and how both the physical remains and the memory of the deceased were treated, were all worthy of comment. We may question how many actual witnesses there were to many of the deaths that are described and how these witnesses would have really described what they had seen; although we should not forget that there could be a deliberate element of drama and staging in some death scenes. The death of the emperor Galba, as reported by Tacitus, acknowledges variations in the known accounts.

1.53 *Tacitus,* Histories *1.41*

History: early 2nd c. AD. Galba was murdered and succeeded by Otho in AD 69.

For the fate of Galba's body see **4.51.**

> His last words have been variously reported according to whether men hated or admired him. Some have said that in an entreating tone he asked what he had done wrong, and begged for a few days to pay the bounty. The more general account is that he voluntarily offered his neck to the assassins, telling them to hasten and strike if it seemed for the good of the country. To those that killed him it mattered little what he said.

In many cases the literary accounts of the deaths of famous people were tailored to fit the character or the author's purpose, or both. In general, and in simplified terms, a good life meant a good death, a bad life a bad death. Augustus and Brutus both died in very different circumstances, but met their ends well (**1.54** and **1.55**), reflecting the positive side of how they had lived their lives. In contrast to these 'good deaths' are the descriptions of the final moments of the empress Messalina (**1.56**) and the emperor Nero (**1.57**). Neither, despite their treacherous actions, was prepared for what was coming and both lost their composure.

1.54 *Plutarch,* Brutus *52–3*

Biography: 2nd c. AD. Events of 42 BC.

Brutus, a champion of the Republic, was one of the conspirators against Julius Caesar. He committed suicide after defeat by Marc Antony at the Battle of Philippi.

> Then after taking the hand of each, with a cheerful expression he said that he was filled with a great joy because not one of his friends had proved false, and as for Fortune, he blamed her only for his country's sake. He believed that he was to be envied more than the victors, and not only in the past but even today, since he was leaving behind him a reputation for virtue which his conquerors, for all their arms or their wealth, could not match; and the world would come to know that wicked and unjust men who put to death the good and the just were unfit to rule. Then after begging them to save themselves, he walked a little distance away with two or three of his friends, among whom was Strato, who had been one of his closest friends since they had studied rhetoric together. He placed Strato next to him, and then grasping with both hands his naked sword by the hilt, he fell upon it and died ... [Plutarch notes that Strato was respected for his role in the suicide] ... When Antony found Brutus' body, he ordered it to be wrapped in the most costly of his scarlet cloaks, and afterwards when he heard that the cloak had been stolen, he had the thief put to death. The ashes of Brutus he sent home to his mother Servilia. As for Porcia, Brutus' wife, both Nicolaus the philosopher and Valerius Maximus relate that she now longed to die, but was prevented by her friends who kept a strict watch on her. So she snatched up some live coals from the fire and swallowed them, keeping her mouth closed, and so suffocated and died.

1.55 Suetonius, Augustus 99

Biography: early 2nd c. AD. Augustus died an old man in AD 14.

> On the final day of his life, Augustus asked every now and then whether there was any public disturbance outside on his account. He called for a mirror, and had his hair combed and his falling jaws set straight. After that he called in his friends and asked whether it seemed to them that he had played his role in the comedy of life aptly, adding the phrase, 'Since I've played my part well, all clap your hands and dismiss me from the stage with applause'. Then he sent them away, but while he was asking some new visitors from Rome, about the ill daughter of Drusus the Younger, he suddenly died as he was kissing Livia and saying these last words: 'Goodbye, Livia, never forget our marriage!' Thus he was blessed with an easy death and one such as he always longed for. For whenever he had

heard that anyone had died quickly and painlessly, he prayed that he and his might have a similar 'euthanasia', for that was the term he used to use. He gave a single sign of wandering before he breathed his last, calling out in a sudden terror that 40 young men were carrying him off. And even this was a premonition rather than a delusion because that number of soldiers of the Praetorian Guard carried him out to his lying-in state.

1.56 Tacitus, Annals 11.37–8

History: early 2nd c. AD.

Messalina, the third wife of the emperor Claudius, was accused of adultery and treason in AD 48. Narcissus was one of several influential freed slaves in the emperor's court.

Narcissus rushed out of the room and ordered the centurions and the attending tribune to carry out the execution, as if this was the emperor's order. Euodus, one of the freedmen, was appointed to watch and see that it was done. Hurrying to the gardens ahead of the rest, he found Messalina lying on the ground with her mother Domitia Lepida sitting beside her. The mother had been estranged from her daughter while she had prospered, but she was now overcome with pity by Messalina's final need, and was advising her not to wait for the executioner: life was over and all that could be sought was decency in death. But in that heart, corrupted by lust, there was no place for honour. Messalina was crying and complaining in vain when the door was driven open by the force of the men. The tribune stood over her in silence and the freedman abused her with many servile insults. Then for the first time she saw her situation as it was and picked up a dagger. In terror she was putting it to her throat and her breast, without success, when the tribune ran her through. The body was left with her mother.

1.57 Suetonius, Nero 49

Biography: early 2nd c. AD. Events of AD 68, when Nero was declared a public enemy by the Senate and fled Rome.

At last, while his companions all urged him to save himself as soon as possible from the indignities that threatened him, he ordered them to dig a grave at once, of the right size for his body, and collect any bits of marble that they could find and at the same time bring water and wood for the disposal of his corpse. As these things were done he wept and said again and again: 'What an artist is dying!' While he hesitated, a letter was brought to Phaon by one of his couriers. Nero snatched it from the man's hands and read that, having been pronounced a public enemy by the Senate, he would be punished in the ancient fashion. He asked what this punishment was, and he learned that the criminal was stripped naked, fastened by the neck in a wooden fork, and then beaten to death with rods. Terrified, he seized two daggers which he had brought with him and having tried the points of each of them put them down again, saying that the fated hour had not yet come. Then he begged Sporus to weep and wail and then begged one of the others to set him an example by taking their life first. He blamed himself for his cowardice with words such as these: 'To live is a scandal and shameful; this does not become Nero, does not become him; one should be firm at such times; come pull yourself together.' And by now the horsemen who had orders to take him alive were at hand. When he heard them he anxiously said: 'Hark to the sound I hear! It is the trampling of swift-footed horses.' [*Iliad* 10.535], and with the help of his secretary, Epaphroditus, drove a dagger into his throat. He was half dead when a centurion rushed in and pretended that he had come to help him by placing a cloak to the wound. Nero gasped: 'Too late! This is fidelity!' With these words he died with eyes so set and bulging from their sockets, that everyone that saw him shuddered with horror. He had made his companions promise, first and above all else, that no one was to have his head, but to arrange somehow that he be buried unmutilated. And this was granted by Icelus, Galba's freedman.

Such was the nature of Roman public life that taken in isolation the literary descriptions of the deaths of the famous would suggest that few people shared Augustus' fate and died peacefully in their beds! But whatever the cause of death, it could be deemed good or bad by how those involved handled themselves and the situation. To face death with courage and dignity, to show consideration and concern for loved ones, to utter a few last apt words or pithy statements, to be mourned by survivors and for your body to be treated well, and even honoured by enemies, was a good end (**1.54** and **1.55**). To prevaricate about facing your death, to think only of yourself, to chatter nervously, to weep uncontrollably and to be largely unmourned was a bad end which could be compounded by corpse abuse and damnation (**1.56**, **1.57** and **1.59**). However, some 'bad' characters were allowed to show bravery and resolve in the face of death. Otho, an inadequate emperor, committed suicide with dignity and was greatly mourned by his troops (**1.58**). And even some of the great and the good (for example, Pompey and Cicero), although meeting their end bravely, could be unprepared and unable to avoid subsequent abuse of their corpse (see **3.42** and **4.50**).

DEATH IN ANCIENT ROME

1.58 Suetonius, Otho 11–2

Biography: 2nd c. AD. Otho committed suicide in AD 69 following his defeat by Vitellius.

See also Tacitus, *Histories* 2.46–49, and Chapter 5.

> He said: 'Let's add one more night to life', these were his actual words. He left the door of his room open until a late hour, and allowed all to speak with him who wished to come in. After quenching his thirst with a glass of cold water he took up two daggers and having tried the points of both of them, put one of them under his pillow. Then closing the doors he slept very soundly. When he awoke at dawn he stabbed himself with a single stroke under the left breast. To those who rushed in at his groans he first concealed and then revealed the wound. He died and was buried at once, for such were his orders ... [Suetonius describes Otho's physical appearance] ... I think that it was because of his habits that his death, which was so little in tune with his life, became such a great marvel. Many of the soldiers who were present kissed his hands and feet as he lay dead, weeping bitterly and calling him the bravest of men and the best of Emperors; and afterwards they killed themselves close to his pyre. Many of those who were absent too killed one another from sheer grief on hearing the news. In short the majority who had hated Otho bitterly while he was alive praised him to the skies when he was dead; and it was even commonly believed that he had killed Galba not so much for the sake of ruling as of restoring the Republic and freedom.

How a death was defined and characterized also might alter with changing political regimes and changing reputations. The demise of the emperor Claudius is a case in point. Allegedly poisoned by his wife and her son, Claudius was buried with full honours and deified in order to secure the succession for Nero. However, later during Nero's reign Claudius, including his final moments, was lampooned for comic impact by Seneca. This was an end far removed from, and in stark contrast to, the élite ideal of Seneca's own death (**1.45**).

1.59 Seneca, Apocolocyntosis 4

Satire: 1st c. AD. Attributed to Seneca the Younger. The action takes place in 'heaven', immediately after the death of Claudius (AD 54).

> But as for Claudius, they ordered everyone 'to carry him out from the house with rejoicing and solemn-speaking'. And he did gurgle his spirit out, and from then on ceased to have the appearance of life.

44

He was listening to some comic actors when he died, so you know I have good reason to fear them. The final words he was heard to say in this world, after he had let out a great sound from that part by which he found it easier to speak: 'Oh dear, I think I've shit myself.' Whether he did or not, I don't know, but he certainly shat up everything else.

2

MORTALITY AND MEMORY

Introduction

Mortality rates in Rome and its empire were high. Poor sanitation, disease, epidemics, famine, malnutrition and warfare would have taken their toll (Parkin 1992: 93; Chapter 1). Death was ever present. Even if an individual was strong and healthy, those around, especially the young and the old, were vulnerable. Death, which removed parents, spouses, siblings, children and friends, must have constantly redefined people's lives. We can note, for example, that Ausonius (4th c. AD) dedicated a series of poems (*Parentalia*) to his dead relatives who included his grandparents, parents, uncle, aunt, brother, two sisters, wife, son and grandson. How did people cope with the frailty of life and their own impending death? And how did they prepare practically for their ultimate demise?

The material in this chapter presents attitudes to death and how these shaped attitudes toward life. For some the sting of death may have been mitigated by spiritual or religious beliefs which informed how they lived life and awaited death. Understanding the nature and extent of such beliefs is complex and is explored further in Chapter 6. Here the emphasis falls more on philosophical views about mortality and also some of the practical preparations for death that concerned the living. It is worth noting that for many, plans for death may have focused more on an earthly legacy than preparing spiritually (or even philosophically) for the life hereafter. People did explore the moral issues raised by death and the role of the gods, Fortune and Fate, and may have feared the process and pain of dying, but death could also be viewed as a relatively matter-of-fact part of life.

The sources presented in this chapter are varied; sooner or later everyone was forced to confront their mortality, thus thoughts and practical concerns about death are relatively commonplace. For some, life was very much for the living, something to be enjoyed and savoured before the onset of oblivion. You could not cheat death, but you could have a good time trying! For others, the prospect of oblivion (and uncertainty about the afterlife) meant that life was an opportunity to prepare for the great unknown; thus the prospect of death, especially its inevitability, became the chief motivation to live a sensible and thoughtful life. For the practically minded, preparing for death meant composing a last will and testament that protected their interests and those of their family. Wills were also closely associated with various strategies devised to preserve individual memory. In élite culture in particular there was a drive to leave a suitable legacy for posterity. People sought to preserve their name and control how they would be remembered in this world. However, the best laid plans could still come to naught since memories and monuments could easily be subverted, destroyed or simply forgotten.

This chapter does not focus on the legal technicalities of making a will, but more on why people were motivated to make wills, how wills impacted upon relationships between the dying and the living, and how the testator's hopes for posthumous memory might be enshrined in the will. The promotion of memory and the role of monuments is a central theme in the chapter. Recent work has focused on the role of the past in Roman society, and the manipulation of public monuments and collective remembrance (for example, Cooley 2000; Edwards 1996; Favro 1996; Gowing 2005; Zanker 1988). Controlling how the past, and individuals from the past, should be remembered was a symbol of power. The living could be acutely conscious of constructing a suitable posthumous memory; they thought about how future generations would think of them. Examination, for example, of the senatorial decree condemning Piso has thrown new light on the importance of being remembered and what happened when things went drastically wrong for a high-status individual (**2.59**). But the desire to be remembered was not just the preserve of the wealthy élite; thousands of simple epitaphs from across the Roman world stand witness to the significance attached to preserving and remembering the names of the dead.

Born to die

The traditional view was that a person's lifespan was preordained; either the Fates (three sister goddesses known as the Moirai) were spinning an individual's thread that would snap at the appointed moment, or your time of death was written in the stars. We see these ideas represented in literature, where they were generally not well developed and became a standardized cliché for approaching death. There was a frequent sense of irony that Fate could be about to act while its victim remained blissfully ignorant, or a play on the idea that you could strike a bargain, however temporary, with the powers-that-be.

2.1 *Martial*, Epigrams 4.73

Poetry: late 1st c. AD.
    For 'the threads of life' see also **3.11**.

47

When Vestinus was sick, passing his final hours, on the point of going through the waters of Styx, he begged the Sisters as they unwound the final threads to delay a little in spinning the black strands while, already dead to himself, he lived for his dear friends. Such an unselfish prayer moved the harsh goddesses. Then, having distributed his ample wealth, he withdrew from the light, believing that after this he was dying an old man.

Fortune, as well as Fate, was personified as a goddess. These deities were to be thanked and blamed in life according to whether things went well or badly. At death these deities could be seen as cruel, striking down the good, and in epitaphs references to Fate and Fortune could become vehicles for the anger of the bereaved. Such complaints may represent commonplace expressions rather than be indicative of belief in actual life-controlling forces or beings. Indeed, as well as anger there could be resignation to the vagaries of Fate or Fortune; whatever an individual did and believed in they would die anyway, and everyone to come would share this end.

2.2 CIL VI 11743

Epitaph: 2nd or 3rd c. AD. Rome (via Appia). Sarcophagus.
  = *CLE* 1498; Lattimore 1962: 156.

> To the spirits of the departed Lucius Annius Octavius Valerianus. I escape. I flee. Goodbye Hope and Fortune. There will be no more prayers from me, so have your sport with others.

2.3 CIL I 1219

Epitaph: 1st c. BC. Rome.
  = *CLE* 185; *ILS* 7976; Courtney 1995: n.21.

> Here lie the bones of Prima, slave of Pompeia. Fortune pledges many things to many people, but pays up to none. Live for the day and the hour, for nothing is held in perpetuity. The gift of Salvias and Heros.

Even if people did not believe that their death was preordained by the Fates, Fortune or cosmology they still had to confront the inevitable fact that life, whoever or whatever created it and controlled it, entailed death. The need to accept that death was unavoidable was a common theme in all genres. Statements of the obvious such as Horace's 'you are doomed to die' (Horace, *Odes* 2.3.4) underlined human frailty and vulnerability. Death could not be escaped (by anyone) and by acknowledging and accepting the shortness of life people could be inspired to believe in the primary importance of investing in the here and now.

2.4 Horace, Odes 1.11

Poetry: late 1st c. BC.
The Babylonian numbers were astrological calculations.

> Do not ask, Leuconoë, for we cannot know, what end the gods have dedicated for me and for you, or examine the Babylonian numbers. It is better to endure whatever it will be, whether Jupiter grants us more winters or whether this is the last, which now weakens the Tuscan Sea upon the opposing rocks. Be wise, strain the wine and since life is short, cut back far-reaching hopes! Even while we speak, envious time has fled. Seize the day, putting little belief in tomorrow.

The brevity of life and the inevitability of death were frequently coupled with the fact that death was a great leveller. Young or old, rich or poor, all would die. This could be a form of consolation since even the great and powerful could not escape death (see Chapter 5). This theme is represented, for example, in the poetry of Horace (2.5) and the philosophical writings of Marcus Aurelius, composed more than a century later (2.6), and is further echoed in epitaphs (2.7, 2.8). The irony is apparent: even the mightiest men could not cheat death (2.9); money and power were no protection.

2.5 Horace, Odes 1.28, 15–20

Poetry: late 1st c. BC.
Proserpine (Persephone) was the wife of Hades (Pluto) and queen of the underworld; she was thought to cut a lock of hair from those about to die.
Compare also Horace *Odes* 2.3 and 2.14, and see **3.39**.

> But everyone waits for the same night and must travel once the road of death. Some the Furies give as a spectacle for cruel Mars; the greedy sea is the sailor's end. Without distinction the burials of old and young are pressed together; no head escapes cruel Proserpine.

2.6 Marcus Aurelius, Meditations 4.48 and 9.33

Philosophy (Stoic): 2nd c. AD.
Helice (Greece) was destroyed by an earthquake in 373 BC; Pompeii and Herculaneum (Italy) were destroyed in the eruption of Vesuvius in AD 79.

> Think constantly of how many doctors, now dead, used to knit their brows over the sick; of all the astrologers who seriously predicted the deaths of others; of the philosophers who spoke so endlessly on death or immortality; of the great commanders who killed thousands; of the tyrants who wielded the power of life and death with

such terrible arrogance, as if they were immortal; of the whole cities which have died entirely, Helice, Pompeii, Herculaneum, and innumerable others. After that, think one by one of each of your own acquaintances; how one buried another, only to be laid out himself and to be buried by another; and all this in a brief time. In short, note how ephemeral and trivial human life is; yesterday a drop of semen, tomorrow a handful of ashes. So pass this little period of time with regard to Nature, and then go to your rest contented, just as an olive falls when it is ripe, blessing Nature for producing it and thanking the tree on which it grew.

All that you see will soon perish and those who see its passing will soon perish too; and then what difference will there be between one who lives to the greatest age and the baby that dies in its cradle?

2.7 CIL IX 2128

Verse epitaph: 1st c. AD. Beneventum (Benevento, Italy).
= *CLE* 83; Lattimore 1962: 257.
The father held a post (*augustalis*) in the Imperial cult, one of the highest accolades available to a freed slave. His son was free born and had no restrictions on his public career and attained the highest posts in local government.

> Caius Acellius Syneros, the freedman of Caius and Lucius, an *augustalis* and merchant, made this for himself and his wife Calpurnia Phyllis, daughter of Spurius, and for his son Caius Acellius Vementius, son of Caius of the Falernian voting tribe, an *aedile, praefectus, duovir, quinquennalis* and *praefectus fabrum*.
>
> You are human, stop and contemplate my tomb, young man, in order to know what you will be. I did no wrong. I performed many duties. Live well, for soon this will come to you.

2.8 CIL XI 6243

Epitaph: 2nd c. AD. Fanum Fontunae (Fano, Italy).
= Lattimore 1962: 257.

> Marcus Valerius Artemis, freedman of Marcus, architect, and Herennia Maxima, his wife. The place of burial was given by Proculus. Traveller, passer-by, what you are I was; what I am now you will be.

2.9 Propertius, 3.18, 11–28

Elegiac poetry: late 1st c. BC. A lament to Marcellus.

Marcellus, who died in 23 BC, was the son of Augustus' sister, Octavia, and the emperor's heir. Attalus, king of Pergamum, invented a method for weaving cloth of gold. For Cerberus and Charon see Chapter 6. For poetic laments see Chapter 5.

Compare also *Aeneid* 6, 882–5.

> What profit did he get from birth or virtue or by having the best of mothers, or being welcomed into Caesar's home? Or only a moment ago the waving awnings in the crowded theatre, and everything brought about by his mother's hands? He is dead, and his twentieth year stands unhappy: such a bright day closed in such a small circle.Go now, lift up your soul, and imagine your triumphs, enjoy the whole theatre standing in applause, outdo Attalus' cloths, and let the great games shine with gems. You will give all these glories to the flames. But all must still go there, high and low: though evil, this way is travelled by all: the triple-headed barking hound [Cerberus] must be entreated, the common boat of the grim old man [Charon] must be boarded. Though a cautious man may conceal himself in iron or bronze, death will still drag out his hidden head.

For some, however, the arbitrary nature of death and the fact that it took the undeserving as well as the deserving could test their faith or at least their patience. We may question (see Chapter 6) how active people's beliefs really were, but in a time of crisis occasioned by death 'the gods' (including Fate and Fortune as noted above) were a common target for rhetorical blame or doubt.

2.10 Ovid, Amores 3.9, 35–8

Poetry: late 1st c. BC. The poem is about the death of the poet Tibullus.
For a further extract from this poem see **5.62**.

> When evil fate kills good men, forgive my words, but it tempts me to deny that the gods exist. Lead a religious life and you still die. Observe the rites piously and you will still be dragged from the temple to the tomb.

Eat, drink and be merry

Mortality may have shaped life, but life was also for the living. The prospect of death coupled with uncertainty about what lay beyond the grave (see Chapter 6) could promote a *carpe diem* attitude, influenced in part by Epicurean philosophy (Grottanelli 1995). If life was short it might as well be enjoyed. After all, no one was immune. The monuments of the emperors may have been designed to advertise power and stake a claim on divine immortality, but ultimately they emphasized human frailty (**2.11**). The flippant, and sometimes tongue-in-cheek, belief was that any day might be the last, so it should be enjoyed by indulging in the pleasures of life such as the baths, sex, food and especially wine.

2.11 *Martial*, Epigrams 5.64

Poetry: late 1st c. AD.
  For the Mausoleum of Augustus, see **4.20** and **4.21**.

> Pour in, Callistus, two double measures of Falernian [wine]; and Alcimus dissolve the summer's snow; let my wet hair be rich with excessive amomus [shrub], and my temples weary beneath the woven roses. For the Mausoleums close by command us to live, for they teach us that the very gods can die.

2.12 *Petronius*, Satyricon 34

Satirical novel: 1st c. AD. At his extravagant dinner party the freed slave Trimalchio makes no doubt exaggerated but stock piece comments on the brevity of life.
  Compare Virgil, *Copa* 35–8.

> Immediately glass jars carefully sealed with gypsum were brought in, with labels fixed to their necks, which said, 'Falernian wine, of Opimius' vintage, 100 years old'. While we were examining the labels, Trimalchio clapped his hands and said, 'Alas! Wine lives a longer life than poor man. So let's be merry. Wine is life. I present real Opimian. I didn't put out such good stuff yesterday, though better people were dining.' So we drank admiring each luxury in great detail. A slave brought in a silver skeleton, constructed in such a way that its joints and backbone could be moved and bent in all directions. He threw it down on the table once or twice so its flexible parts formed several poses, and Trimalchio said: 'Alas, for us miserable lot, all that man is is nothing. So we will all be after the underworld takes us away. So let us live well while we can.'

Dinner parties and banquets with their over-indulgent elements could be a favoured venue for *memento mori*, with images of death, such as the skeleton, adorning cups and mosaics. These served to remind the diners that death was never far away (Dunbabin 2003: 132–5; see also **3.57–3.59**). Similarly, epitaphs could give the dead a voice, enabling them to warn the living not only of the shortness of life, but also of the importance of making the most of the time available. In such Epicurean visions a good life lived tended to be one filled with the pleasures of the flesh.

2.13 CIL VI 15258

Epitaph: 1st c. AD. Rome.
  Compare *CIL* XIV 914.

> He lived 52 years. To the spirits of the departed Tiberius Claudius
> Secundus. Here he has everything with him. Baths, wine and Venus
> [i.e. sex or love] corrupt our bodies, but they make life – baths, wine
> and Venus. Merope, freedwoman of Caesar made this for her dear
> companion, herself and their family and their descendants.

2.14 CIL VI 18131

Epitaph: 1st or 2nd c. AD. Rome.
  = *CLE* 244; *ILS* 8155a; Courtney 1995: n. 169.
  Compare Cicero, *Tusculan Disputations* 5.101.

> To the spirits of the departed. Titus Flavius Martialis lies here. I
> have with me what I have eaten and drunk, I have lost what I left
> behind. He lived for 80 years. In front the tomb measures 5 feet,
> into the field ... [damaged]

2.15 CIL III 293

Epitaph: 1st c. AD. Pisidian Antioch (Turkey).
  = *CLE* 243; Lattimore 1962: 262.

> Titus Cissonius, son of Quintus, of the Sergian voting tribe, a
> veteran of *legio V Gallica*. While I lived I drank freely. You who live
> drink. The tomb was made by his brother Publius Cissonius, son of
> Quintus, of the Sergian voting tribe.

Live well and die well

Petronius' mock philosophizing on the frailty of life reflected (and parodied) that it was in the genre of philosophy that much discussion on the
meaning of life and death was found (**2.12**). For some philosophers the
prospect of death was a lifelong and life-defining concern; as Plato had put
it 'the whole life of a philosopher is a preparation for death' (Plato, *Phaedo*
67D). There were different philosophical viewpoints on how death should
be faced and how mortality should influence life. Most serious philosophers of whatever doctrine (including Epicureans) believed that the inevitability of death implied a responsibility to live life seriously, sensibly and
virtuously with a philosophical resignation that death would come to all

alike. Time was infinite whereas human life was not, so in the overall scheme of things it mattered not how long a life was.

2.16 *Lucretius,* On Nature *3, 1087–94*

Philosophical (Epicurean) poem: 1st c. BC.
  See also Diogenes Laertius, *Epicurus* 10.125.

> By prolonging life we do not lessen the period of death, nor can we take anything from death so that we will be dead for less time. Finally although by your continuing to live you complete as many generations as you can, eternal death will still be waiting for you; and he whose life ended today will be dead no less long than he who died many months or years ago.

Ancient philosophy often sought to demystify death and challenge the traditional superstitions that surrounded it. Questions of if and how the soul survived death exercised great minds (see Chapter 6), but the great thinkers were generally agreed that since death could not be escaped there was little point in dreading it as an evil.

2.17 *Epictetus,* Discourses *1.27.7*

Philosophy (Stoic): Late 1st or early 2nd c. AD.

> When death appears to be an evil, we ought to have at hand the argument that evils should be avoided, but that death is necessity. For what can I do, or where can I fly from it? ... [it is best to think rationally of death] ... Show me the country, show me the people to whom I may go, for whom death does not come: show me a magic charm against it. If I have none, what do you wish me to do? I cannot escape death, but can I not escape the dread of it? Must I die lamenting and trembling?

The letters and works of Seneca the Younger contain numerous philosophical considerations about death, based on Stoic beliefs. To what extent others shared Seneca's views or were influenced by Stoicism is uncertain. Nevertheless, in his letters to Lucilius (an Epicurean), written in his final years, we can catch glimpses not only of how philosophy shaped Seneca's own attitudes toward death, but also how important the subject was in philosophical debate; a debate that many among the élite would have been familiar with through the philosophical dimensions of their education and private studies. Seneca contemplated his own death and also considered how others faced theirs, and from this formulated some ideals by which both to live and die. Seneca advocated an accepting view: we all know we are going to die, but not necessarily when, so we need to be prepared; 'You do not know when death awaits you: so be ready for it everywhere' (*Letters* 26.7). The inevitability of death meant that it was important to accept rather than fear the situation and live life well. Seneca viewed death as a process; from the day we are born we are dying, and although the means by which life ends may be different, the end is one and the same (*Letters* 66.43). Everyone is thus equal in death and so it does not matter for how long one lives but the quality of the life (*Letters* 93.3–4). Seneca claimed to have 'looked upon every day as if it were my last' (*Letters* 93.6) and firmly believed that moral philosophy could teach men how to die, acknowledging that his own resolve in facing death came from such philosophy (*Letters* 82). A good death, bravely and resolutely met, could be a measure of virtue and a moral example, as would become epitomized by Seneca's own death by enforced suicide (**1.45**).

2.18 Seneca, Letters *1.2; 49.10–11; 61.2–4*

Philosophical (Stoic) letters: *mid* 1st c. AD.

What man can you show me who puts any value on his time, who evaluates each day, who understands that daily he is dying? For we are mistaken when we look forward to death; the greater part of death has already passed. Whatever time is behind us death holds.

What am I to do? Death is following me, and life is running out; teach me something with which to meet these troubles. Bring it about that I shall no longer try to escape from death, and that life may not escape from me. Give me courage to face difficulties; make me calm in the face of the inevitable. Loosen the confines of my time. Show me that a good life is not defined by its length, but by the use we make of it; also that it is possible, or even usual, for a man who has lived long to have lived too little. Say to me when I go to sleep: 'You may not wake again!' And when I wake: 'You may not go to sleep again!' Say to me when I go out: 'You may not return!' And when I return: 'You may never go out again!' You are mistaken if you believe that only on a sailing trip is there a small space between life and death. In all places the distance between them is the same. It is not everywhere that death shows itself to be near; yet everywhere it is near.

Before I became old I tried to live well; in old age, I shall try to die well; but dying well means dying freely. See to it that you never do anything unwillingly. That which is bound to be a necessity if you rebel, is not a necessity if you desire it ... [Seneca emphasizes the need for acceptance of what will be] ... We must reflect upon our end without sadness. We must prepare for death before we prepare for life. Life is well enough furnished, but we are too greedy with regard to its furnishings; to us something always seems to be lacking, and will always seem lacking. To have lived long enough does not depend upon our years or upon our days, but upon our minds. I have lived my dear Lucilius, long enough. I have had enough; I await death.

Making a will

Preparing for death involved practical as well as spiritual and philosophical considerations. Importance was placed on leaving an estate in good order, providing for and protecting loved ones and also ensuring the memory of the testator. The most efficient tool to facilitate these ends was the making of a will. For those with little to leave a will was probably an irrelevance; the laws dictated that the nearest and dearest, especially any children, would automatically inherit the little that the deceased did own, provided, that is, he was free and a Roman citizen. In addition non-citizens, slaves, women in some circumstances and citizens who were under *patria potestas* (a father's power), under age, insane, condemned as criminals or deaf and dumb were unable to make wills (see Champlin 1991: 42; Crook 1970: 120–1). The making of a will assumed a certain level of education or understanding of Roman culture and was probably the preserve of a wealthy, mainly male, minority (Champlin 1991: 41–59). For those with sufficient property, to die intestate was regarded as a failing of duty to the individual, his family and friends.

2.19 Plutarch, Cato 9.9

Biography: early 2nd c. AD.
   Cato the Elder (244–149 BC) was a statesman and author renowned for his traditional views.

> As for regrets, Cato said that there were only three things in his life which he regretted. The first was to have entrusted a secret to a woman, the second to have paid his ship's fare to a place instead of walking there, the third to have remained intestate for a whole day.

A will was a formal document. It had to be written in Latin, follow certain conventions of form, content and language, be witnessed by seven witnesses and then sealed. The majority of wills were written in anticipation of death rather than on the deathbed itself. People may have been forced to revise them frequently or add codicils as their circumstances and the circumstances of those around them changed. Certainly, revisions close to the time of death were common and could occasion interest (see, for example, Cicero, *Letters to Atticus* 12.18). The main beneficiaries of a will were generally the immediate family of the deceased, especially the children. A testator would need expressly to disinherit children if they were not named as heirs or the will could be declared invalid. The will was also a means of making provision for a spouse and rewarding friends and ex-slaves with gifts and legacies. As such, the will was a means to facilitate people's wishes. Some joked that it was the only time that a Roman told the truth (**2.20**); it could be a vehicle to express praise and blame, to insult and abuse. A will was a mirror of character (**2.22**). The testator was supposed to write with care and caution, to weigh decisions carefully and thoughtfully and thereby reveal his or her true nature. Seneca suggests a certain pleasure in it (**2.21**). Considering how to dispose of property, who would benefit and how, could almost be a comfort in the face of death.

2.20 *Lucian,* Nigrinus *30*

Satirical dialogue: 2nd c. AD.

Nigrinus was a philosopher, possibly invented by Lucian.

> Next he mentioned another human comedy, played out by those who busy themselves with life beyond the grave and with last wills. He added that sons of Rome speak the truth only once in their whole lives (meaning in their wills), in order that they may benefit from the fruits of their honesty! I could not help interrupting him with laughter when he said that they want to have their mistakes buried with them and to leave their stupidity on record, to this end some of them leave instructions that clothes, valued in life, be cremated with them, others that servants stay by their tombs, and here and there that gravestones be garlanded with flowers. They remain foolish even on their deathbeds.

2.21 *Seneca,* On Benefits *4.11.4–6*

Philosophy (Stoic): AD 63.

> When we have reached the very end of life, and are making our wills, do we not assign benefits to others that will give us nothing? How much time is spent, how long do we consider in secret how much to leave and to whom! For what difference does it make to whom we leave our property since we cannot expect any return? Yet we never give anything more care, or take such pains in making our decisions … [Seneca suggests that the prospect of death makes people wiser judges of character] … We search for those most worthy people to inherit our possessions, and there is nothing that we arrange with more scrupulous care than deciding what is to be done with what does not concern us. Yet, by the heavens, a great sense of satisfaction comes when we think: 'I shall make this man richer, and, by

increasing his wealth, I shall add lustre to his high position.' Indeed if we give only when we expect some return, we must all die intestate!

2.22 *Pliny the Younger,* Letters 8.18. 1–3

Letter (to Fadius Rufinus): late 1st c. AD.

> The common belief that a man's will is a mirror of his character, is certainly not true, for Domitius Tullus appears a much better man since his death than he did during his life. Although he had encouraged those who paid court to him to believe that they would be his heirs, he has left his estate to his niece whom he had adopted. He also left a great many considerable legacies to his grandsons and to his great- granddaughter. In fact the whole will is a demonstration of his affection for his family; which is to be admired since it was not expected of him. The affair has been talked about a good deal, and various opinions expressed. Some accuse him of being false, ungrateful and forgetful, and in attacking him as if they were disinherited family, reveal their own dishonest designs. Others applaud him for disappointing the hopes of these shameless men whom, considering the nature of the times, it is wise to deceive.

A will was a way of expressing feelings toward and opinions of the living. It gave the dead a voice from beyond the grave, and what the dead said could matter a great deal to the living. Even the all-powerful emperor Augustus put great store by how he was evaluated in the wills of his friends. Augustus was not chasing money, but suitable praise from his peers (**2.23**). Augustus acted well, only accepting bequests from people that he knew and safeguarding the interests of the testator's children. For the élite, naming the emperor in the will reflected their sphere of contact; the emperor was in principle their peer and 'friend'. However, under more tyrannical emperors there may have been a more pragmatic motivation for naming the emperor heir (**2.24**).

2.23 *Suetonius,* Augustus 66.4

Biography: early 2nd c. AD.

> Augustus demanded that the affection that he showed his friends be reciprocated, both in life and in death. For, although he was no legacy-hunter, and in fact could not bear to accept anything from the will of a stranger, he was still very careful in weighing the final opinions of his friends. He concealed neither his disappointment if the bequest was thrifty or was without words of praise, nor his pleasure if he was praised with gratitude and affection. But whenever legacies or shares in inheritances were left him by men, of whatever standing,

who had children, he either conceded them at once to the children or if they were under age kept the money, paying it back with interest when they assumed the toga of manhood or married.

2.24 *Tacitus*, Agricola 43

Biography: AD 98.
Agricola, the father-in-law of Tacitus, died in AD 93.

> In his [Domitian's] manner and appearance he made a show of grief; his hate no longer made him anxious and he more easily hid his joy than fear. It was well known that on reading the will of Agricola, which named Domitian co-heir with his good wife and faithful daughter, he was delighted at the honour and distinction. His mind was so blinded and corrupted by incessant flattery that he did not see that it is a bad emperor who is made heir by a good father.

Others were less subtle in how they used the will to express their misgivings about people or politics. To leave someone a trifling legacy or to omit their name altogether from the will was to create a well-considered insult (for example, Tacitus, *Annals* 3.76). Some wills went a stage further and abused or vilified the living. Abuse of the emperor or powerful individuals was probably unusual, although not unheard of (Champlin 1991: 16). Most testators contained their criticisms to their own smaller sphere. The ultimate testamentary punishment of disinheritance specifically of children was also rare, but the will might identify slaves that were never to be freed, or ex-slaves who were not to be interred in the tomb (**4.31** and **6.32**). In extreme cases of acrimony an enemy might receive a rope as an insulting bequest, the implication being that he should hang himself.

2.25 *Martial*, Epigrams 4.70

Poetry: late 1st c. AD.

> Ammianus' dying father left his son in his last will nothing except a dry rope. Who would have thought, Marcellinus, that Ammianus would be upset at his father's death?

In principle the will may have been a vehicle of truth, but it was one tempered by practical realities such as the need to protect the living, to do the right thing, to repay favours and to ensure that people thought well of the testator even if the testator did not think well of them (Champlin 1991: 18). A good will reflected well on both the testator and the living survivors.

2.26 CIL VI 10230, 4–19

Inscription: 1st c. BC. Rome. The inscription refers to the will of Murdia and probably records the eulogy delivered at her funeral by her son.
= *ILS* 8394.
For eulogies see Chapter 3.

> She made all her sons equal heirs, and gave her daughter a share as a legacy. Her maternal love was demonstrated by her affection for her children and the equal shares she gave them. She bequeathed a set sum of money to her [second] husband so that the dowry, to which he was entitled, should be increased by her good judgement of him. Recalling the memory of my father [her first husband], and influenced by that and by her own sense of what was right, she bequeathed me a legacy, not to show preference for me and offend my brothers, but because remembering my father's generosity, she thought she should return to me what she had, by her husband's judgement, received from my father's estate, so that after preserving these things in her use, they might be restored to my ownership. This was usual of her. Her parents gave her in marriage to worthy men. Her obedience and honour upheld her marriages; as a wife, she won praise by her virtues, was loved for her loyalty and was left the more honoured for her discretion. After death her fellow citizens were in consensus in praising her, since the provisions of her will showed both her gratitude and faithfulness towards her husbands, her equality towards her children, and her sincere righteousness.

Inheritance-hunters

For those with property the will and its contents gave them a certain power over those around them both before and after death. Its contents might be private, but the will might be spoken of freely and could be changed regularly. Who was to inherit, and how much, might be a topic of conversation and speculation. A testator could say one thing and do another or change his mind altogether. Wills might be opened and read by the testator to prove what their intentions were or to gain the praise and affection of the beneficiaries before death. Petronius has Trimalchio read out his will at a dinner party so that his household can hear how he intends to treat them (**2.56**). The power of the will is also represented in the literary commonplace of the inheritance-hunter (*captator*). These individuals allegedly preyed on the dying, on men and women who were stereotypically childless, old and rich, trying to win their favour, in the hope of being named heir in the will. Some authors noted, in exaggerated and comical form, that being childless brought certain advantages in the shape of more 'friends' and more gifts.

2.27 *Plautus,* The Swaggering Soldier *705–9*

Comic play: late 3rd or early 2nd c. BC. The words are spoken by the old man
Periplectomenus.
  Compare Juvenal, *Satire* 6.37.

> What do I need children for? I have plenty of relatives. I live
> comfortably and happily as I am; I live as I please, I do as I like; and
> on my death my relatives will have my property to share between
> them. They'll soon be at my house, taking care of me, seeing how I
> am, and whether they can do anything for me. They come already as
> a matter of fact, before daybreak, asking how I've slept. My children
> are all the people who send me presents.

2.28 *Petronius,* Satyricon *116*

Satirical novel: 1st c. AD. The heroes of the novel have just arrived in the city
of Croton (southern Italy).
  Compare Plutarch, *Moralia* 497C, 'many at any rate, who had many
friends and much honour, the birth of one child has made friendless and
powerless'. See also Lucian, *Dialogues of the Dead* 16–19.

> In this city literary studies are not celebrated, eloquence has no
> place, frugality and purity do not achieve reward or praise, but
> know that all of the men you see in this city are divided into two
> classes. Either they are the prey of legacy-hunters or they are
> legacy-hunters. In this city no one raises children, because anyone
> who has heirs of his own is not invited to dinner or admitted to the
> games; he is deprived of all advantages and lives in ignominy. But
> those who have never married and have no close relatives, attain
> the highest honours; they alone are considered courageous, or even
> good. You will enter a town that is like a plague-stricken field,
> where there is nothing but corpses to be torn to pieces and crows to
> tear them.

To win favour the *captator* (a noun derived from fishing; Champlin
1991: 87) might give the testator (their victim) gifts, or apply praise and
flattery or tend the sickbed or offer sexual favours. Such behaviour was
widely condemned and as Seneca makes clear there was little to excuse the
scavenging ways of the legacy-hunter (**2.29**). However, the stereotypical
legacy-hunter was also a source of fun and exaggerated anecdotes, especially since the victim of his plans was often perceived as little better, in
moral terms, than the *captator* (**2.30**).

2.29 Seneca, On Benefits 4.20.3

Philosophy (Stoic): AD 63.

> I call someone ungrateful who sits at the bedside of a sick man
> because he is about to make a will, who finds time to think of inheri-
> tances or legacies. Though he may do everything that a good and
> dutiful friend ought to do, if his mind is filled by the hope of gain, he is
> only a legacy-hunter and is angling for a reward. Like birds that feed
> upon carcasses, staying close by diseased animals that are ready to
> fall, so such a man is attracted by death and hovers about the corpse.

2.30 Horace, Satires 2.5, 10–30

Satirical poetry: late 1st c. BC.

> You must use your skills to catch old men's wills. If one or two are
> clever enough to bite the bait off the hook and escape, you must not
> give up hope and abandon the craft even though disappointed. If a
> legal case, either small or great, comes up, support the party who is
> rich and childless, although he's a rogue and has the audacity to
> accuse a better man; despise the citizen who has the superior case
> and character, if he has a son at home or a fertile wife.

Arguably the most famous *captator* in Latin literature is Regulus as he is
characterized in the letters of Pliny the Younger. Regulus' antics included
criticizing doctors for prolonging someone's life after he had had himself
written into the will, tricking another testator with superstitious nonsense,
and asking for the clothes that one testator was wearing as a legacy. Regulus
is painted as a monster by his political rival Pliny, but the latter can hardly be
described as an impartial witness.

2.31 Pliny the Younger, Letters 2.20. 7–8

Letter (to Calvisius Rufus): late 1st c. AD.

> Velleius Blaesus, a man of consular rank, and noted for his immense
> wealth, in his last illness wished to make some alterations to his will.
> Regulus, who had recently worked at placing himself in favour,
> hoped to get something from the new will, and accordingly
> approached the doctors, and implored them to use all their skill to
> prolong the poor man's life. But after the will was signed, Regulus
> changed his character and tone: 'How long,' he said to the very same
> doctors, 'do you intend keeping this man in suffering? Since you
> cannot save his life, why do you begrudge him the happy release of

death?' Blaesus died, and, as if he had overheard every word that Regulus had said, left him nothing.

It has been argued that chasing wills was a widespread phenomenon (Hopkins 1983: 239), but this view has been challenged. Undoubtedly the *captator* was a figure of hate; such schemers and flatterers were perceived as evil, and it was extremely insulting to be so described, but this does not mean that the *captator* was commonplace. Perception was key. An individual might be characterized as a *captator* by critics (**2.31**) or a loyal and genuine friend by supporters. Furthermore, the *captator* became a stock literary character and social stereotype who served as a powerful example of the negative effects of wealth on Roman society, especially greed and selfishness (Champlin 1991: 94–102). By contrast there is less criticism of the testators who, after all, had the final say, and most of whom may have been far from vulnerable innocents. How common, and perhaps more importantly how successful, inheritance hunting was is difficult to gauge. In literature the *captator* could be thwarted, with the testator having the last laugh (**2.22**, **2.31** and **2.32**).

2.32 Martial, Epigrams 2.26

Poetry: late 1st c. AD.
See also Martial, *Epigrams* 5.39; 6.63; 11.44; 12.56; 12.90.

Naevia gasps for air, she has a dry cough and she repeatedly spits into your lap. Bithynicus, do you believe that you have made good? You are mistaken. Naevia is flirting not dying!

Wills and memory

An important function of the will was its role in memory promotion. For most testators this memory promotion centred on the family, freed slaves and slaves. These were the people that the testator both expected and wanted to be remembered by. Ensuring the continuity and security of the family was a major concern of wills, as we have seen, and in part, at least, this was motivated by the idea that an individual lived on through his or her children and that it was the family who were the guardians of memory. Testators also looked to the beneficiaries of wills to dispose of their bodies and mark their graves and thereby provide a focus for their remembrance. The heir would generally be in charge of the funeral and the will could include stipulations as to its nature and cost. Seneca, for example, requested a simple affair (**1.45**). Generally, wills contained more detailed requests about the tomb than the funeral. The funeral was a matter of ritual and decency, but a tomb could be an expensive drain on the estate (Champlin 1991: 171). Some people foresaw this, anticipated death and built their own tomb (see below). Others used their wills to make specific requests on tomb location, budget and design, and made stipulations about the role of the living in remembering the dead. The onus fell on the heirs to follow the testator's wishes.

2.33 Digest (Alfenus Varus) 35.1.27

Legal text: 6th c. AD (late 1st c. BC).

> A man wrote in his will that he wanted a monument built for himself like that of Publius Septimius Demetrius on the via Salaria; if this was not done, his heirs would pay a large fine. When it was discovered that there was no monument to Publius Septimius Demetrius but that there was one to Publius Septimius Dama, which it was suspected was the one that the testator intended as the model of his own memorial, the heirs asked what sort of monument they should build and, if they built none because they could not identify the intended model, would they incur the penalty? The reply was that if it could be established which monument the testator intended, even if he had misdescribed it, they should build on the model which he thought he had identified; if, however, the testator's wishes could not be established, the penalty would not have force because the model never existed which he had ordered them to use. However they would still have to erect a monument appropriate to the wealth and standing of the deceased.

2.34 AE 1945, 136

Epitaph: 2nd c. AD. Rome (Vatican necropolis). This extract from the will of the tomb founder was inscribed on a marble panel located above the tomb door.

> From the triple codicils of Popilius Heracla. Caius Popilius Heracla to his heirs, greetings. I ask and order and commit to the faith of you, that you build me a tomb on the Vatican hill near the circus, next to the tomb of Ulpius Narcissus, for 6,000 sesterces, of which Novia Trophime will pay 3,000 sesterces and her co-heir 3,000 sesterces. I wish my remains to be placed there and also those of my wife, Fadia Maxima, when the time comes. I charge my freedmen and freedwomen to maintain the tomb cult. This shall apply to those who will be freed in my will and those freed thereafter; and the same applies to the freedmen and freedwomen of Novia Trophime and to the descendants of those named above. They will be allowed access to the tomb to make sacrifices.

Epitaphs often recall that a tomb or grave-marker was made according to the will of the deceased (*ex testamento*). Heirs were eager to prove that they had discharged their duties, burying the dead decently and honouring specific requests. Similarly, heirs might record how much money had been spent on the tomb. Such statements either advertised the generosity of the heirs or confirmed a budget that had been stipulated in the will.

2.35 CIL VI 1374 and Figure 1

Epitaph: late 1st c. BC. Rome (via Ostiensis). The monumental tomb, in the form of a pyramid, was constructed during the reign of Augustus. The pyramid stands more than 36 metres high and is built of concrete faced with blocks of white Italian marble. The dedicatory inscription found on both the east and west faces names Caius Cestius Epulo. On the east side a smaller inscription notes that the tomb was built in accordance with the will of the deceased. The pyramid survived due to its incorporation into the 3rd c. AD Aurelianic city wall.

> Caius Cestius Epulo, son of Lucius, of the Poblilian voting tribe, praetor, tribune of the People, member of the Board of Seven in charge of public feasts.
> The work was completed in 330 days under the authority of his heirs.

Figure 1
The Pyramid tomb of Caius Cestius Epulo, Rome.

2.36 CIL VIII 2815

Epitaph: 2nd or 3rd c. AD. Lambaesis (Tazoult, Algeria).

The deceased was a standard-bearer (*signifer*) in the legion. Costs were recorded fairly frequently in epitaphs from Lambaesis and are also found in a few epitaphs from Italy, but elsewhere this information was far from standard; see Duncan-Jones 1982: 99–101.

> To the spirits of the departed Publius Aufidius Felix, *signifer* of *legio III Augusta*. He lived 47 years. Manilia Arbuscula, his mother, and Aufidius Quartus and Aufidius Amarantus, his brothers and heirs, made this for him who deserved it, at a cost of 1,200 sesterces.

Testators could also attempt to prevent the sale or division of the tomb, or restrict access to those who bore the family name such as freed slaves and their descendants (**4.30–4.32**). The testator might request that the tomb should be equipped with seats, dining areas, wells, and soft furnishings to be used by the living when they visited the tomb (**2.37**). The will could also address how the tomb was to be maintained. A guardian or custodian might be appointed to protect the tomb (**2.20** and **2.56**) and income generated from associated gardens used for the upkeep (**4.33–4.35**). By inscribing the terms of a will onto a tomb (or statue base and so forth) the testator had his or her wishes made public, thereby binding the living to the dead.

2.37 CIL XIII 5708, 1–15

Epitaph: late 1st or early 2nd c. AD. Territory of the Lingones (Langres, France).
= *ILS* 8379. See Le Bohec 1991.

> My wishes are that the memorial shrine should be completed according to the plan I left. The shrine is to contain a recess, in which there is to be put a seated statue of myself, made of the finest imported marble or else of the best bronze, at least 5 feet in height. Just inside the recess there is to be a couch, with two seats on either side of it, all made of imported marble. There are to be covers kept there, which are to be spread out on the days when the memorial shrine is opened, and there are to be two rugs, two dining cushions of equal size, two woollen cloaks and a tunic. In front of this building is to be placed an altar, carved with the finest decoration from the best Luna marble, and in this my bones are to rest. The shrine is to be closed with a slab of Luna marble, in such a way that it can be both easily opened and shut again. The care of the shrine and the orchards and ponds is to be supervised by my freedmen Philadelphus and Verus, and money shall be supplied for rebuilding and repairs should any of these suffer

damage or destruction. There are to be three landscape gardeners and their apprentices, and if one or more of them die or are removed others are to be substituted in their place.

Heirs, however, were not always the best guardians of memory. The hapless testator may have selected heirs who were unreliable or at least slow to honour their commitments.

2.38 Pliny the Younger, Letters 6.10

Letter (to Lucceius Albinus): early 2nd c. AD.
Verginius Rufus, who suppressed the revolt of Vindex in AD 68, was Pliny's friend and mentor.
See also **2.58**.

> I have been visiting my mother-in-law at Alsium [Alzia, Italy], at the villa which once belonged to Verginius Rufus. The place renewed all my grief and longing for that great and excellent man. This was where he lived in retirement, calling it the nest of his old age. Wherever I looked I missed him and felt his absence. I wished to see his tomb, but regretted it afterwards. It is still unfinished, not through any difficulty in the work, for it is very modest, even humble, but through the neglect of the man in charge of it. I was filled with indignation and concern that the remains of a man whose fame filled the whole world, should lie neglected for ten years after his death without a name or inscription. And yet he had directed that the divine and immortal deed should be recorded on his tomb:
>
> > Here lies Rufus, who once defeated Vindex and set free the imperial power
> > Not for himself but for the good of his country.
>
> Faithful friends are so rare and the dead so soon forgotten that we ought to build our own monuments and anticipate all the duties of our heirs. Which of us has no reason to fear what has happened to Verginius? His eminence makes the wrong more shameful and more notorious.

The tomb was a focus for memory, but there were other ways that the will, in particular, could seek to keep the name of the testator alive. One way to promote memory was to make donations or set up foundations that benefited the community. Only the very wealthy could indulge in such testamentary benefactions and grand gestures of public philanthropy. The most extravagant testamentary bequests were cash gifts to the populace. Julius Caesar left the people of Rome money and some gardens as a public park (Suetonius, *Julius Caesar* 83). Agrippa, Augustus' heir and right-hand man, was just as generous, giving the people of Rome money, gardens and a bath building (Cassius Dio 54.29.4). These expensive gestures symbolized the power of these leading men, but such donations could also be politically useful in buying support for their successors and survivors. Legacies to fund public works, to build, restore or embellish structures used by the public such as temples, theatres, libraries and baths, could be perceived as particularly enduring.

2.39 *Pliny the Younger,* Letters *10.75 and 10.76*

Letters (to and from the emperor Trajan): early 2nd c. AD.

Pliny was serving as the emperor's special representative in the province of Bithynia. The will, of which Pliny had been appointed heir, sought to honour the emperor, benefit local inhabitants and promote the memory of the deceased. Heraclea and Tium were cities in Pontus, near the Black Sea.

Pliny to the Emperor Trajan

Julius Largus of Pontus, Sir, a person whom I have never seen nor heard of until recently, but presumably relying on your opinion of me, has entrusted me with administering his last example of loyalty towards you. He has left me in his will his estate upon trust, and after receiving 50,000 sesterces for my own use, to pay over the remainder to the cities of Heraclea and Tium, either for the erection of public buildings to be dedicated in your honour or for the institution of athletic games to be held every five years and to be called by your name. I am to choose which scheme I think best. I thought I should bring this to your attention so that I may receive direction as to which alternative to select.

Trajan to Pliny

In his wise choice of trustee you would have thought that Julius Largus knew you personally. Consider then what will suit the conditions of both places, and also what will perpetuate his memory, and make your own decision accordingly.

2.40 CIL V 5262

Honorary inscription: early 2nd c. AD. Comum (Como, Italy). Pliny the Younger remembers his home town in his will. The inscription served to celebrate, commemorate and remember Pliny's life as well as his donations.

Caius Plinius Secundus, son of Lucius, of the Oufentina voting tribe, consul, augur, propraetorian legate of the province of Pontus and Bithynia, sent to that province with consular power, following a decree of the senate, by the emperor Caesar Nerva Trajan Augustus

Germanicus, conqueror of Dacia, father of his country. He was curator of the channel and banks of the river Tiber and of the sewers of the city, prefect of the treasury of Saturn, prefect of the military treasury, *praetor*, tribune of the plebs, *quaestor* of the emperor, *sevir* of the Roman *equites*, military tribune of *legio III Gallica*, *decemvir* for judging cases. He ordered in his will that baths be constructed from [amount lost] sesterces and that an additional 300,000 sesterces be used for their decoration and another 200,000 sesterces for their upkeep. He also bequeathed 1,866,666 sesterces to the municipality for the support of his one hundred freedmen, the income from which he wished to put toward a banquet for the urban plebs thereafter [...] While alive, he gave 500,000 sesterces for the support of boys and girls of the urban plebs, and he gave 100,000 sesterces for the library and its upkeep.

More modest were testamentary gifts to the community of statues of the gods, the emperor or of the testator, or one-off bequests to buy grain for the people or subsidize their use of the public baths. More complex, but arguably of greater longevity, were foundations; bequests that were invested and the income then used to fund regular benefactions. These might finance games or shows or the distribution of money, oil or food or the upkeep of public buildings. The beneficiaries of these foundations might be restricted to members of a *collegium* or the local magistrates or *augustales*.

2.41 CIL XI 5745

Inscribed statue base: 1st c. AD. Sentinum (near Sassoferrato, Italy).
    The month Germanicus was September; it was renamed in honour of Germanicus see **2.63**.

To Gaius Aetnius Naso, son of Gaius, of the Lemurian voting tribe, honoured with a public horse in five decuries, prefect of the first cohort of Germans, military tribune of *legio I Italica*. He ordered in his will that this be set up; also to the citizens of the municipium of Sentinum he gave 120,000 sesterces for a banquet to be given on the 17th of the kalends of Germanicus [August 16].

2.42 CIL X 5056

Inscribed statue base: mid 1st c. AD. Atina (Atene Lucana, Italy).
    For a bequest of baths for the use of the public, see *Digest* 32.35.3.

To Titus Helvius Basila son of Titus, *aedile*, *praetor*, proconsul, imperial legate, he bequeathed to the people of Atina 400,000 sesterces; out of the income from this bequest their children are to be given grain until they reach adulthood, and thereafter 1,000 sesterces each. His daughter, Procula, set this up.

Some foundations were explicitly linked to the cult of the dead by paying for libations, dinners and flowers at the tomb. These offerings were often connected to the festivals for the dead or the birthday of the deceased and depended not just on money but on the continuing goodwill of others, such as freed slaves and local dignitaries. There were mutual benefits to these arrangements, but we can wonder for how long they lasted and the extent to which, like threats in epitaphs (**4.53** and **4.54**), they were legally enforceable. Whatever the nature of his or her bequests, the testator was trying to strike a bargain with the living; money, property and philanthropic gestures could buy memory preservation and a sense of immortality.

2.43 ILS 6468

Inscribed statue base: 2nd c. AD. Peteleia (Strongoli, Italy).
  For the *Parentalia* see Chapter 6.
  Compare D'Arms 2000; Dixon 1992b.

Manius Megonius Leo, son of Manius, grandson of Manius and great-grandson of Manius of the Cornelian voting tribe, *aedile*, *quattuorvir* of the lex Cornelia, *quaestor* of public funds, patron of the municipality, *quattuorvir quinquennalis*. The *decuriones*, *augustales* and people set up this bronze statue on account of his merit.

Taken from his will: 'If a standing statue of me, with stone foundation and marble base, like that which the *augustales* set up to me, near the one set up by my fellow citizens, is erected in the upper forum I promise that I will give 100,000 sesterces to the municipium. On the condition that the income from this is used as written below. Every year on my birthday, which is March 23rd, 300 denarii is to be distributed from this money for a feast of the *decuriones*; the remainder is to be divided between those present. On the same condition on the same occasion every year I wish to give 150 denarii to the *augustales* and one denarius to the citizens of the town, and on the *Parentalia* 50 denarii ... To you the best of citizens, I beg and ask by the health of the immortal emperor Antoninus Pius and his children that you will maintain my wishes and distributions forever and that you will inscribe all of this section of my will on the statue base I have asked you to set up to me, so that it might be better known to our descendants, or that it might serve to remind those who would be generous to their homeland.'

Monuments and memory

Foundations, benefactions, tombs and epitaphs all sought to promote the memory of the deceased, to confer some sort of immortality. Chapter 6 explores varied views on life after death and the difficulty of assessing whether individuals actually believed in the afterlife, but for many people the focus appears to have fallen on being remembered in this life rather than on preparing for the hereafter. Prompting memory, getting the living to remember in an active fashion, was important, although not all agreed as to how this should be achieved. Ulpian stated that a monument existed 'to preserve memory' (*Digest* 11.7.2.6), but what was the best, the most appropriate and most enduring monument? The Latin for monument (*monumentum*) could refer not only to an imposing structure, be it a tomb, statue or building, erected to commemorate a person or event, but also to a noteworthy piece of writing or a collection of writings.

2.44 Varro, On the Latin Language 6.49

A study of language: late 1st c. BC.
  Previous to this extract Varro considers the derivation of the Latin words for remember and memory, relating them to *manere* 'to remain'.

> From the same is *monere* 'to remind', since he who 'reminds', is like a memory. So also the *monimenta* 'memorials' which are on tombs, and in fact alongside the road, that they may *admonere* 'admonish' the passers-by that they themselves and the readers too were mortal. From this the other things written and done to preserve *memoria* 'memory' are called *monimenta* 'monuments'.

Roman public life drew heavily on memories of the past. Deciding who or what would be remembered was an aspect of power and authority. Rome was filled with mnemonic triggers that recalled and celebrated Rome's past and her leading citizens. Buildings, statues and amenities promoted the memory of those whose names were attached in the explanatory inscriptions. To contribute to the urban fabric was a way of buying memory, although it was even better to earn memory through actions that might lead to the public vote of the cost of *monumenta*. A monument symbolized not just success, but an enduring reputation. For the leading male citizens, of both Republic and Empire, reputation (*fama*) was of fundamental importance (**2.45**). To have a good reputation in life and for this to persist for posterity could be a driving ambition. Immortality, conveyed by fame, could offer consolation for the lack of an afterlife.

2.45 *Pliny the Younger,* Letters *9.3. 1–2*

Letter (to Valerius Paulinus): late 1st or early 2nd c. AD.

> Others may think differently, but in my opinion a truly happy man is one who lives in anticipation of a good and lasting reputation, and is confident of future glory in the eyes of posterity. If I did not have in view the reward of immortality, I would prefer an easy life of complete retirement to any other. For everyone, I think must evaluate these two points: that fame is imperishable and man is mortal. Those who are motivated by the former will lead a life of work and effort; those who are motivated by the latter will resign themselves to quiet repose, and not wear out their life with vain endeavours.

People were surrounded by the past, lived in the present and anticipated the future. The élite were supposed to be inspired by their forebears to create their own equally worthy legacies. But at the very least they could ensure that, through their life and actions, the family name survived.

2.46 *Cicero,* Tusculan Disputations *1.14.31*

Philosophical dialogue: 45 BC.

> Having children, the promotion of a name, the adoption of sons, the careful writing of wills, the very burial monuments, the epitaphs – what meaning do they have except that we are also thinking of the future?

For the élite the path to immortality lay through deeds that would enhance their reputation. These would ensure enduring monuments; not just honorary statues, grand buildings and tombs, but also great works of literature. Literary texts, if you wrote them or had them written about you, were vehicles for immortality (**2.47**). Writers preserved memory, but also decided what to remember and how it should be remembered (Gowing 2005: 10). Reading history in particular could be the equivalent of looking at a monument (**2.48**).

2.47 *Cicero,* Letters to his Friends *5.12.1 (22)*

Letter: 55 BC. Cicero wants Lucceius to compose a history of his achievements.

> I am inflamed, by an unbelievably strong desire, for which I think I should not be blamed, that my name should gain lustre and frequent praise in a history written by you. You have often promised me, it is

true, that you mean to do this, so I hope you will forgive my impatience. The quality of your writing, of which I had always held the highest hopes, has exceeded my expectations, and has taken such a hold of me and has so fired my imagination, that I want to see my achievements on record in your writings as quickly as possible. The thought that posterity will speak of me and the hope of a chance at immortality urges me on, but so too does the desire of enjoying in my lifetime an authoritative expression of your judgement, the evidence of your kindness, and the charm of your literary talent.

2.48 Livy, Preface 10

History: late 1st c. BC or early 1st c. AD.

Here Livy makes explicit the connections between text, monument and memory; see Jaeger 1997; Gowing 2005: 22–3; Miles 1995.

This is what is especially healthy and fruitful in the study of history, that you look upon examples of every kind as though they were set on an illustrious monument. From there you can choose for yourself and your state what to imitate and what, foul in both its beginnings and result, to avoid.

The past was perceived as important because it defined the present, and as such it needed to be revered and respected, especially by the aristocratic élite. Orators could be regarded as the best preservers of memories, especially since they were well-versed in mnemonic techniques (Small 1997: 95–131). Words preserved and promoted the past and transmitted historical memory. It was a recurrent literary *topos* that words (of whatever genre) were a more effective monument than monuments crafted in other materials. Cicero in his letter to Lucceius also notes that a well-written volume can achieve more 'than all the portraits and statues under the sun' (*Letters to his Friends* 5.12.7). Equally, it was frequently noted that words had the power and the potential to be immortal. A building might be reduced to rubble, but a great poem or history would last forever. This is the equivalent of the effects of Shakespeare's 'sluttish time' (*Sonnet 55*, 4) and is a theme that cross-cuts Latin genres. It is best and most famously encapsulated in an ode by Horace (**2.49**), but writers of philosophy, epigrams and biographies could also justify their efforts and subject matter by reference to the enduring power of the written word.

2.49 Horace, Odes 3.30, 1–9

Poetry: late 1st c. BC.

Horace is adapting Pindar, *Pythian* 6.6–18. Compare also Virgil, *Aeneid 9*, 446–9.

I have made a monument more lasting than bronze and higher than the Pyramid that marks a royal grave. Neither wasting rain, nor the violent north wind can destroy it; nor the countless years, nor the passing of time. I shall not die completely, but a great part of me will escape death. On and on shall I grow, refreshed by the praises of posterity.

2.50 Ovid, Metamorphoses 15, 871–9

Poetry: late 1st c. BC or early 1st c. AD. These are the final lines of the poem.
  Compare Ovid, *Tristia* 3.3, 78–80; Propertius, *Elegies* 3.2, 18–27; Martial 10.2, 7–12.

And now the work is done, which neither the anger of Jupiter, nor fire, nor sword, nor the gnawing tooth of time shall ever erase. Let that day, that only has power over this mortal body, come and end the uncertain span of my years. Yet the better part of me will be borne, immortal, far beyond the distant stars. Wherever Rome's power extends, over the conquered lands, I will be spoken of by men's lips and, famous for all time; if the prophecies of poets have any truth, I shall live.

2.51 Seneca, Consolation to Polybius 18.2

Philosophical consolation: *c.* AD 43. Seneca consoles Polybius on the loss of his brother.

And also extend the remembrance of your brother by some monument in your writings; for this is the one work in human achievements that no storm can harm, nor age destroy. All others, those that are constructed in stone and masses of marble, or building up on high huge mounds of earth, do not last for long, for they themselves will also perish; but the memory of genius is immortal.

2.52 Pliny, Letters 3.10. 6

Letter (to Vestricius Spurinna and Cottia): early 2nd c. AD. Pliny intends to publish a eulogy to the recipients' son.

It is difficult for you to concentrate on this at a time of suffering. However if a sculptor or painter were producing a portrait of your son, you would tell him what features to express or re-do, so I hope you will guide and direct me in producing this enduring likeness which shall, if you are pleased to think it, last for ever.

To champion literary texts was not to reject other forms of monument. For the successful man praise by a great writer might be the most enduring of a whole package of memorials that could include statues, buildings, public donations, benefactions and a tomb. Cicero may have longed to be remembered by and in history, but he himself became almost obsessive about creating a memorial shrine for his deceased daughter (**4.28**). Pliny the Younger tells that Silius Italicus regularly visited the tomb of Rome's greatest poet, Virgil, treating it as if it were a temple (*Letters* 3.7.8). Words had their place and role, but stone structures could have a more tangible and immediate impact. Indeed physical monuments could make maximum use of a range of communicative dimensions, words, through inscriptions, forming an essential element. To memorialize effectively, a monument needed a name attached. Cicero said 'by reading [epitaphs] I refresh my recollection of the dead' (Cicero, *On Old Age* 7.21). For many people epitaphs were their only written record; the option of writing great poetry, history or biography, or having such things dedicated to them or written about them was limited.

2.53 Tacitus, Agricola 46

Biography: AD 98.
Compare Tacitus, *Annals* 16.6 and Seneca, *Letters* 21.5.

> All that we have loved and admired in Agricola remains and will remain in the hearts of men, in eternal time, in the records of history. Many will be engulfed in oblivion as if they had no name or fame. But Agricola, whose story is told for posterity, will survive.

For the majority a funerary monument was the only available method to keep oblivion at bay. If a life would not be remembered for deeds and donations, if no inscription would recall the name in the centre of town, there was always the suburban cemetery (Hope 2001; Mouritsen 2005). Not everyone could afford a grandiose monument, but many strove to leave some form of marker to spare them, if only temporarily, from anonymity in death. Requests for tombs in wills have already been noted; for some a more satisfactory solution was to plan even further ahead. Pre-death action removed responsibility from heirs, who might be unreliable. Building a tomb before death was one way of ensuring that you got what you wanted, that the memorial was in the right place, or of the right type and right price. Many epitaphs contained expressions such as *vivus fecit* (he/she made it living), meaning that the person commemorated had built, or at least had commissioned, the memorial themselves.

75

2.54 CIL V 1365

Epitaph: 2nd c. AD. Aquileia (Italy). A stele decorated with a *patera* and rosettes.
    = *IA* 1450.
    See also **2.7**, **2.57** and **6.46**.

> Sardia Artemisia made this while living for herself and for Cantius Proculus, a very good husband, and Cassia Secundina, a very sweet daughter.

2.55 CIL VIII 4387

Epitaph: 1st or 2nd c. AD. Seriana (Algeria).
    = *ILS* 8074.

> Sacred to the spirits of Titus Caninius Saturninus aged […], who during his life arranged to have a monument made for himself and Saturnina Ninis and his well-deserving son, of the form and measurements of the tomb of Obstoria Bellica and Petronius Verecundus, for 200,000 sesterces.

To decide the details of one's memorial before death suggests careful consideration of how one wished to be remembered; that the identity projected into posterity by the tomb was rigorously selected. This process is parodied by Petronius who has the *nouveau riche* freedman Trimalchio give precise instructions about his tomb. The details which Trimalchio explores provide an insight into how funerary monuments operated; decoration, size and design are fundamental in grabbing the attention of the passer-by (see Chapter 4). The tomb portrays aspects of Trimalchio's life, his wealth, generosity, pleasures and family. Spectators are supposed to be drawn by these images, as well as an amenity function in the form of a sundial, to read and remember the name of Trimalchio.

2.56 Petronius, Satyricon 71

Satirical novel: 1st c. AD.

> Everyone began thanking their master for his kindness, when he became serious and ordered a copy of his will to be brought in, which he read aloud from beginning to end while the household sobbed. Then looking at Habinnas, he said, 'What have you to say, my dear friend? Will you build my monument the way I have directed? I ask you earnestly to put up around the feet of my statue my little dog, some wreaths, scent bottles, and all the fights of

Petraites [a gladiator], so that your kindness will bring me life after death; and I also want the monument to be 100 feet in front and 200 feet into the field. For I would like to have all kinds of fruit around my ashes and lots of vines. After all, it's a mistake for a man to adorn the house he lives in and not worry about the one he'll occupy for much longer. So above everything else I want this added to the inscription, "This monument does not go to the heir". I shall certainly take care in my will that I am not injured when I'm dead. I'll appoint one of my freedmen to be caretaker of my tomb and prevent people from running up and shitting on it. I'd like you to put some ships in full sail on the monument, and me sitting in my robes of office on a platform, wearing five gold rings and distributing money from a bag in public; for you know I gave a dinner worth two denarii a head. I'd like you to show a dining hall and all the people there enjoying themselves. On my right put up a statue of Fortunata, holding a dove, and leading her little dog tied to her belt; and my dear little boy, and big jars sealed up with gypsum so the wine won't spill. And carve me a broken urn with a boy crying over it. And a sundial in the middle, so that anyone who looks at the time, like it or not, will read my name. As for the inscription, think carefully whether this seems appropriate to you, "Here lies Gaius Pompeius Trimalchio Maecenatianus, elected to the Augustan college in his absence. He could have been an attendant to any magistrate in Rome, but he refused. God-fearing, brave and faithful, he grew from very little and left 30,000,000. He never heard a philosopher. Farewell, Trimalchio, and to you."

Trimalchio may represent a caricature, but surviving memorials set up by freed slaves suggest that this group could take a particular interest in how they were commemorated at death, celebrating their new-found citizen status and their position within the community (Zanker 1975; Kleiner 1977; Kockel 1993; Whitehead 1993; and also the cautionary note in Hackworth Petersen 2006). These men (and women) could have mixed identities and experiences since even those who attained great wealth were still stigmatized by their former slavery. A freedman could rarely aspire to the public reputation (*fama*) so lauded by Pliny the Younger (see Letters 7.29 and 8.6, for when one did and the consternation caused). Nevertheless even if a freed slave found setting up his statue in the forum almost impossible there were no such restrictions in the cemetery.

2.57 AE 1986, n.166a and Figure 2

Tomb: 1st c. AD. Pompeii (Porta Nocera necropolis).
  = D'Ambrosio and De Caro 1983: 23 OS.

The tomb consists of a niche holding three statues. The central female statue is probably the patron (that is the former owner) of the founder of the tomb, and the two male statues to either side the founder and his erstwhile friend. The original epitaph, beneath the niche, was updated by the addition of the title *augustalis* (a distinguished office for a freed slave) and then by a second inscribed panel telling of a change in friendship. Overall the scale and décor of the tomb suggest the wealth, success and social standing of the former slave.

> Publius Vesonius Phileros, freedman of a woman, an *augustalis*, built this monument while living for himself and his family. For Vesonia, daughter of Publius, his patron, and for Marcus Orfellius Faustus, son of Marcus his friend.
>
> Stranger, stop a short while if it is not inconvenient, and learn what to avoid. This man whom I believed was my friend, I am giving up. A case was maliciously brought against me; I was charged and legal proceedings begun. I give thanks to the gods and to my innocence that I was freed from this distress. May neither the household gods nor the gods below accept the man who lied about our affairs.

Figure 2
The Tomb of Publius
Vesonius Phileros,
Pompeii.

How best to be remembered, which monument (text, statue, tombstone, donation) to choose, and how and by whom it should be produced and promoted, touched the lives of many people, if to varying degrees. However, perhaps only in élite circles, where the options were near limitless, was there any debate about the true nature and value of monuments and memory. There is some evidence that fashions changed across the centuries in how the wealthy (and to some extent the moderately wealthy) chose to be remembered (von Hesberg 1992; Mouritsen 2005; Woolf 1996). The grandiose funerary memorials of the late Republic may have seemed less appropriate under the Empire, and as memorials became accessible to a wider social mix some among the élite may have dismissed them altogether. Herein perhaps lay one of the comforts of immortal literature; anyone (well, almost anyone) could buy a tombstone or commission an epitaph, but not so a great literary work. Equally a modest tomb, or even no tomb at all, could be perceived as more appropriate than some sort of ostentatious and crass display.

2.58 Pliny, Letters 9.19

Letter (to Cremutius Rufus): early 2nd c. AD.

Pliny is responding to comments about the unfinished tomb of Verginius Rufus (2.38). Frontinus was an author and general, who held the consulship in AD 73, 98 and 100.

Compare Tacitus (*Annals* 4.38), where Tiberius decries monuments and honours because he wishes to be remembered for his deeds and reputation.

> In my opinion everyone who has done some great and memorable deed should not only be excused but praised if he wishes to ensure the immortality he has deserved, and seeks to perpetuate his everlasting remembrance by the words of his epitaph. And I cannot easily think of anyone who has performed such great achievements as Verginius and spoken so modestly of it ... [Pliny continues to stress Verginius' modesty] ... Now let us consider Frontinus, on the very point in which you found him more moderate and reserved. Frontinus forbade any monument to be set up, but with what words? 'The cost of a monument is superfluous; my memory will endure if my life has deserved it.' Is there less vanity, do you think, to put on record for all to read that your memory will endure, than to inscribe in two lines your achievements in a single place? However, it is not my intention to criticize Frontinus but to defend Verginius; though there could be no better defence of him for your ears than a comparison between him and the man you prefer. My own feeling is that neither should be blamed, for both hoped for fame although they sought it by different paths, one by claiming the monument which he deserved, the other by appearing to despise it.

Destroying memory

Monuments preserved memory, but not everyone could claim a monument by right. Many were no doubt financially unable to leave any tangible memories behind; in the short term they were remembered by their nearest and dearest, but in the long term they had no permanent monument. For others, memory could be compromised or even actively destroyed. Criminals and traitors were cast out in death; their bodies could be denied decent burial (see Chapter 4) and any form of monument. For those in authority, including the emperors, controlling memory was a means of exerting power. A regime, or individual ruler, could choose to champion, ignore or promote the memories of predecessors and deceased contemporaries, a fate that could affect both men and women. The ultimate sanction was to condemn the memory of the deceased. There was a repertoire of penalties for suppressing the memory of a public enemy; although these were not fully legally recognized, they are often now known as *damnatio memoriae*. Statues could be defaced and toppled (Varner 2001a, 2004), *imagines* (see Chapter 3) banned from public display, names chiselled out of inscriptions and property confiscated. This represented organized and orchestrated forgetting rather than remembering. One of the most famous cases involved Cnaeus Calpurnius Piso who, on 10 December AD 20, was posthumously condemned by the Senate on a charge of treason. Rome may have been the venue that mattered in terms of suppressing the memory of Piso (Bodel 1999a: 45), but his damnation was widely published across the empire. The decree aimed to erase the name and memory of Piso, the complete opposite of the senatorial ideal of achieving a reputation worthy of remembrance by posterity. It would be as if Piso had never existed.

2.59 Senatorial decree concerning Cnaeus Piso 73–85

Extract from an inscribed senatorial decree: AD 20. Found in Spain.

= Eck, Caballos and Fernández 1996; see also Griffin 1997; Potter and Damon 1999.

The text of the decree was probably sent to the governor of Baetica who would have then arranged for its publication across the province. Piso, who had been implicated in the death of the emperor Tiberius' nephew Germanicus, had committed suicide at the prospect of loss of honour and property. The senatorial decree dishonoured his memory.

Compare also Tacitus, *Annals* 3.17–18. For Germanicus see **1.1, 2.60** and **5.6**.

> That no mourning on account of his death be undertaken by the women by whom he should have been mourned according to ancestral custom if this decree of the Senate had not been passed; and that statues and portrait masks of Cnaeus Piso, wherever displayed, be

removed; and that those who at any time belong to the Calpurnian family or who are related to that family by blood or marriage will act rightly and properly if they take care that if anyone of that family or any of those related by blood or marriage to the Calpurnian family has died and is to be mourned, that the portrait mask of the elder Cnaeus Piso not be carried among the rest of the portraits masks with which they customarily celebrate the processions at those funerals; and that his portrait mask not be placed among the portrait masks of the Calpurnian family; and that the names of the elder Cnaeus Piso be removed from the inscription of the statue of Germanicus that the *sodales Augustales* erected to him in the Campus Martius next to the Altar of Providence; and that the property of the elder Cnaeus Piso be confiscated with the exception of the lands which were in Illyricum.

We can contrast the damning of Piso with the many honours bestowed upon the deceased Germanicus. Piso's alleged victim, and great favourite with all, was to be remembered in many different and varied ways. Copies of the Senate's decree recording these honours have been found in Spain and Italy and are also summarized by Tacitus (2.60). Suspicions may have been raised about the extent of the emperor's grief (5.6), but in public Germanicus was to be remembered in grand style. Piso was to have no public monuments to his memory, Germanicus many.

2.60 *Tacitus*, Annals 2.83

History: early 2nd c. AD. Events of AD 19.

Compare *Tabula Siarensis* (see Crawford 1996, n. 37–8), an inscribed record of the decree. Tacitus records only a dozen of the 27 honours listed in the Tablet. For the differences between the two and how Tacitus uses the honours as the finale to his recounting of the stormy relationship between Tiberius and Germanicus, see González 1999: 129.

Affection and ingenuity competed in devising and decreeing honours to Germanicus. His name was to be sung in the hymn of the Salii; curule chairs with oak garlands over them were to be set up for him wherever the priests of the augustales had right of place; his image in ivory was to lead the procession in the Circus games; no flamen or augur, except from the Julian family, was to be chosen in the room of Germanicus. Arches were built at Rome, on the banks of the Rhine, and on Mount Amanus in Syria, with an inscription recording his achievements, and how he had died for his country. There was to be a monument in Antioch, where he had been cremated, a mound at Epidaphna, where his life had ended. The number of his statues, or the places in which they were honoured, could not easily be counted.

When it was proposed that a golden shield of remarkable size be placed among the portraits of the leading orators, Tiberius declared that he would dedicate one himself, saying that it would be one of the customary kind, similar to the rest, for eloquence was not discerned by fortune, and it was sufficient distinction to be among the old masters. The equestrian order renamed the seats in the theatre known as 'the juniors' after Germanicus, and arranged that on the 15th of July the procession should follow behind his portrait. Many of these honours still remain; some were dropped at once, or have lapsed with time.

A damned memory was still a memory. Piso may have been disgraced but people would still recall his infamy, just as with time they would forget to honour Germanicus so rigorously (2.60). Indeed, a political regime might seek to control public memory, to destroy or promote public monuments, but it could not control what people actually remembered or how different groups characterized the dead.

2.61 Suetonius, Domitian 23

Biography: early 2nd c. AD. Events of AD 96.
For the fate of Domitian's body see 3.25.

The people received the news of Domitian's death with indifference, but the soldiers were deeply grieved, and at once began to call him Domitian the God; they would have avenged him, but they lacked leaders. However, they did achieve this a little later by their insistent demands for the execution of his murderers. The senators, on the other hand, were so overjoyed that they raced to fill the senate house where they were uncontrolled in their abuse of the dead emperor, using the most insulting and bitter language. They even sent for ladders and had his shields and images torn down before their eyes and dashed to the ground. Finally, they decreed that all his inscriptions should be erased and all memory of him obliterated.

Those who fell from favour, and not all were publicly damned, could become controversial figures in Roman public life. Power changed hands and posthumous reputations could be restored or re-evaluated. Cicero is a case in point. In 43 BC Cicero was proscribed by the triumvirs; he was hunted down, assassinated and his head and hand cut off for display in the Roman Forum (4.50). This was an infamous end to a great life, and one that future generations would feel uncomfortable with. Cicero came to be remembered not as an enemy of the state, but as a victim of Marc Antony (who would himself become the enemy), while the role of the future emperor Augustus in the proscriptions was conveniently suppressed (Gowing 2005: 44–8). Cicero was remembered for his eloquence and his writings, rather than for the fervour of his political beliefs that led to his death. Ultimately, Marc Antony could not condemn the reputation of Cicero to oblivion.

2.62 *Velleius Paterculus 2.66.1–5*

History: 1st c. AD.

Compare Lucan's anger at Rome's failure to honour the grave of Pompey, whose fame cannot be marred by such ill treatment, *Civil War* 8, 835–65.

> Marc Antony, you achieved nothing – the sheer indignation that bursts forth from my mind and my heart forces me to exceed the bounds I have set for my work. I say, that by offering a reward for the destruction of those divine lips and famous head and by encouraging people with blood money to murder a man who was once saviour of the Republic and a great consul, you achieved nothing. You took from Marcus Cicero some anxious days, a few senile years, a life that with you in power as triumvir, would have been more miserable than death. But you did not so much rob him of the fame and glory of his deeds and his words but rather you increased them. He lives and he will live in memory for all time.

Outstanding men such as Cicero left many monuments behind them; writings, the writings of others, public benefactions, and their political actions (mistakes and all) preserved and promoted their memories. There was an ever-present paradox that monuments were seen as permanent and enduring, but their meaning and use was changeable (Fowler 2000: 211). Posthumous reputations were open to manipulation; who was remembered and how could change with the political regime. So for example, those condemned by one emperor might be reintegrated and rehabilitated by another. Memories, and the monuments that conveyed memory, could be reinvented as well as destroyed. Following his succession, the emperor Gaius (son of Germanicus; **2.60**) made a great show of reclaiming the remains of his relatives who had been banished and executed by his predecessor, the emperor Tiberius. It was under Tiberius that Piso had been damned (**2.59**) and Tiberius' own reputation now rested in the hands of his successor.

2.63 *Suetonius, Gaius 15*

Biography: early 2nd c. AD. Events of AD 37.

Gaius' mother, Agrippina the Elder, had been banished by Tiberius to the island of Pandataria in AD 29, where she starved herself to death in AD 33. Gaius' brother Nero was exiled and died in AD 31. For Gaius see also **1.1**, **2.41** and **6.53**. The Mausoleum was the mausoleum of Augustus, see **4.20** and **4.21**. For Tiberius' reign of terror see **4.49**.

Gaius tried to incite men's devotion by courting popularity in every possible way. Shedding many tears he delivered a funeral speech for Tiberius to the assembled crowd and gave him a magnificent burial. But at once he set off for Pandataria and the Pontian Islands to bring back the remains of his mother and his brother; and during stormy weather too, to make his filial duty more noticeable. He approached the ashes with reverence and placed them in urns with his own hands. With no less theatrical effect he brought them to Ostia in a bireme with a standard raised in the stern and from there up the Tiber to Rome. He had the urns carried to the Mausoleum by the most distinguished members of the equestrian order on two biers, in the middle of the day, when the streets were busy. He established annual funeral sacrifices and in addition games in the Circus in honour of his mother, providing a carriage to carry her image in the procession. In memory of his father he renamed the month September Germanicus.

The paradox existed that condemnation of memory could ultimately make that memory more famous (Hedrick 2000: 94). This was especially true for those who could be characterized as victims, and those who could be remembered for their talents or services to the state. Try as they might, the powerful could not control the future.

2.64 Tacitus, Annals 4.35

History: early 2nd c. AD. Events of AD 25.
Aulus Cremutius Cordus was prosecuted for writing a history in which he praised Brutus and Cassius, the assassins of Caesar.

Cremutius then left the senate, and starved himself to death. The senators ordered his books to be burned by the aediles. But copies survived, hidden and then republished. This makes one deride the folly of those who believe that a despotic act in the present can destroy the memories of the future. On the contrary, genius that is punished increases its authority. All that foreign kings or the imitators of their cruelty achieve is their own ruin and glory for their victims.

3

FUNERALS

Introduction

Funerals act as transitional rituals. Death dislocates the deceased and the bereaved from their usual roles in the social structure, placing them in a liminal state. The deceased person has left the world of the living, but the corpse is still present; simultaneously, the bereaved are isolated, often marked out (for example, by dress) and excluded from full participation in the community. Funerals serve both to reintegrate the bereaved into and separate the dead from the world of the living. Rituals can also bring together different members of a society while also allocating, and thus reinforcing, roles according to status, wealth, age and gender. As such, funerals can bind and unite a society, providing an opportunity to demonstrate common beliefs and core values.

For the Roman period, reconstructing the events immediately before and after death, the preparation of the body and the funeral itself involves drawing together a multitude of pieces of evidence. There are few literary accounts of deathbed rituals and funerals; people rarely comment upon or describe in detail what to them is standard behaviour and common knowledge. Thus many of the textual extracts given below are little more than snippets, often casual comments made by authors, that unwittingly illuminate funerals. So if it weren't for Pliny the Elder's encyclopaedic listing of Roman trivia we might not know that cypress branches symbolized mourning (**3.52**) or that the eyes of the dead were opened prior to cremation (**3.43**). The relevant texts are of varied form and origin and combining them together to construct an impression of the rituals is a problematic process. Take Virgil's *Aeneid*, for example, which includes various descriptions of the deaths and funerals of Italians, Trojans and Carthaginians and includes rare insights into the washing and preparation of the corpse (**3.17** and **3.18**). To what extent does this long poem centred on Rome's distant and mythical past reflect the ritual practices current in Rome in Virgil's own day? Equally, uncertainty over why things were done the way they were was common; many of the rituals described were anachronistic; this was the way it had always been done, regardless of present practical requirements or spiritual beliefs. Other forms of evidence do complement the available literature. There are some sculpted reliefs that depict deathbed scenes and the display of the body and these provide invaluable evidence, but are few in number. Archaeology, on the other hand, provides a wealth of material from the funeral process, especially in terms of how the body was disposed of (cremation or inhumation) and the inclusion of grave-goods. Yet interpreting this material evidence and reconstructing and understanding the rituals and human actions that created it remains problematic.

Despite the patchy nature of the evidence, certain aspects of the ritual process can be pieced together: the funerals of the élite (Price 1987; Bodel 1999b); the significance of the *imagines* (Flower 1996); the role of undertakers (Bodel 2000); the purpose of *collegia* (Patterson 1992); the construction of a pyre (Noy 2000a). Nevertheless the danger remains that we will merge together primary sources and secondary interpretations to create a composite picture of a Roman funeral that may never have been a reality. That is to say that the evidence often comes from such varied sources and periods that it is not possible to produce a definitive description. The details of funeral customs may have varied considerably between period, region and ethnic group, as well as by economic and social status and so, for example, funerals in Roman Judaea or Roman Britain or Roman Egypt would have had their own distinctive features. The following compilation of sources aims to illuminate and identify some broadly 'Roman' elements in how the body was prepared, the death marked and the body disposed of, but cannot provide a complete or universal account of funeral rituals practised in the Roman period.

Planning, instructions and cost

Proper and decent disposal of the dead was perceived as important and was legislated for. It was the duty of the heir to carry out the funeral unless the will of the deceased specified otherwise. The fact that the Digest of Roman Law considers who should pay for the funeral and who could make a legitimate claim on the estate for funeral expenses suggests that disputes and uncertainties could arise. One thing that the law does make clear is that burial took priority; it was best for the dead to be buried at their own expense.

3.1 Digest (Ulpian) 11.7.12.2–4 and 11.7.14.6

Legal text: 6th c. AD (3rd c. AD).

> The praetor says: 'Where money is spent on a funeral, I shall give an action for its recovery against the person concerned.' This edict was issued for a good reason, so that someone who organizes a funeral may claim his expenses. This ensures that corpses are not left unburied and that nobody is buried at a stranger's expense. The

person chosen by the deceased ought to arrange the funeral. If he does not do so, there is no penalty, unless he has been left something as a reward for arranging it; in that case, if he has not followed the wishes of the deceased, he is excluded from the reward. But if the deceased made no provision concerning his funeral and the role of arranging it has not been given to anybody else, then it falls to the heirs named in the will.

What is fair in a particular case depends upon the rank of the person being buried, the circumstances, the occasion, and also on good faith, so that no more should be charged than was actually spent, and if the expenditure was excessive the full amount should not be charged for; for consideration should be taken both of the resources of the person on whom the expense is incurred and of the estate which is unreasonably being used up to an excessive extent.

How often people had recourse to law over funeral expenses is difficult to judge. For the majority who were disposed of simply, issues of finance may have had little relevance; those that survived them just did the best they could. Some people did anticipate the financial worries associated with death by joining a burial *collegium*. This was a type of club into which members made regular contributions. The *collegium* would then pay the expenses of the funeral and provide a tomb. These *collegia* had a social side with regular meetings, internal hierarchies and an enjoyment of 'good wine'. The membership of such *collegia* appears to have been predominantly male; for some members the comradeship offered by the society may have stood in place of family.

3.2 CIL XIV 2112, 20–41

Inscription: AD 136. Lanuvium (Italy).
  See Friggeri 2001: 175–6.
  For a burial society being dissolved due to lack of support see *CIL* III 924–7.

It was voted unanimously that anyone who wishes to enter this society shall pay an entry fee of 100 sesterces and an amphora of good wine and shall pay monthly fees of 5 asses. It was voted also that if anyone has not paid his fees for six months in a row and he then meets death, his claim to burial shall not be upheld even if he has provided for it in his will. It was voted further that upon the death of a member of the society who has regularly paid his fees, there will be due to him 300 sesterces from the treasury. From this amount 50 sesterces will be deducted as a funeral fee to be distributed at the pyre [among the mourners]; the funeral, furthermore, will be performed on foot. It was voted also that if any member dies more than 20 miles from this town and notice is received, three men chosen from the society will be required to go to that place and to arrange for his funeral. They will be required to render a true and honest account to the members, and if they are found guilty of any fraud they shall pay a fourfold fine. They will be given money for the funeral expenses for the deceased, and each in addition will be given 20 sesterces for travel expenses there and back ... [the society will pay expenses to those who bury a member] ... It was voted further that if any slave member of this society dies, and his master or mistress unfairly refuses to hand over his body for burial, and he has not left written instructions, a funeral ceremony will be held for an image of him. It was voted also that if any member takes his own life for whatever reason, his claim to burial shall not be considered. It was voted as well that if any member of this society becomes free, he is required to donate an amphora of good wine.

The fact that such clubs existed suggests that funerals were not cheap. *Collegia* might gain the financial support of wealthy patrons, and the heads of large households could also encourage burial for servile members on the *collegium* model (Patterson 1992). Nevertheless *collegia* still needed regular contributions by members and the budgeting this required may have been beyond the means of the extremely poor and the destitute. It seems likely that many people, especially those with no funds or family, would have gone to their graves in a very simple and basic fashion. In literature we only tend to hear of funeral costs on particularly extravagant occasions. Pliny the Elder (*Natural History* 33.135) tells of a freedman who died in 8 BC who left a fortune in his will, specifying that 1,100,000 sesterces was to be spent on his funeral, while it has been calculated that the 1,000,000 asses allocated for a funeral held in 152 BC (**3.5**) would have supported 800 peasant farmers at subsistence level for a year (Walker 1985: 12). Some epitaphs do record sums of money expended in funeral costs and these range from 500,000 sesterces to 96 sesterces (Duncan-Jones 1982: 128). However, it is often unclear whether these sums refer to the cost of the monument, the funeral or both (**2.36**, **3.29** and **3.62–3.64**). Toward the end of the 1st c. AD the emperor Nerva introduced a funeral grant (*funeraticium*) of 250 sesterces for the Roman plebs. We do not know how long this was paid for or exactly who was eligible (Hopkins 1983: 208). It was probably a short-lived scheme, although in times of crisis assistance with burial might still be given.

3.3 *Scriptores Historiae Augustae*, Marcus Aurelius *13.3*

Biography: 4th c. AD. Events of AD 168.

There was such a great epidemic that the dead were carried out on wagons and carts. At this time, also, the emperors ratified very strict laws on burials and tombs, in which they forbade anyone to build a tomb where he wished, a law which is still in force today. Thousands were carried off by the disease, including many of the leading men, for the most prominent of whom Antoninus set up statues. His goodness of heart was so great too that he ordered funeral ceremonies to be performed for the common people at public expense.

In evaluating the cost we should not lose sight of the fact that organizing a funeral was not just a financial matter, but a familial and emotional duty. Family members wished to be at the deathbed and to fund (if they could afford it) and attend the funeral; it was both their responsibility and part of the mourning process.

3.4 Cicero, In Defence of Cluentius 27

Speech: 66 BC. Cicero is defending Cluentius against a charge of poisoning brought by Oppianicus.

Here Cicero is blackening the name of Oppianicus' family by implying that it was wrong (and suspicious) for a mother to be excluded from her son's final rites.

The very same day the boy, who had been seen in public at the eleventh hour enjoying good health, was dead before nightfall; and before dawn the next day the body had been cremated. As for his mother, she heard of her terrible bereavement by common gossip, before any member of Oppianicus' household had given her the news. At one and the same moment she heard that her son was dead and that it was too late for her to take part in his funeral. Overwhelmed with grief, she went immediately to Larinum and performed the funeral rites all over again, although he was already buried.

Some people may have left specific instructions concerning the arrangements of their funeral. However, Roman wills, which would be the expected avenue, rarely contained such information (Champlin 1991: 171). Instructions may have been transmitted orally or informally to family and friends.

3.5 Livy, Summaries 48

History: late 1st c. BC or early 1st c. AD. Events of 152 BC.

Marcus Aemilius Lepidus was consul, censor and principle senator during the 2nd c. BC.

Compare Seneca's request for a simple funeral (**1.45**). For the *imagines* see **3.65** and **3.66**.

Before he died, Marcus Aemilius Lepidus, who had been chosen to be leader of the senate by six pairs of censors, ordered his sons that they should carry him out for burial on a bier covered with linen but with no purple; and that for the rest of his funeral they should spend no more than a million asses, since the funerals of great men were made noble not by the expense but by the spectacle of the funerary masks [*imagines*].

3.6 Propertius 2.13b, 1–8

Elegiac poetry: 1st c. BC.

The poet is addressing his lover Cynthia, and gives details as to the funeral he would prefer, or more accurately prefer not to have, thus providing insights as to what others might expect to receive at death and the instructions that might be left with loved ones.

Attalus of Pergamum invented a method for weaving golden cloth, see **2.9**.

Therefore, whenever death shall close my eyes, hear the instructions for my funeral which you should observe. Do not let my funeral procession make its way with many masks, nor let there be a trumpet making a vain lament for my end. Do not allow a bed with an ivory pillow to be prepared for me, nor let my dead body lie on a bier embroidered with gold of Attalus. Let there be no procession of incense bearers, but only the humble rites that mark a poor man's funeral.

Undertakers

The family could take responsibility for many parts of the funeral rites but there were professional undertakers available to help (if the bereaved could afford their services). Libitina was the goddess of funerals; she was not worshipped as such but was associated with a grove in Rome, outside the Esquiline Gate, which provided a base for undertakers (*libitinarii*) and where items for burial could be purchased (Bodel 2000: 136–7; 2004). Among the specialists were *pollinctores* who took their name from the practice of placing powder on the face of the deceased to conceal the discolouration of death; *vespillones* who carried coffins and corpses; *fossores* who were grave diggers; and *ustores* who were corpse burners. A *dissignator* might also organize and direct the funeral procession. Contact with the dead made the undertakers an ill-omened and little-respected element of the population. No one looked forward to seeing an undertaker.

3.7 Horace, Epistles 1.7, 3–7

Poetry: late 1st c. BC.

> You show patience when I'm ill; so show patience when I fear becoming ill, when the heat that ripens the first figs brings the undertaker [*dissignator*] out with his black-dressed attendants, when fathers and fond mothers are pale with fear for their children.

3.8 Martial, Epigrams 1.47

Poetry: late 1st c. AD.
See also Martial, *Epigrams* 1.30 and 2.61.

> Diaulus was a doctor until recently; now he's an undertaker's assistant [*vispillo*]. What the undertaker does the doctor used to do.

Those employed in undertaking were of low social status; they were slaves who were despised for their sordid association with the dead. Yet undertaking could be a profitable industry and this added to the negative connotations of the profession since the undertaker gained profit from the grief, misfortune and loss of others (Bodel 2000: 140).

3.9 Valerius Maximus 5.2.10

Memorable deeds and sayings: 1st c. AD. Events of 43 BC.
Aulus Hirtius and Caius Vibius Pansa were killed at Mutina in conflict with Marc Antony. The undertakers showed respect by unusually waiving their fee. See also **4.44**.

> Those who practised undertaking at that time promised the use of both their equipment and their own services without charge, because the two had fallen fighting for the Republic, and by persistent request forced their point that provision of the accessories for the funeral procession be awarded to them for one sesterce. The condition attached to the contract adds to their credit rather than reduces it, in that those who lived for nothing but profit despised profit.

An inscription from the colony of Puteoli sets out regulations for funerals which were normally contracted out to firms of professional undertakers (**3.10**). The same firms were also involved in the punishment and execution of slaves. The inscription suggests some of the taboos surrounding death and the marginal status of those employed in handling dead bodies. By the early Empire it would seem that death was becoming increasingly professionalized, with a need for the relationship between undertakers and clients to be legally acknowledged (Bodel 2004).

3.10 AE 1971, n.88. Column 2, 1–23

Inscription: late 1st c. BC or early 1st c. AD. Puteoli (Pozzuoli, Italy). A record of the regulations concerning funerals that was to be displayed in the undertakers' premises.

= Hinard and Dumont 2003; Gardner and Wiedemann 1991: 25.

To the contractor or to his partner, when anyone abandons [a body] he shall pay a fine of 60 sesterces per corpse, and the magistrate shall enforce judgement for recovery of this sum according to the law of the colony. The workers which shall be provided for this task are not to live on this side of the tower where the grove of Libitina is. They are to take their bath after the first hour of the night. They are not to enter the town except to collect or dispose of corpses, or to inflict a punishment, and then when they enter or are in the town, each of them must wear a colourful cap on his head. None of them is to be over 50 years of age or under 20, nor have any sores, nor be one-eyed, maimed, lame, blind or branded. The contractor should have no less than 32 workers. If anyone wishes to have a male or female slave punished privately, he who wishes to have the punishment inflicted shall act as follows. If he wants to use the cross or fork, the contractor must supply the posts, chains, ropes for floggers and the floggers themselves. The person having the punishment inflicted is to pay the workers who carry the fork, the floggers and the executioner 4 sesterces each. The magistrate shall give orders for such punishments as he hands out in his public role, and when orders are given the contractor is to be ready to inflict the punishment. He is to provide the cross and supply without charge nails, pitch, wax, tapers and anything else that is necessary. If he is ordered to remove the corpse with a hook, the workers are to be dressed in red and ring a bell while dragging away the body, or bodies if there are several. Anyone who wishes to use any of the services listed in this regulation is to notify, or have notification made to the public contractor or to his partner or to the person responsible for the matter concerned, or, if he is absent, to such premises as the contractor shall have hired or established for the work of funeral director, as to the day, place and nature of the service he wishes to have performed. Once notice is given, then the contractor or the person responsible shall carry out the commission for the person who gave notice first, and then for any others in order of receipt of notice; unless notice is received for the funeral of a decurion, or for a mass funeral, since these are to be given precedence. The order of the rest of the funerals, however, shall be followed. They are to send those things whose supply is required by this regulation and supply what is to be supplied. If notice is given of a hanged man, the contractor is to act and remove the body within the hour. The same is true for a male or female slave. If notice is received before the tenth hour, removal is to be done the same day; if after the tenth hour, then before the second hour the following day.

The moment of death

Roman funeral rituals were a process that both removed the deceased from the world of the living and guided the behaviour of the bereaved survivors. The dying might attempt to exert individual preferences (by will, personal instructions or financial savings) and the bereaved to distance themselves by employing undertakers, but events from deathbed to grave were supposed to follow a certain pattern and people conform to expected roles. The process began with the moment of death, which was itself imbued with idealized expectations. How people faced death, well or badly, was a common theme in Latin literature (**1.53–1.59**). However, few of these literary accounts probably resemble the reality of dying for the majority of the population. Most of the sources represent the wealthy, largely male élite, and the deaths are often notable because they entail violence, murder, execution, death in battle or suicide (see Chapter 1). Mundane deaths are little commented upon. There are some exceptions. The Letters of the Younger Pliny, for example, contain some descriptions of the illnesses and demise of his friends and their relatives. These letters often refer to legacy-hunters who haunted the deathbeds of the wealthy (**2.31**) or focus on the bravery of the dying person in the face of illness (**1.18** and **5.27**). Deathbed behaviour is idealized and the emphasis is on meeting death well rather than on the pain and suffering which must have characterized the final moments of many. The poet Statius also idealizes the deathbed, but in his description of the final moments of Priscilla he does capture some of the discomforts and uncertainties of death (**3.11**), the suffering of the dying woman, the numbing of her senses, the bewilderment of her husband and a general sense of sadness and despair.

3.11 Statius, Silvae 5.1, 155–98

Poetry: late 1st c. AD. The poem was written in memory of Priscilla, the wife of Abascantus, who served the emperor Domitian.
    For Statius' laments see Chapter 5.

> On all sides the dark snares of death surround the poor woman; the Sisters' [the Fates] harsh threads are tightened, and only the final part of the exhausted thread remains. The crowds of slaves and the doctors' hard-working skills bring no relief to her suffering. Those present still look hopeful, but she notes her husband weeping ... [the husband begs the gods to save her] ... Now her face falls, and her

eyes take their final glances, her ears are dulled, except she recognizes only her husband's voice. Returning from the midst of death, her mind sees only him. She embraces him tightly with frail arms, as her lifeless eyes meet his. Not with the final light but with her dear husband does she prefer to fill her eyes. Then dying she comforts her true love ... [Priscilla comforts her husband] ... As she says this she slips away, and without reluctance sends her dying breath into her husband's mouth and he closes her eyes with his dead hand. But the young man's heart is inflamed with a mighty grief and he fills his empty home with a fierce shout.

The sources provide us with some insights into the customs, or at least expected behaviour, associated with the deathbed. To die well it was important to be surrounded by family. Statius has the dying Priscilla attended by her husband, friends, slaves and doctors (**3.11**); Livia was at Augustus' side (**1.55**) and sadly not at that of her son Drusus (**5.5**). A relative or close friend should hear the last words, and give a final kiss to catch the last breath of the deceased, before closing the dead person's eyes and calling out their name (*conclamatio*). The perfect and moving death scene was occasionally even idealized in funerary art (**3.12**). However, it is ironic that some of the best insights into the moment of death, and funeral rituals in general, come from situations that did not conform to the ideal; situations where family members were ignorant of an impending death, or individuals were isolated or where the expected norms of behaviour were transgressed (**3.13, 3.14, 3.18, 3.39, 3.41, 3.42, 3.48, 3.49**). People were deprived, or worried that they would be deprived, of the desired familiar elements that would make for a good, or at least a better, death and funeral. Deviation from the norm (that is the élite well-to-do norm) could be striking and even abhorrent.

3.12 *Figure 3: A child's deathbed*

Front panel of a marble sarcophagus: late 2nd c. AD. Rome (now in the British Museum). 47 x 105 x 40 cm.
    = Walker 1990: n.6.
    A dead girl lies on a high-backed couch (*kline*). Beneath the couch are a dog and a foot stool with the girl's slippers. Mourners flank the couch. The two seated figures, both holding their heads in grief, may represent the girl's parents. Closest to the couch are three female figures with their arms either outstretched or held up. This gesture may represent the *conclamatio,* or the calling out of the name of the deceased with arms upraised, that was supposed to follow closely after a death. For similar examples see Huskinson 1996, figure 3.

Figure 3 A marble sarcophagus depicting a child's deathbed, Rome. Photograph: copyright British Museum.

3.13 Ovid, Tristia 3.3, 37–46

Poetry: early 1st c. AD. Ovid is in exile and thus removed from his family. Compare **3.49**.

> So far away, then, on an unknown shore will I die, and the very place will make my fate unhappy. My body will not grow weak upon a familiar couch, and when I am close to death there will be no one to weep; my wife's tears will not fall upon my face adding brief moments to my life. I will not utter final words, nor with a final lament will a loved hand close my failing eyes. Instead without funeral rites, without the honour of a tomb, this head will lie unmourned in a barbarian land.

3.14 Lucan, Civil War 3, 737–47

Poetry: 1st c. AD.

Argus is a casualty on his father's ship during a naval battle between Caesar's forces and the ships of Massilia (49 BC). His father views it as an unnatural thing, especially in the context of civil war, for a son to predecease his father and therefore commits suicide rather than perform the final rites for his son.

> The son, at the sight of his father, raised his falling head and failing neck; no voice came from the opening of his throat, he could only seek a kiss with a silent look and invite his father's hands to close his eyes. When the old man recovered from his shock and cruel grief

began to take hold, he said 'I will not waste the time granted by the ruthless gods, but will use it to cut this old throat. Argus forgive your miserable father for refusing your last embrace and final kiss. The warm blood is still flowing from your wounds and you lie there still breathing; it is still possible that you will survive me'.

Dramatic displays of grief might accompany the death or the moments immediately after; wailing, the tearing of clothes, the beating of breasts, scratching of cheeks, pulling of hair and the discoloration of the latter with dirt and ashes (**3.15**, **3.20**). However, a death might also be accompanied by a shocked and disbelieving silence, before the wailing commenced.

3.15 Virgil, Aeneid 12, 604–11

Epic poetry: late 1st c. BC. The queen of the Latins has committed suicide, believing Turnus, her preferred choice of husband for her daughter, to be dead at the hands of Aeneas.
See also *Aeneid* 10.840–5.

> When the unhappy women of Latium heard of this disaster, her daughter Lavinia was the first to tear her golden hair and rosy cheeks. The whole household was in a frenzy of grief around her, and their lamentations echoed through the palace. From there the sad news spread through the whole city and hearts sank everywhere. Latinus went with his clothes torn, dazed by the death of his wife and the downfall of the city, soiling his grey hair with handfuls of dirt and dust.

3.16 Lucan, Civil War 2, 21–8

Poetry: mid 1st c. AD. Lucan is describing the impact of civil war on the inhabitants of Rome and compares it with the powerful and private moment for the bereaved before the public displays of grief begin.
Compare Catullus 64.349–351.

> Men restrained their lamentations and a deep silent grief overtook the people. Just as at the moment of death a household is shocked and speechless before the body is lamented over and laid out, and before the mother with dishevelled hair calls her maids to beat their breasts with cruel arms; the mother still clings to the limbs stiff with the loss of life and the still face with eyes fierce in death. She feels no fear, but not yet grief; not thinking she wonders at her loss.

Preparing the body

After the death the body needed to be prepared for the funeral. As noted above, initially the eyes were closed, the name of the deceased called out and the household began its display of grief. The body may have been moved to ensure that all signs of life were gone (Servius, *On Virgil's Aeneid* 6.218), before being washed in warm water. The body was then anointed, dressed, and garlanded by the women of the house or male *pollinctores* (**3.17**, **3.18** and **3.20**). A plaster cast mould of the face of the deceased may have been made at this stage, perhaps for use in subsequent portraits. A few examples of these death masks have been found interred with the deceased, but most masks were probably taken while people lived and were used for statue production rather than as part of funerary ritual (Carroll 2006: 37–9), with the exception that is of the *imagines* of the élite (see below).

3.17 Virgil, Aeneid 6, 218–20

Epic poetry: 1st c. BC. Preparations prior to the funeral of the Trojan Misenus.

> Some lit fires beneath the cauldrons to boil water and they washed and anointed the cold body of their friend and lamented. When they had wept enough, they placed him on the bier and covered him with his own purple robes.

3.18 Virgil, Aeneid 9, 485–90

Epic poetry: 1st c. BC. Lamentation of the mother of the Trojan Euryalus. Compare *Aeneid* 4, 671–89.

> So now you lie in a strange land, and your body is prey for the dogs and the birds of Latium! I am your mother and did not lead your funeral procession; nor close your eyes, nor bathe your wounds, nor cover you with the robe I have been weaving for you day and night with what speed I could, finding in my loom some comfort for the cares of age.

The dishevelled appearance of the mourners and their dark clothing contrasted with the appearance of the deceased. The corpse would be dressed in the best clothes available. Male citizens would have worn their togas. Juvenal joked that in his day nobody wore a toga except after death (*Satire* 3, 171). For the poor a simple shroud of cloth or old clothes would have sufficed. Martial (*Epigrams* 9.57.8) speaks of the 'yellowing gown of a dead pauper', but if possible the emphasis was on display, expensive clothes for the body and, where applicable, the insignia of office (**3.58**; and Cicero,

On the Laws 2.24.60). Once dressed, and prior to the funeral, the body was laid on the funeral couch (*lectus funebris*) in the atrium of the house, or at least somewhere suitable for its display. Perfumes would be burned and flowers, symbolizing the fragility of life, scattered around the corpse. Laments and dirges may have been spoken or sung and a coin placed in the mouth of the deceased to pay the ferryman (**1.22**). For the poor the display of the corpse was unlikely, and bodies were probably disposed of rapidly. But for the wealthy, and the moderately wealthy, the exhibition of the dead was a display of status.

3.19 Figure 4: Relief from the tomb of the Haterii

Funerary relief: late 1st c. AD. Rome (via Labicana), now held in the Vatican museums.

= Sinn and Freyberger 1996: n. 5.

Several ornately carved panels survive from the tomb which may have belonged to a building contractor by the name of Haterius. On this panel a deceased woman is laid out on a bed with a double mattress. The bed is surrounded by torches and at the foot is a flute player. Behind the bed a male figure holds out a garland toward the deceased and two female figures beat their breasts. At the bottom of the scene in front of the bier, and shown in smaller scale, are further mourning figures. To the right of these are three figures wearing the pointed caps of recently freed slaves.

Figure 4 Relief from the tomb of the Haterii, Rome. Photograph: copyright Alinari.

3.20 Lucian, On Funerals 11–15

Satirical essay: 2nd c. AD. An exaggerated description of the preparation of the body, its display and the dramatic laments of the survivors.

Note this is set in a Graeco-Roman context, although Lucian does go on to claim that 'the same stupid custom prevails everywhere' (*On Funerals* 21).

Compare Persius, *Satire* 3.98–106.

Then they wash them (as if the lake in Hades was not large enough for people there to wash in). Having anointed the body, which is already speeding to decay, with fine perfumes, and crowning it with beautiful flowers, they lay the dead in state, dressed in splendid clothes, which, most likely, are thought to stop them from getting cold on the journey and from being seen naked by Cerberus. Next come cries of distress, wailing women, weeping everywhere, the beating of breasts, tearing of hair and blood marked cheeks. Sometimes clothing is torn into strips and dust sprinkled on the head. And so the living are more pitiable than the dead, for they roll repeatedly on the ground and beat their heads against the floor, while the dead man, calm and handsome, elaborately garlanded with wreaths, lies in a lofty and exalted state, decorated as if for a pageant. Then his mother, or even his father, comes forward from among the crowd of relatives and throws himself upon the body. For let us imagine that a handsome young man is upon the bier, to make the drama more moving. The father makes strange and foolish cries, to which the dead man would answer if he could speak. In a plaintive tone, dragging out every word, he says, 'Dearest child, you are gone from me, dead, taken before your time, leaving me behind all alone and grieving, before marriage, before having children, before serving in the army, before working the farm, before reaching old age! Never again will you walk the streets at night, or fall in love, or get drunk at parties with your young friends.' He will say these things and more in the same tone, believing that his son still needs and wants this sort of thing after death, but cannot get it. But this is nothing. Many have sacrificed horses, concubines, and even servants, with their dead, and burned or buried clothing and other personal items, as if the dead would use them or benefit from them down below. But the old man who mourns in this fashion with all the melodramatic ranting that I have described, and more besides, probably does not do it on his son's account. For he knows that his son will not hear him, however loud he shouts. Nor is it on his own account since it would be enough to think these things and have them in mind without shouting; nobody needs to shout at himself. So it is on account of the others present that he talks this nonsense.

The funeral procession

The body had to be transported from the home to the site of cremation or the grave since this would be located without the town walls. Friends and family followed the body. The splendour of the cortège (*pompa*) depended on the status of the deceased and their family and the ultimate destination of the body. For funerals of the élite the body was taken to the *Forum Romanum* for the funeral speech (see below) and may have been accompanied by much pomp. Most bodies were probably taken direct to the cemetery and any rites were conducted at the grave or pyre. The funeral procession could be a noisy spectacle. Musicians led the way with trumpets, horns and flutes announcing the presence of the corpse (**3.6**, **3.58**, **3.61** and **3.70**; Pliny, *Natural History* 10.121; Suetonius, *Julius Caesar* 84).

3.21 Figure 5: Relief of a funeral procession

Funerary relief: mid 1st c. BC. Amiternum (Aquila, Italy). Held at the Museo dell'Aquila.

The panel depicts a funeral cortège. The linear progression of the event is represented not horizontally but vertically by stacking groups of participants. The deceased lies on a bier with a double mattress that is shouldered by eight pallbearers. Around the bier is a canopy decorated with the moon and stars. Behind the bier follow nine mourners, the lowermost carrying a container, probably for incense. Immediately in front of the bier are two women, possibly hired mourners, one pulling at her hair, the other with her arms upraised in grief. Two tiers of musicians head the procession, including three horn players and four flute players.

Figure 5 Relief of a funeral procession, Aquila. Photograph: copyright Alinari.

Funeral processions originally may have been held at night, hence the role of torches (see **Figure 4**), although the torches may have been 'magical protectors' (Rose 1923: 194). By the mid Republic night-time funerals were the norm only for children.

3.22 *Servius,* On Virgil's Aeneid *11, 143*

Commentary on Virgil: 4th c. AD.

> And it is the custom of the Romans to carry children out for burial at night by the light of torches so that the house does not go into mourning at the funeral rites of a minor.

3.23 *Seneca,* On the Shortness of Life *20.5*

Philosophical (Stoic) treatise: *c.* AD 49.
  See also Seneca, *Madness of Hercules* 849–74.

> No one keeps death in sight, no one holds back from far-reaching hopes. Indeed some men even arrange things that are beyond life, great masses of tombs and dedications of public works and gifts for their pyres and ostentatious funeral rites. But, in truth, the funerals of such men ought to be led by the light of torches and wax tapers, as if they had lived only the shortest time.

3.24 *Tacitus,* Annals *13.17*

History: early 2nd c. AD. Events of AD 55. The emperor Nero rapidly disposes of the body of his stepbrother, Britannicus.
  Compare **3.4**.

> The same night united Britannicus' death and pyre. Indeed preparations for his modest funeral had already been made. His remains were buried on the Campus Martius [in the mausoleum of Augustus] in a terrible rain storm ... [Tacitus notes the outrages to which the boy had been subjected] ... Nero defended the speed of the funeral by an edict referring to the traditional custom of removing these untimely deaths from the public gaze and not prolonging things with speeches and processions.

The body was transported by means of a bier (**Figure 5**). This could be a simple structure of wood or might be elaborately decorated with ivory panels and bronze handles (Noy 2000a: 39–40). For the poor, a combined stretcher and coffin was used called the *sandapila*. Use of a *sandapila*, with its narrow shape and lowly bearers, could be an insult (sometimes in jest) to the well-to-do or those with social aspirations.

3.25 Suetonius, Domitian 17

Biography: early 2nd c. AD. Events of AD 96, following the assassination of the emperor Domitian.

The hasty burial and the use of a *sandapila* added to the indignity of his end. See also **2.61**.

> The body was carried away on a common bier [*sandapila*] by under-takers [*vespillones*] who bury the poor, and was cremated by his nurse Phyllis at her suburban estate on the via Latina. She secretly carried the ashes to the Temple of the Flavians and mixed them with those of Julia [Domitian's niece], daughter of Titus, who had also been one of her charges.

3.26 Martial, Epigrams 2.81 and 8.75

Poetry: late 1st c. AD.

> Zoilus, your litter may be more spacious than a litter with six bearers, however since it is yours, Zoilus, it is a pauper's bier [*sandapila*].

> [Having fallen down] What was Gallus to do, how was he to move? Only one little slave attended the large master, so emaciated that he could barely carry a small lamp. Chance came to the wretch's rescue and brought help. Four branded men were carrying a corpse of low status, the unhappy pyre receives thousands like it, and the feeble slave begged them humbly to carry the lifeless body where ever they wished. The load is changed and the great bulk squashed into the narrow bier [*sandapila*] and carried high.

The *sandapila* was carried by four bearers of servile status, whereas those who could afford it were placed on a bier carried by eight bearers, drawn from members of the family of the deceased. It was an honour for sons, close relatives and heirs to carry the dead. The more distinguished the deceased the more distinguished the bearers might be (**3.27**). Freed slaves, especially those who had been freed by the will, might also be used as bearers. Some sources suggest that slaves might be freed via the will to swell the numbers of those following the deceased to the graveside (**3.28**). Indeed the emperor Augustus placed a limit on the number of slaves that could be freed in a last will and testament. For the funeral to be well attended was, to some at least, a symbol of worldly prestige and success and on a few occasions was boasted of in epitaphs (**3.29**).

3.27 *Valerius Maximus 7.1*

Memorable deeds and sayings: 1st c. AD.

Quintus Metellus Macedonicus, consul in 143 BC, was a prominent general and politician in the 2nd c. BC. Pliny the Elder adds that among his bearers were a praetor, three ex-consuls and one ex-censor, a distinction that 'singly have fallen to a few' (*Natural History* 7.44).

See also Cicero, *Tusculan Disputations* 1.25.85.

> This life was followed by an end to match it. Metellus, having lived a great span of old age, died a gentle death amid the kisses and embraces of his dearest children, and his sons and sons-in-law carried him though the city on their shoulders and placed him on the pyre.

3.28 *Dionysius of Halicarnassus,* **Roman Antiquities 4.24.6**

History: late 1st c. BC.

> I know of some men who have allowed all their slaves to be freed after their death, in order that they might be called good when they were dead and that many people might follow their biers wearing their caps of liberty.

3.29 *CIL VI 6221*

Epitaph: mid 1st c. AD. Rome (Columbarium of the Statilii)

> [name lost] here he lies. 130 companions conducted his funeral at a cost of 900 sesterces. Maximus, Helicon and Daphnus made this.

Those following the body of the deceased would have been distinguished by their mode of dress. Plutarch notes that sons covered their heads when escorting their parents to the grave, while daughters had their heads uncovered and hair unbound (Plutarch, *Roman Questions* 14). The colour for the dress of the bereaved was black or dark. Horace (**3.7**) refers to the black clothes of undertaker's assistants. Tacitus speaks of people donning dark mourning clothes following the death of Germanicus (Tacitus, *Annals* 3.2; see also Juvenal, *Satires* 3.212). Cicero also speaks of dark clothing and its unsuitability in certain contexts. It seems that black was suited to the funeral and procession but not to the banquet held later, at which white was the expected colour.

3.30 Cicero, Against Vatinius 30–2

Speech: 56 BC.

Cicero alleges that Publius Vatinius wore inappropriate clothes at the funeral celebration which Quintus Arrius held in honour of his father. Vatinius was making a political protest by offending his host and violating religious custom (Heskell 1994: 141).

See also Horace, *Satire* 2.3.86. For white as the colour of mourning see Plutarch, *Moralia* 270.

> Another thing I should also like to learn from you: what was your plan, what was your intention, in being present in a dark toga [*toga pulla*] at the funeral banquet given by my friend Quintus Arrius? Have you ever seen, ever heard of anyone presenting himself on such occasion in such dress? What example, what custom made you do it? ... [Cicero continues to question Vatinius' behaviour] ... Although so many thousands were reclining at table, and the master of the feast himself, Quintus Arrius, was all in white, you took yourself to the Temple of Castor in funeral clothes, with Gaius Fibulus and your other evil spirits in black [*atratus*].

Laments and speeches

The exact nature of the rituals or ceremonies performed once the grave was reached is unclear. Was there some sort of equivalent of a religious service? Did words and actions follow a predetermined pattern? We know that, for those with friends and family to mourn them, a funeral speech (*laudatio*) was a common element. These speeches may have developed from dirges (Kierdorf 1980). It was the traditional role of women to wail at the funeral, and to raise dirges and laments which may have been accompanied by music (**3.31**). Note how tributes were sung at Caesar's funeral (**3.68**). By the late Republic, hired professionals, mainly women, monopolized the displays of extreme grief, while praising the deceased in a speech became the preserve of male relatives (see below). The hired mourners were performers who were expected to make a dramatic show of grief, adding to the spectacle of the funeral (**3.32**).

3.31 Varro, On the Latin Language 7.70

A study of language: 1st c. BC.

See also Varro, *On the Life of the Roman People* 3.110.

> *Praefica* 'praise-leader', as Aurelius writes, was a woman from the grove of Libitina who was hired to sing the praises of the dead man in front of his house.

3.32 *Horace,* The Art of Poetry *429–33*

Poetry: late 1st c. BC. Here Horace is distinguishing between a poet's false and true friends.

> He will grow pale over them; he will even let tears fall from his friendly eyes, he will dance and thump the ground with his foot. As those hired to weep at a funeral say and do almost more than those who grieve from the heart, so the man who mocks is more moved than a true admirer.

For the majority of the population any commemorative speech would have been made at the grave or pyre and probably focused on the family and its loss. Lucian's account of a father's lament for his son is evocative (**3.20**). It needs to be noted that this was written for satirical effect and as part of the 'lying-in-state', but it still evokes, in exaggerated form, the types of things that may have been said about the deceased. Lucian's account can be contrasted with Polybius' description of an élite Republican funeral (**3.65**). Whereas Polybius emphasizes the celebration of public duty and service, Lucian parodies a more personal sense of loss. The difference is due to genre, but may also reflect shifting attitudes between Republic and Empire from the public to private spheres (see Bodel 1999b). Indeed, for the élite of the Republic the funeral speech would have been made by a close relative in the forum and could contain an overt political element, praising both the deceased and the family. Under the emperors the speeches for great men were often delivered by fellow great men, blunting the role of the speech as a political tool of the surviving family. However, in both Republic and Empire part of the act of commemorating the deceased could be the preservation of the speech for posterity; eulogies could be recorded and published, as could more cathartic poetic laments for the dead (see Chapter 5). These writings became part of the historical legacy of the great and the good (see Chapter 2).

3.33 *Pliny the Elder,* Natural History *7.139–40*

Natural history: 1st c. AD. Pliny is quoting from a eulogy delivered more than 200 years earlier.
Lucius Caecilius Metellus died in 221 BC. His son became consul in 205 BC.

> Quintus Metellus in a speech that he delivered in final praise of his father Lucius Metellus the pontiff, who had been consul twice, Dictator, Master of the Horse and a land commissioner, and who was the first person to display elephants in a triumphal procession having captured them in the first Punic War, has left it in writing that his father had achieved the ten greatest and best things which

wise men spend their whole lives seeking. He had wished to be a first class warrior, the best of orators, the bravest of commanders; to be in charge of important matters and held in great honour; to possess supreme wisdom and be regarded as the most eminent member of the senate; to obtain great wealth in an honourable way; to leave many children; and to be the most distinguished person in the state. He had achieved these things and no one else had done so since Rome was founded.

Elements of the funeral speech could also be incorporated into the inscriptions that adorned funeral memorials. Two long inscriptions honouring women, Turia (so-called) and Murdia (**2.26**), appear to preserve elements of such speeches. These women were well-to-do so we can question how representative these eulogies are, but the general tone of praising the dead and bemoaning their loss may well capture the overall nature of such eulogies. We can contrast the nature of these speeches with Tacitus' summary of the speech given by Nero in honour of Poppaea (**3.41**); Tacitus implies that Poppaea had no genuine virtues to be praised!

3.34 CIL VI 1527, 31670 (Laudatio Turiae), left hand column, 27–36

Inscription: late 1st c. BC. Rome.
  = *ILS* 8393; Wistrand 1976; Ramage 1994.
  The exact identity of the woman described is uncertain, but she belonged to the senatorial classes during the triumviral period. The inscription appears to record a eulogy delivered by the husband. As well as praising the woman's virtues and loyalty to her family, the inscription also details elements of her life story, including how she helped save her husband during the proscriptions.

> Marriages as long as ours are rare, marriages that are ended by death and not by divorce. We had the good fortune to live together without argument for a full forty years. I wish that our long marriage had come to its final end through something that had happened to me instead of you; it would have been more just for me, who was older, to yield to fate. Why should I mention your personal virtues: your loyalty, obedience, affability, good nature, industry in working wool, adherence to religion without superstition, simplicity of dress and modesty of appearance? Why speak about your love for your relatives, your devotion to your family? You have shown the same care to my mother as you did to your own parents, and ensured an equally peaceful life for her as you did for your own relatives. You have countless other virtues in common with all Roman matrons, worthy of that name. It is

your very own virtues that I claim for you; few people have possessed such virtues or been known to possess them. Fate has made such hard tests rare.

Cremation and inhumation

Different methods for the disposal of the corpse were known of and practised during the Roman period. Lucretius asserts that bodies could be inhumed, cremated or embalmed and for a philosopher who believed that death was not an evil it all amounted to the same thing (3.35). However, most people did care about what happened to their bodies and to those of their loved ones, as the fear of corpse abuse so well indicates (1.58, 3.37, 3.40 and 4.49–4.51). Equally, how a culture treated its dead could be seen as one of its characteristic features (3.36); thus an aspect of Roman identity was how the dead were disposed of.

3.35 Lucretius, On Nature 3, 870–93

Philosophical (Epicurean) poetry: 1st c. BC.

> When you find a man complaining at his lot, that after death he will either rot away in the grave or be destroyed by flames or the jaws of wild beasts, be sure that his words do not ring true ... [people imagine that they can still feel after death] ... He does not see that in real death there will be no other self alive to mourn his own loss; no other self standing by to feel pain at the agony he suffers lying being mauled or burned. For if it is really an evil after death to be mauled by the jaws of animals, I cannot see why it is not painful to roast in the hot flames of a funeral pyre, or to lie embalmed in honey, stifled and stiff with cold, on top of an icy rock, or to be crushed under a heavy weight of earth.

3.36 Cicero, Tusculan Disputations 1.45.108

Philosophical dialogue: 45 BC.
  Compare Lucian, On Funerals 21.

> The Egyptians embalm their dead and keep them in the house; the Persians even cover them with wax before burial, so that the bodies may last for as long as possible; it is the custom of the Magi not to bury the bodies of their dead unless they have first been torn to pieces by wild animals.

The most basic requirement, in terms of disposal, was that the corpse should be covered with earth or, in the case of cremation, that a fraction of it (*os resectum*) was removed prior to incineration for later burial. The exact significance of severing a bone in the rite *os resectum* is unclear, and Varro implies that it may have been connected to the purification of the living rather than the dead (**3.38**; Graham forthcoming). For the dead it was a covering of earth that ensured the deceased a respected place of burial (*locus religiosus*).

3.37 Cicero, On the Laws 2.22.55–57

Dialogue on law: *c.* 43 BC.

Cyrus was a Persian king and conqueror of the 6th c. BC; Xenephon (5th c. BC) was his biographer. Numa was the legendary second king of Rome (*c.* 715–673 BC). The tomb of the Cornelii Scipiones still survives off the via Appia and contains stone sarcophagi of the 2nd and 1st c. BC. Sulla (see **1.27** and **3.61**) and Marius were rivals for power in Rome during the 80s BC, although Marius died from natural causes in 86 BC. Ennius was a playwright and poet who wrote a eulogizing poem to Publius Cornelius Scipio Africanus (died 184 BC).

It is not necessary for me to explain when the family mourning is ended, what type of sacrifice of a sow is offered to the Lar, in what way the severed bone [*os resectum*] is buried in the earth, what are the rules in regard to the need to sacrifice a sow, or when the grave becomes a grave with the protection of religion. But in my opinion the most ancient form of burial was that which according to Xenephon, was used for Cyrus. For the body is returned to the earth, and placed and laid to rest as if its mother's covering were drawn over it. The same rites, according to tradition, were used for our own King Numa in that tomb which is not far from the altar of Fons, and we know from our own memory that this method is used by the Cornelian clan. The victorious Sulla ordered the remains of Marius, which had been buried, to be thrown into the river Anio, for he was motivated by a hatred more cruel than he could have entertained if he had been as wise as he was bitter. Perhaps it was through fear that the same might happen to him that Sulla, for the first time in the history of the patrician Cornelii, ordered his body to be cremated. For Ennius says of Africanus, 'Here is he laid'; and accurately so for 'laid' is used of those who are buried. However, their places of burial do not really become graves until the rites are performed and the pig is killed. And the expression that is now used concerning all who are buried, that is that they are 'laid in the earth', was then confined to those cases where earth was cast upon the bodies and covered them, and this custom is confirmed by the laws of the pontiffs. For until earth is placed upon the remains, the place where a body is cremated is not religious.

3.38 Varro, On the Latin Language 5.23

A study of language: late 1st c. BC.

> And because *humus* 'soil' is *terra* 'earth', therefore a dead man who is covered with *terra* is *humatus* 'inhumed'. For when a Roman is cremated and then buried and clods of earth are not thrown over the grave, or if a bone of a dead man has been kept to purify the family, the household remains in mourning. In the latter case the bone is purified by a covering of earth.

Inadequate burial, for the corpse to be abandoned and uncared for, was an insult to the dead. Proper burial was associated with religious belief, especially since the spirits of those who had not received sufficient rites might wander and menace the living (see Chapter 6). To bury the dead with due care and attention was also to remove a potential source of pollution and to act with compassion and humanity (Ulpian, *Digest* 11.7.14.7). Even a token burial of just a few handfuls of earth could suffice and be of great significance.

3.39 Horace, Odes 1.28 (2), 10–6

Poetry: late 1st c. BC. Horace imagines an unburied drowned sailor addressing a passer-by.
See also **2.5**.

> Do you believe that this neglect is a small wrong, when afterwards it will harm your children? Perhaps the need for burial and recompense for a similar wrong may await you some day. I shall not be left with my prayer unanswered, and for you no offering shall make amends. Although you are eager to be going, it will not take long. Throw over three handfuls of earth, then hurry away.

Both inhumation and cremation were practised in Rome and the provinces. The early laws enshrined in the Twelve Tables (*c.* 450 BC) assumed that both rites were possible. By the 1st c. BC cremation appears to have been the most commonly practised rite in Rome, although inhumation was retained by some of the older families. Why cremation became more popular at this time is unclear; ancient commentators note the precedent set by Sulla and issues surrounding the desecration of inhumation graves (**3.37** and **3.40**). Cremation was to become so standard that any variation was seen as unusual (**3.41**).

3.40 Pliny the Elder, Natural History 7.54.187

Natural history: 1st c. AD.
  For Sulla see **1.27**, **3.61** and **3.37**.

> Cremation is not actually an old custom at Rome: formerly bodies
> were buried. However, cremation was adopted after it became
> known that the bodies of those fallen in foreign wars were some-
> times dug up again. Many families, however, still observed the old
> rites; for example, it is recorded that no one in the Cornelian family
> was cremated before Sulla the dictator who requested this because,
> having disinterred the body of Gaius Marius, he was afraid that
> others might do the same to him.

3.41 Tacitus, Annals 16.6

History: late 1st c. AD. Events of AD 66, the disposal of the emperor Nero's
wife, Poppaea.
  The Julian mausoleum was the tomb of Augustus, see **4.20** and **4.21**. See
also **3.44**. Compare **5.44** where inhumation is described as a Greek custom.

> The body was not cremated in the Roman fashion, but in the tradi-
> tion of foreign courts was embalmed by stuffing with spices and
> then was interred in the Julian mausoleum. However a public
> funeral was held. The emperor himself on the rostra and in the
> absence of real virtues, praised her looks, her parenthood of a
> deified infant, and other gifts of fortune.

While cremation flourished in the 1st c. BC and 1st c. AD in Rome and
many parts of the empire, there were exceptions. There were no laws against
inhumation; the Jews of Rome probably continued to practice inhumation
(Noy 1998) and from its beginnings the Christian community always practised inhumation, and denied that it was an innovation. Inhumation was
probably always used in some parts of Italy and elsewhere in the empire,
especially in the east (Morris 1992: 48–53). The overall shift back toward
inhumation started at Rome in the early 2nd century AD and spread to the
provinces. During the 3rd c. inhumation came to be virtually universally
practised (Morris 1992: 68). The exact reasons for the change remain
unclear, but a change in fashion rather than a change in beliefs seems most
likely (Nock 1932), although the belief systems did accommodate the
change. In inhumation the body was placed directly in the ground, wrapped
in a simple shroud or encased in a coffin made of wood, lead or stone. The
bodies of Jews and early Christians might be placed on shelves (*loculi*) cut in
the rock walls of hypogea and catacombs. Items or grave goods (see below)
might also be placed with the deceased. Large and heavy stone sarcophagi

could be located above ground or within tombs; this was especially the case with ornately decorated examples since the fine sculpture could then be viewed (**Figure 3**).

At the pyre

In cremation the body, still on the bier, was placed on a pyre constructed of wooden logs, each layer being placed at right angles to the previous one (Vitruvius 2.19.5); kindling wood, papyrus and incense might also be added to help the flames take hold (Noy 2000a: 36–8). Prior to the ignition of the pyre, by a close family member, the body may have been kissed and anointed (**1.52** and **3.42**). The eyes of the deceased were also opened (**3.43**).

3.42 Lucan, Civil War 8, 729–58

Epic poetry: mid 1st c. AD. Pompey was murdered in Egypt in 48 BC.
  Lucan imagines the disposal of Pompey and what he was deprived of, thereby providing insights into pyre construction and cremation.

He prayed 'Fortune, here lies your Pompey. He does not request a costly pyre heaped with incense to give off a rich smoke of eastern perfumes to waft up to the stars. Nor does he ask that noble Romans should carry on their shoulders the father of his country; nor that the trophies won in his triumphs should be displayed; nor that the forum should be filled with sorrowful music; nor that a whole army should drop its arms and march round the burning pyre. But grant to Pompey the simplest bier of a pauper's funeral and put the mutilated body on unfed fires. Do not let the unlucky body lack wood or a sordid man to light the pyre. Be content, you mighty gods, that Cornelia does not lie prostrate with dishevelled hair, does not embrace her husband and order the torch to be lit. Pompey's unhappy wife, although not far from the shore, is unable to pay her last tribute to the dead.' When he had said this the young man saw at a distance a weak fire that was burning an uncared for and unguarded corpse. ... [Cordus disturbs the cremation] ... Cordus filled his lap with burning embers and rushed back to the corpse, which as it lay upon the shore had almost been carried away by a wave. He scraped away some sand and in a narrow trench quickly placed pieces of a broken boat that he had gathered at a distance. That noble corpse was not placed on oak beams, the limbs did not lie on a platform. The flames that engulfed Pompey's body did not lie beneath him but beside him.

3.43 *Pliny the Elder,* Natural History *11.55.150*

Natural history: 1st c. AD.

> There is an important sacred rite among the Romans to close the eyes of the dying and to open them again on the pyre, for customs suggest that it is not right for the eyes to be seen by a human at the final moment and that it is also wrong for the eyes not to be displayed to the heavens.

Pyres could be elaborate, at least for those with money and status, and Pliny the Elder suggests that they could even be painted (Pliny, *Natural History* 35.49). The pyres of the emperors were large, multi-layered structures designed to turn the cremation into an eye-catching spectacle (**3.69**). An element of expensive display could be the use of perfumes and incense in the pyre; these assisted combustion and also disguised odours.

3.44 *Pliny the Elder,* Natural History *12.41.83*

Natural history: 1st c. AD.
For Poppaea see also **3.41**.

> Luxury has made them [cinnamon and cassia] sacred even at people's deaths. They are thought to have been made by the gods for burning with the dead. Those knowledgeable about the matter have said that more than a year's supply was burned by the Emperor Nero on the last day of his wife Poppaea. It is estimated that throughout the entire world every year as much is given at funerals, heaped and piled in honour of the corpse, as is given little by little to the gods.

3.45 *Statius,* Silvae 2.6, 84–93

Poetry: late 1st c. AD. A lament for a favourite slave of Flavius Ursus.

> No servile flames for you. The fire consumed fragrant forests of incense and saffron, and cinnamon stolen from the Phoenix, and the juices that drip from Assyrian herbs, as well as your master's tears. Only these did the ashes consume, and the pyre did not stop drinking them. Nor was the wine that quenched the ashes, nor the smooth onyx that guarded his bones more welcome to the unhappy shade than these tears.

3.46 Martial, Epigrams 10.97 and 11.54

Poetry: late 1st c. AD.
Compare also Statius, *Silvae* 2.1.159–62.

> When the insubstantial pyre was being built with papyrus that was
> soon to be burned and his tearful wife was buying myrrh and cassia.
> When the grave, the bier and undertaker [*pollinctor*] were prepared,
> Numa put me down as heir. He recovered.

> Shameless Zoilus, empty your dirty pockets of the unguents and
> the cassia and the myrrh smelling of funerals and the half-cremated
> frankincense you took from the pyre and the cinnamon you
> snatched from the Stygian couch.

Pyres could be located at sites, within the cemetery (or within a specific
grave enclosure), designated for the purpose (a *ustrina* or *ustrinum*).
Permanent *ustrina*, quadrangular or circular in shape and built of tiles or
stone walls, have been found in urban cemeteries (Polfer 2000: 31). The
ustrina for the enormous pyres of the emperors could become monuments
in their own right in addition to the place of burial (Boatwright 1985;
4.20). The alternative to a *ustrina* was for the pyre to be located at the
actual site of interment (*bustum*), although direct archaeological evidence
for this practice is rare (Weekes 2005: 22–5).

3.47 Servius, On Virgil's Aeneid *11,201*

Commentary on Virgil: 4th c. AD.
Compare Festus, *On the Significance of Words* 29.

> The place is called *bustum* where the deceased is cremated and his
> bones are buried next to it. Others say that, when a man is cremated,
> if he is not buried in the same place, it is not a *bustum* but an
> *ustrinum*.

Items such as pots, glassware, jewellery, food and small animals might be
placed with the body or thrown into the pyre. Similar items might also be
placed with the ashes if these were subsequently buried, and are also found in
inhumation burials. In origin it must have been believed that these items
would accompany the deceased to the afterlife and, in the case of coins, might
pay the ferryman's fee or symbolize wealth (Stevens 1991). Evidence for such
offerings or sacrifices comes from archaeological analysis of cremation burials
and pyre debris. For example, the pyre debris from a 3rd c. cremation at York
suggests that a body held in a coffin on a bier was burned on a pyre made from
coal and wood with a chicken, three pots and a glass vessel; what remained

113

had been collected and placed in an urn (Wenham 1968: 31). From Roman London the pyre debris from cremation graves suggests the presence on the pyre of pottery (amphorae, drinking vessels and beakers), glass (vessels and beads), nails (from coffins, the bier or shoes), copper alloy (from jewellery and dress accessories), carved bone (hairpins, needles, pins), wood (including inlay from a decorated box and a comb), animal bones (mainly pig and chicken), pulses and cereals (Barber and Bowsher 2000: 67–76). Status display, cultural differences and the continuation of pre-Roman practices can sometimes be demonstrated by the excavation of the remains of such pyre items. However, much pyre debris and graves of the Roman period contain little or no evidence for such offerings or grave-goods. Excessive disposal of property on the pyre (or in the grave) was viewed as extravagant by some ancient commentators (2.20 and 3.20) or characteristic of certain cultural groups, especially the Gauls (Noy 2000a: 42).

3.48 Pliny the Younger, Letters 4.2. 3–4

Letter (to Attius Clemens): late 1st c. AD. The death of the son of Regulus. For Regulus see 2.31. Compare Statius, *Silvae* 2.1.157–66.

> Now that his son is dead he expresses his loss in an extravagant manner. The boy used to own a number of ponies for riding and driving, dogs both big and small, and many nightingales, parrots and blackbirds. Regulus had all these slaughtered around the pyre. This was not grief, but a parade of grief.

To facilitate adequate burning the pyre would have stayed alight and been tended for some hours (Weekes 2005: 16–22); for a corpse to be half-burned was insulting for the dead and offensive to the living (Noy 2000b). Once the fire had burned down the pyre was drenched with wine (3.50), the remains of bones and ashes collected and placed in a container (3.45 and 3.50). Analysis of cremation burials from Roman Britain suggests that the collection of the remains may not always have been thorough, with little consigned to the container. The fate of the other ashes (and bones) and the significance of their apparent non-burial remains unclear (McKinley 2000). In some cases could the collection of the remains be little more than a token gesture? Were some remains divided and buried in different locations? Literary texts provide no explanations for this apparent lack of care, instead emphasizing the ideal scenario of the gathering of the remains and their delivery to the closest female relative prior to burial.

3.49 Tibullus 1.3, 5–8

Elegiac poetry: 1st c. BC. Tibullus imagines his death without his mother and sister to perform the essential rites.

See also **5.43**; and compare **3.13**.

> Black Death keep away, I pray. I have no mother here to gather up
> the burned bones to her grieving breast; no sister to put Assyrian
> perfumes on my ashes and weep beside the grave with dishevelled
> hair.

3.50 Virgil, Aeneid 6, 226–8

Epic poetry: late 1st c. BC. The funeral of Misenus, a drowned Trojan warrior.

> After the ashes had fallen in and the fire died down, they washed the
> remains and the thirsty embers in wine, and Corynaeus covered with
> a bronze urn the bones which had been collected.

The container for the ashes could be a pottery urn, glass vase, lead canister, marble ash-chest or ossuary altar. The latter were free-standing, but the other receptacles could be buried directly in the ground with a marker of stone, wood or pottery (**Figures 8, 19** and **20**) indicating the spot, or could be placed in a niche located in the wall of a house tomb, enclosure or columbarium (**Figures 6, 10** and **15**).

3.51 Figure 6: The Columbarium of Pomponius Hylas

Tomb interior: 1st c. AD. Rome (near the Porta Latina).

This is a small subterranean burial chamber, the walls and ceiling of which are decorated with painted stucco. It takes its name from a mosaic inscription found in the stairwell (not shown) naming Pomponius Hylas, but it was probably originally built for those whose remains were buried in the central niche (to the right of the figure). This niche contains two large lidded urns and an inscription on a marble panel beneath names Granius Nestor and Vinileia Hedone. Other smaller niches had urns sunk into them to hold cremated remains; many of the lids that covered the remains also survive.

After the funeral

After the funeral a sacrifice of a sow to Ceres (*porca praesentanea*) took place at the grave (**3.37**) and on the day of the funeral a meal may have been consumed, or offerings of food made to the dead. The evidence for this initial feasting at the grave is ambiguous and the meal, known as the *silicernium*, may have occurred later. Festus, who epitomized an earlier work 'On the Significance of Words' by Verrius Flaccus, suggests that the *silicernium* was food that 'purged the family of their grief' (Festus 294 (Paulus 417)) without elaborating on when it was held. After the funeral there were days of rest and mourning (*feriae denicales*) for the bereaved. The state of mourning was

Figure 6 The Columbarium of Pomponius Hylas, Rome.

marked by a cypress branch outside the door of the house of the family of the deceased.

3.52 Pliny, Natural History 16.60.139

Natural history: 1st c. AD.

[The cypress] is difficult to grow, bears no useful fruit, has sour berries, bitter leaves, and a strong smell; even its shade is unpleasant and its timber is so poor that it almost belongs to the class of shrubs. It is consecrated to Dis; and so placed outside the doors of houses as a sign of mourning.

On the ninth day after burial cleansing rituals, a sacrifice and a feast (*cena novendialis*) near the tomb brought this period of mourning to a close. Archaeological discoveries of food remains from cemeteries and graves suggest that food associated with funeral rituals could be varied; traces of bread, meat, cereals, fruit and nuts are all attested (Carroll 2006: 71–4). However, apart from remains clearly cremated on the pyre, it is impossible to know which food stuffs were offered to the dead and which were consumed by the living. The dead were supposed to join in the feasting at the ninth day feast and subsequent festivals, if only symbolically (see Chapter 6). Simultaneously, it is likely that the food offered to the dead, its type and presentation, served to separate further the dead from the living (Feldherr 2000: 212; Lindsay 1998: 73). Food and drink given to the dead could be viewed as polluted, although the offerings might be a source of temptation for the hungry homeless (**3.53**). The simplicity of the food offered to the dead meant that a comparison with it could also be a way of insulting people's style of entertaining (Tacitus, *Annals* 6.5; Juvenal, *Satires* 5.85). Certain foods were associated with offerings made to the dead and thus could take on negative or ominous connotations (**3.54**).

3.53 Catullus 59

Poetry: 1st c. BC.
  Compare Tibullus 1.5.53 (a starving woman looking for food in a graveyard).

> Bononia Rufa, who sucks off Rufulus, the wife of Menenius, she whom you have often seen in graveyards grabbing her dinner from the pyre; when she was running after a loaf rolling out of the fire, was thumped by the half-shaved slave of the undertaker.

3.54 Plutarch, Crassus 19

Biography: early 2nd c. AD. Events of 53 BC, prior to the Roman defeat by the Parthians.

> Besides this, it happened that when the rations were distributed to the soldiers after the crossing of the river, lentils and salt came first, which are considered by the Romans to be symbols of mourning, and are used as offerings to the dead.

Feasts held after the funeral may have been extravagant, providing an opportunity for the living to display status and entertain peers and social inferiors, even if the offerings given to the dead remained modest. For the poor any feasting may have been limited, but the events could still take on a party atmosphere. The Twelve Tables (*c.* 450 BC) sought to prevent these funeral feasts becoming too boisterous by prohibiting continuous drinking rounds (Cicero, *de Legibus* 2.24.60). One of Trimalchio's dinner guests arrives late and drunk after attending a funeral feast (**3.55**). Alternatively, an heir might insult the deceased by not inviting everyone to the banquet or by spending too little on the funeral rites in general (Persius, *Satires* 6, 33–7; Suetonius, *Tiberius* 37.3). Indeed it is worth remembering that funerals and the following events were social occasions (**3.56**).

3.55 Petronius, Satyricon 65

Satirical novel: 1st c. AD. Habinnas has just arrived at Trimalchio's dinner party.

Note the reference to the 5 per cent inheritance tax. Habinnas goes onto describe an extravagant feast.

> It was really splendid. Scissa was having a funeral feast on the ninth day in honour of her poor dear slave whom she had freed on his deathbed. And I think she will have a large profit to record with the 5 per cent tax collector because they reckon he was worth 50,000. Still it was a pleasant affair, even if we did have to pour half our drinks over his bones.

3.56 Ovid, The Art of Love 3, 429–32

Poetry: late 1st c. BC.

The mythological Andromeda was fastened to a rock as an offering to a sea monster. She was rescued by Perseus.

> What less did fettered Andromeda have to hope for than that her tears would attract a lover? Often a husband is sought for at a husband's funeral; it is fetching to have dishevelled hair and mourn without restraint.

People who attended funerals and the ninth day feast hoped to be well fed and entertained in payment for their presence and commemoration of the deceased. There was an expectation that the dead would have a good send off. This expectation could gain a macabre twist with people not just planning their final parting and party but trying to enjoy it all, and the attention, while still alive (**3.57** and **3.58**). Such mock funerals could also serve the more serious purpose of acting as a *memento mori*, a reminder that all men will die (see also Chapter 2); a point that one of the more bloodthirsty emperors made to his dinner guests by employing funeral paraphernalia to entertain them and make them feel suitably uncomfortable (**3.59**).

3.57 Seneca, Letters 12.8

Philosophical letter: mid 1st c. AD.

Pacuvius was governor of Syria under Tiberius.

For Seneca's beliefs about how best to face death see **2.18**.

> Pacuvius, who by his long presence made Syria his own, used to celebrate a burial rite in his own honour, with wine and a funeral feast, and then would have himself carried from the dining room to his

chamber, while eunuchs applauded and sang in Greek to musical accompaniment 'He has lived his life, he has lived his life!' Thus Pacuvius had himself carried out every day. Let us do from a good motive what he used to do from a bad motive; let us go to our sleep with happiness and gladness; saying 'I have lived ...'.

3.58 Petronius, Satyricon 77–8

Satirical novel: 1st c. AD. The freed slave Trimalchio thinks about and enacts his own funeral.

'Meanwhile Stichus, bring me the clothes in which I mean to be carried out. And some ointment, and a sample from that jar which is to be poured over my bones.' In a moment Stichus had fetched a white shroud and dress into the dining room and Trimalchio asked us to test whether they were made of good wool. Then smiling he said, 'Mind neither mouse nor moth damages them, Stichus; otherwise I will burn you alive. I want to be carried out in splendour, so that everyone calls blessings down on me.' At once he opened a jar of ointment and anointed us all and said, 'I hope that I shall like this as much when I'm dead as I do when living.' Besides this he ordered the wine to be poured into a bowl, and said, 'I want you to think that you've been invited to the *Parentalia*.' The thing was becoming really sickening, when Trimalchio, now deep in a disgusting drunken state, had a new set of performers, some trumpeters, brought into the dining room. He propped himself on a pile of cushions and stretched out along the couch saying, 'Imagine that I am dead. Play something nice.' The trumpeters broke into a loud funeral march. One man in particular, a slave of the undertaker who was the most respectable man in the party, blew so loudly that the whole neighbourhood was roused.

3.59 Cassius Dio 67.9.1–3

History: late 2nd or early 3rd c. AD. Events of late 1st c. AD.

On another occasion he [Domitian] entertained the leading men among the senators and knights in the following fashion. He prepared a room that was pitch black on every side, ceiling, walls and floor, and made ready bare couches, also black, resting on the uncovered floor. Then he invited in his guests alone at night without their slave attendants. At first he set beside each of them a slab shaped like a gravestone, bearing the guest's name and also a small lamp, such as hang in tombs. Next, attractive naked boys, likewise painted black, entered like phantoms, and after circling the guests in an awe-inspiring dance took up positions at their feet. After this, set before the guests were all the things that are commonly offered at the sacrifices to departed spirits, all of them black and in black dishes. As a result every single one of the guests feared and trembled, constantly expecting his throat would be cut the next moment, the more so as everybody but Domitian was dead silent. It was as if they were already in the realms of the dead, and the emperor himself spoke only upon topics relating to death and slaughter.

Public funerals

A public funeral, voted by the Senate, paid for by the treasury and to which all citizens were invited, was a great honour reserved for the great and the good who had served Rome well (Wesch-Klein 1993). It is notable, however, that soldiers, at least the rank and file, who made the ultimate sacrifice for Rome were not honoured in this fashion (see Chapter 4). Cicero reveals some aspects of how and why individuals were considered for the honour (**3.60**), while the funeral of Sulla, held at public expense, provides a striking and extravagant example (**3.61**).

3.60 Cicero, Philippic 9. 7.17

Speech: 43 BC.

Servius Sulpicius Rufus had died of natural causes while on an embassy to Marc Antony. In proposing a statue in the Forum and public burial Cicero was implying that Sulpicius had died in the service of the state and at the hands of the enemy (however indirectly), thereby blackening Antony's name.

> The Senate has before now shown its authority by conferring the distinction of public funerals on brave men; now it is the Senate's pleasure that Sulpicius be carried out on the day of his funeral with the appropriate ceremony. For Servius Sulpicius Rufus, the son of Quintus, of the Lemonian voting tribe, well deserves of the State to be honoured with these distinctions. The Senate decrees, and considers it in the interests of the State, that the aediles suspend their edict applying to funerals as regards the expense of the funeral of Servius Sulpicius Rufus, the son of Quintus of the Lemonian voting tribe; and that Gaius Pansa, the consul, assign a space for the burial of 30 feet in all directions on the Campus Esquilinus, or in another place that seems appropriate to him, to receive the body of Servius Sulpicius; and this burial place will be also for his children and descendants.

3.61 Appian, Civil Wars 1.105–6

History: 2nd c. AD. Events of 78 BC.

Sulla himself had denied his political enemies proper burial, had desecrated their graves and banned their *imagines* (**3.37** and **3.40**). Plutarch claims that so many spices were donated that a large figure of Sulla was fashioned out of frankincense and cinnamon; *Sulla* 38.

> Immediately disagreement broke out in the city over his remains; some proposed that his body ought to be brought to Rome in a procession, exhibited in the Forum and honoured with a public funeral ... [Sulla's body was carried though Italy on a golden litter with soldiers flocking to it] ... When the body reached Rome it was carried through the city with great splendour. More than 2,000 golden crowns which had been made hurriedly were carried; these were the gifts of cities and of the legions he had commanded and of individual friends. It would be impossible to describe all the expensive items sent to the funeral. Frightened by the assembled soldiers all the priests and priestesses, in their colleges, the whole Senate and all the magistrates, with their insignia of office, escorted the body. They were followed by the knights and all the legions that fought under Sulla. The soldiers had come together eagerly, all hurrying to take part; they carried gilded standards and shields decorated with silver, of the sort that are still used on such occasions. There were many trumpeters who played alternately melting and mournful tunes. Sulla's praises were raised first by the Senate, then by the knights, then by the soldiers, and finally by the ordinary people. Some genuinely longed for Sulla, but others were just as afraid of his army and his corpse as they had been of him when he was alive.

In the towns and cities of the empire a public funeral could be provided by the local council (*ordo decurionem*) and was usually given to members of that council and their relatives. Inscriptions record the honour and, in some cases, what was provided, such as incense, and additional honours such as statues. Public burial did not include the burial plot and monument unless expressly stated (see **4.11** and **4.12**).

3.62 CIL X 1024

Epitaph: 1st c. AD. Pompeii (Herculaneum Gate necropolis).
  = Kockel 1983: 70–5.

> Aulus Umbricius Scaurus, son of Aulus, of the Menenian voting tribe, *duumvir*. The *decuriones* gave this monument and 2,000

sesterces for a funeral and an equestrian statue to be set up in the forum. His father Scaurus to his son.

3.63 Espérandieu 1929: n.429

Epitaph: 2nd c. AD. Nemausus (Nîmes, France).

To the spirits of the departed Terentia Marcella, daughter of Marcus, priestess of the Imperial cult in the colony of Narbonne. The colony of Nemausus publicly decreed the cost of the funeral and a statue.

3.64 CIL XIV 321

Epitaph: mid 2nd c. AD. Ostia (Italy).
  = ILS 6136.

To Publius Celerius Amandus, son of Publius, of the Palatina voting tribe, elected *decurio* by special decree. The *decuriones* decreed that he be awarded a public funeral with all honours and 20 pounds of incense. His father yielded to this considerable honour. He lived 18 years, 9 months and 8 days. His mother Scantia Lanthanusa, daughter of Spurius, made this.

Elite funerals

The funerals of the élite during the late Republic and early Empire involved the same basic elements as those of other members of society. The body had to be washed, dressed, displayed, carried to the grave, and then disposed of by cremation or inhumation. But through additional touches the funerals of the élite were designed to be memorable spectacles, which often entailed political messages. A fundamental source is Polybius' description of a Republican funeral which placed due emphasis on the public life of the deceased, his relationship with his ancestors and also future generations of the same family (**3.65**). The deceased was located 'in a continuum of past, present and future' (Bodel 1999b: 264). The masks or *imagines* were crucial to the pageantry of the event and were carefully stored and displayed in the family home when not used at funerals. Wearing these masks, actors could bring the dead back to life; something that the mime playing the part of the emperor Vespasian at his funeral did all too well by remembering the late emperor's reputation for stinginess (**3.66**)! The procession of the ancestors allowed the aristocratic family to create a pageant of Roman history that suited its needs and the spectacle also promoted a common heritage between the spectators and their leaders (Flower 1996: 126–7). Indeed, what was important at these events was not what happened at the graveside – the pyre, the grave, the *silicernium* and so forth are not mentioned – what was key was the procession in the city, the display of élite symbols in the heart of Rome and the laudatory speech delivered in the Forum.

3.65 Polybius, 6.53–54

History: 2nd c. BC.

Whenever one of their leading men dies, when the funeral has been arranged, the body is carried with every kind of honour into the Forum to the so-called *rostra*, where it is usually propped up for all to see, but rarely is it laid down. The whole mass of the people stand round to watch, and an adult son if he can be present, or if not some other relative, mounts the *rostra* and delivers a speech about the virtues of the dead man and the successes achieved during his lifetime. As a result the people, not only those who shared in the deeds but those who did not, remember what happened and picture it. Both share the same feelings to the extent that the loss seems not to be confined to the mourners but to be a public one which affects the people. Then after the burial of the body and the performance of the customary rites, they place the image of the dead man in the most public part of the house, keeping it in a wooden shrine. This image is a mask, which is made to resemble closely in both the shape of the face and its colouring the features of the dead man. The masks are displayed during public sacrifices and they compete in decorating them. And when a leading member of the family dies, the masks are taken to the funeral, and are there worn by men, who seem most like the original, both in height and in their general appearance. These men are dressed according to the rank of the deceased: a toga with a purple border for a consul or praetor, an all-purple toga for a censor, and one embroidered with gold for a man who had celebrated a triumph or done something similar. These men all ride in chariots with the rods and axes and other symbols of those in power according to the dignity of rank and station achieved by each man in his lifetime. When they reach the *rostra* they all sit down in order on ivory stools. It is not easy for an ambitious and virtuous young man to see a finer spectacle than this. For who would not be impressed at the sight of the masks of all these men who have won fame in their time, now gathered together as if alive and breathing? What spectacle could be more noble than this? Moreover the man who gives the speech over the man who is about to be buried, when he has finished the eulogy, begins to praise the others present, relating the successes and achievements of each, beginning with the oldest. As a result of this, since the reputation for virtue of good men is constantly renewed, the fame of those who did some noble deed is immortal and the glory of those who have served their country

123

becomes well known and is an inheritance for posterity. But the most important result is that it inspires young men to undergo anything for the common good in the hope of winning the glory that follows the brave deeds of men.

3.66 Suetonius, Vespasian 19.2

Biography: early 2nd c. AD. Events of AD 79.
  Compare Diodorus 31.25.2.

> And when Vespasian died, the leading actor Favor, who wore his funeral mask in the procession and gave the customary imitations of his actions and words, having asked the procurators in front of everybody how much the funeral procession would cost and hearing that it would cost 100,000, said 'Give me 100 sesterces and you can throw me into the Tiber.'

The *imagines* were an important symbol of aristocratic honour. Note how their destruction or banishment from funerary processions could form a part of *damnatio memoriae* (**2.59**). During the Republic in particular the *imagines* could be a source of inspiration to the descendants of these men, a reminder to the élite of the right to rule and ideally the need to do so well (Sallust, *Jugurtha* 4.5). The *imagines* are also suggestive of the entertainment, almost theatrical, element, to these funerals (Sumi 1997); a death was an opportunity to create an eye-catching pageant and spectacle. Cicero notes that the Twelve Tables had attempted to curb funerary expenditure and frivolity (**3.67**). No doubt such laws were invented for and by the élite; they provided norms in a highly competitive society (Flower 1996: 118), but funerals did become more extravagant and the laws had little weight in Cicero's day.

3.67 Cicero, On the Laws 2.23.59

Dialogue on law: *c.* 43 BC.
  Solon was a political and legal reformer in Athens during the 6th c. BC.

> There are other rules, too, in the Twelve Tables, which aim to limit the expense and the mourning at funerals, which were borrowed for the most part from the laws of Solon. The law says, 'Do no more than this: do not smooth the pyre with an axe.' You know what follows, for we learned the Twelve Tables in our boyhood as a required lesson; though no one learns it nowadays. The expense then is limited to 'three veils, a purple tunic, and ten flute players'; the mourning is also limited: 'Women shall not scratch their cheeks, nor have a *lessum* at a funeral'. The older interpreters, Sextus Aelius and Lucius Acilius, admitted that they did not fully understand this,

but suspected that it referred to some kind of mourning clothes. Lucius Aelius thought a *lessum* was a kind of sorrowful wailing, for that is what the word would seem to mean. I incline to the latter interpretation, since this is the very thing which is forbidden in Solon's law. These provisions are praiseworthy and relevant to both the rich and the common people; for it is according to nature that differences in wealth should cease with death.

Elite funerals were just one part of a whole range of commemorative events sparked by a death. In the late Republic a death in the family could provide the perfect opportunity to court public support. Remembering the deceased was important (see Chapter 2), but so was the continuing public profile of the survivors. Distributions of food, public banquets, gladiatorial combats and other forms of entertainment were held, nominally at least, to honour the dead. The year after (58 BC) he held a lavish banquet to commemorate his father (3.30), Quintus Arrius stood for the consulship. Gladiatorial combats first appeared at the funeral of Decimus Junius Brutus Pera in 264 BC (Valerius Maximus 2.4.7). The games originated as a commemorative event, but became the ultimate form of mass entertainment and propaganda. In amongst these shows and feasts the funeral itself, with its public display elements, was not neglected. During the late Republic the funerals of women as well as men were exploited and the opportunity taken to make speeches in the Forum that served the political ends of the family. Julius Caesar, for example, took advantage of the deaths of his female relatives to win popular sympathy and support (Plutarch, *Caesar* 5 and 55.2). Such were the political tensions that could be stirred up at funerals that riots ensued on several occasions (Bodel 1999b: 274–5). The funeral of Clodius led to the burning down of the Senate House (Sumi 1997), while the crowd seized Caesar's body and cremated it in the Forum (3.68). Such transgressions of the normal rites served to highlight uncertain and unstable political times. Caesar's funeral was a theatrical event in which the members of the crowd were far from passive spectators; Antony was able to turn the funeral into 'a political drama' (Flower 1996: 125–6).

3.68 Appian, Civil Wars 2.146–47

History: 2nd c. AD. Events of 44 BC, following the assassination of Julius Caesar.

> After the speech [by Antony] other lamentations were chanted by the people in chorus over the dead with funeral music according to the Roman custom; and his achievements and his fate were recited again. Somewhere, in the middle of these lamentations Caesar himself was supposed to speak, listing by name the enemies he had helped, and referring to his murderers … [the crowd is angered that

the murderers have not been punished] ... Somebody raised above the bier a wax image of Caesar; the body itself, as it lay on its back on the bier, was not visible. The image was turned round and round by a mechanical device, showing the 23 wounds, brutally inflicted on all parts of the body and on the face. This sight seemed so pitiful to the people that they could not stand it any longer. Shouting and lamenting, they surrounded the senate house, where Caesar had been killed, and burnt it down, and rushed about searching for the murderers, who had slipped away some time earlier.

With the transition from Republic to Empire came changes in the nature of élite funeral display. Bodel (1999b) has suggested that in death rituals there was a movement away from the Forum and public spaces to the more intro-verted spheres of the house (the lying-in-state) and the cemetery. The élite did not wish to compete with the emperor who now manipulated the traditional arenas of élite self-definition and public display; the most elaborate funerals were to become the prerogative of the emperor and members of his family. A *iustitium* or cessation of all public and legal business in Rome was declared after an emperor or an important member of the imperial family died. This in effect extended mourning from beyond the confines of the family to all the population. The funeral itself drew upon Republican models for the funerals of the élite. Processions, *imagines*, speeches and spectacle were integral to these events. It was the funeral of the first emperor Augustus that set the precedent for future emperors (3.69). The bier, carried by Senators, was made of ivory and gold, with gold and purple hangings. Several effigies of Augustus, made of wax and gold, were displayed and numerous masks (*imagines*) of his ancestors and illustrious Romans formed the procession. Two orations were given in the Forum. After these the body was carried to the Campus Martius for cremation. The widowed Livia stayed by the pyre for five days and then the bones were collected by members of the equestrian order and placed in the mausoleum (Cassius Dio 56.34–43; Tacitus, *Annals* 1.8). This was not only in extravagance and display of honours the funeral to outstrip all that had gone before, but in the release of an eagle from the pyre also gave basis to Augustus' claims to divinity. In death the emperor ceased to be a mortal and became a god.

3.69 Suetonius, Augustus 100

Biography: early 2nd c. AD. Events of AD 14.
    For the death of Augustus see 1.55; for the mausoleum see 4.20 and 4.21. Compare the funeral of Pertinax (AD 193), Cassius Dio 75.5.

> Though it was decided to set a limit to the honours paid him, he was given two funeral eulogies; one by Tiberius before the temple of the deified Julius Caesar, and another by Tiberius' son Drusus from the

old rostra. After this he was carried on the shoulders of senators to the Campus Martius, where he was cremated. There was even an ex-praetor who swore that he had seen Augustus' spirit, after he had been burned, on its way up to Heaven. His remains were collected by leading men of the equestrian order, barefoot, and wearing unbelted tunics, and then placed in the Mausoleum.

The *apotheosis* process had begun with Julius Caesar (Price 1987: 71–2), and was to become a common posthumous honour for the emperor and members of his family – an honour that could be of great political benefit to the heirs. However, divinity was not bestowed automatically and this was especially the case during the early Empire. It was the decision of the Senate to grant divine honours, usually following convenient reports of people seeing the deceased ascend to heaven. It gave the Senate symbolic power over the emperor (Price 1987: 91). In theory, divinity was an honour only awarded to the deserving, to those who had ruled well. Some among the élite may have retained a level of cynicism; the death of an emperor and the associated rites may not have been taken too seriously or too literally. Indeed it is worth remembering that with elements of spectacle, feasting and the mocking role of mimes, élite and imperial funerals could entail an entertaining and even satirical or carnivalesque element (Bettini 2005; Sumi 2002). It wasn't that unusual for some mourners at a funeral, even that of an emperor, to have a good time.

3.70 Seneca, Apocolocyntosis 12

Satire: 1st c. AD. Claudius ascends to heaven and the gods rather than the Senate decide whether to accept him among their number. Expectations are deliberately reversed; Claudius had been declared a god by the Senate on earth but is rejected by the gods in heaven. Equally the funeral of Claudius is portrayed as a happy rather than a sombre event.
See also **1.59**.

Mercury dragged him, with his neck twisted, down to the under-world, 'from where they say no one returns'. As they passed down-wards along the Sacred Way Mercury asked what was that great procession of men? could it be Claudius' funeral? It was certainly the most beautiful spectacle, with no expense spared, it was clear that a god was being carried to the grave. Trumpets, horn players, a brass band of all sorts, a great crowd, and so much noise that even Claudius could hear it. Joy and rejoicing on every side, the Roman people walking around like free men.

4

THE CEMETERY

Introduction

Funerary monuments are among the most evocative survivals from the Roman world; they number in the thousands and are found in most areas that came under Roman power. These monuments communicated, and continue to communicate, important messages about status, culture, power and identity, as well as attesting to the more personal and private world of grief and family life. Funerary monuments recall the Roman cemetery, its appearance, use and organization, but few actually survive in situ. Many stones were reused in later buildings, or were retrieved with scant regard to context; most are now displayed and stored in museums, lined up in tidy rows or as fragments cemented into walls. Putting these monuments and isolated pieces of stone back into the cemetery and understanding how each memorial related to its environment is not straightforward. Many questions remain unanswered: where was a specific monument situated? how visible was it? how did it compare to adjacent memorials? was it part of a larger group of related memorials? did it mark a cremation or inhumation grave? was it the focus for tomb cult?

Even when removed from context stone memorials, with their words and images, fuel our imagination and provide insights into the visual dimensions of Roman cemeteries. However, we should not automatically prioritize stone in the study and reconstruction of the Roman cemetery (Hopkins 1983: 218). A funerary monument was only one part of how some people were buried, commemorated and remembered. When Roman burial grounds are excavated many of the graves, whether cremations or inhumations, have no surviving surface indicators. Bones, ashes, containers, pots, lamps and coins are often found in high densities, but no or few stone markers. In such cases the original grave markers may have been made from varied materials, many of which were perishable, and in addition we need to acknowledge that many graves may never have been marked at all. This does not mean that a cemetery was not cherished by the community or that individual graves were rapidly forgotten and neglected.

One factor in determining how people were buried and commemorated was geographic region. There were variations across the empire; it comes as no surprise that the cemeteries of Roman Britain did not look exactly the same as those found in Roman North Africa. Recent research has emphasized this regional diversity in practices and customs, while acknowledging that there were some unifying factors, such as mode of burial (cremation or inhumation) and extra-mural burial, that tended to unite the empire (Zanker and von Hesberg 1987; Pearce et al. 2000). The shift from inhumation to cremation and then back to inhumation (see Chapter 3) also highlights that the use, appearance and organization of cemeteries was not chronologically static. As an area for displaying and constructing status and identity the cemetery could go in and out of fashion (MacMullen 1982; Meyer 1990; von Hesberg 1992).

It cannot be disputed that there is a wealth of evidence for Roman cemeteries, such as burials, grave-goods, markers and tombs, but understanding the cemetery environment with all its regional and chronological variations is complex. Reuniting bones and stones is often just not possible. Thus this chapter is limited to exploring some of the characteristic features of the Roman cemetery, its graves and memorials, as well as the aspirations and fears of those who were buried there. I also wish to capture that the Roman cemetery was in many respects a dynamic space, one of change and development, a marginal but still-active zone, a place that could be neglected, but by its presence, hugging the roads, one that could not be completely overlooked. The Roman cemetery was a place of beauty and fears, of hopes and disappointments, a place where the living interacted with the dead and the living with the living.

Urban burial

In the towns of the empire, where death was concentrated, disposing of the dead could be a problem for the urban authorities. Corpses needed to be disposed of properly and hygienically and to ensure this rules and laws were in place. An overriding concern was that the dead should be separated from the living. People were not to be buried or cremated inside towns. Cemeteries were to be located outside the walls.

4.1 *Paulus,* Opinions 1.21.2

Legal text: late 2nd or early 3rd c. AD.

> You are not allowed to bring a corpse into the city in case the sacred places in the city are polluted. Whoever acts against these restrictions is punished with unusual severity. You are not allowed to bury or cremate a body within the walls of the city.

Stipulations concerning place of burial may have arisen from, or in conjunction with, religious scruples, but by the late Republic the practical advantages of separating the living and the dead were apparent. Cicero interprets the early law of the Twelve Tables (*c.* 450 BC) as primarily providing protection to the city from the risk of fire from cremations (**4.2**). We find similar stipulations enforcing extramural burial and cremation in town charters from the provinces (**4.3**). These charters suggest that burial laws were widely given and enforced, the practical benefits of which were taken for granted.

4.2 *Cicero,* On the Laws 2.23.58

Dialogue on law: *c.* 43 BC.

> A law of the Twelve Tables says 'A dead man shall not be buried or burned inside the city'. I suppose the latter is due to the danger of fire.

4.3 Lex Coloniae Genetivae Iuliae seu Ursonensis 73–4

Inscribed town charter: 1st c. AD. Bronze tablets found in 1870–1 in Spain (Sevilla), now held in the Museo Arqueológico Nacional, Madrid.
  = *ILS* 6087; Crawford 1996: 424.
  This is a copy of an earlier charter for the establishment of the colony.
  For a two mile exclusion zone for cremation at Rome see Cassius Dio 48.43.3.

> No one within the boundaries of the town or the colony or within the area marked round by the plough, shall bring a dead person, or bury, or cremate a body there, or build a monument to a dead person. If any person acts contrary to this regulation he shall be condemned to pay to the colonists of the colony Genetiva Julia 5,000 sesterces and he shall be sued and prosecuted for that sum by any person who wishes. A *duumvir* or an *aedile* shall see to the demolition of any monument built, and if, against this law, a dead person has been brought in and buried, they shall make the proper expiation. No one is to construct a new *ustrina*, where a dead person has not been cremated before, nearer to the town than 500 paces. Any one acting against this regulation shall be condemned to pay to the colonists of the colony Genetiva Julia 5,000 sesterces and shall be sued and prosecuted for that sum by any person who wishes in accordance with this law.

Bodies needed to be disposed of outside the town walls and in a suitable fashion. Dumping bodies was unacceptable. The regulations for undertakers at Puteoli suggest that those abandoning bodies should be fined (3.10). Inscriptions from the city of Rome suggest that laws existed to prevent people casually disposing of rubbish and corpses, or at least these laws were aimed at protecting certain suburban areas from being abused in this fashion.

4.4 CIL VI 31615

Inscription: late 1st c. BC. Rome (Esquiline). A boundary stone.
  = $CIL1^2$ 839.

> Lucius Sentius, son of Caius, praetor, has made regulation, by decree of the Senate, about the siting of graves. For the public good. No burning of corpses beyond this marker in the direction of the city. No dumping of rubbish or corpses.
> Take shit further on, if you want to avoid trouble.

Bodies and body parts did turn up in places where they were not expected or wanted, suggesting that some corpses were left unburied or were disposed of inadequately, attracting scavenging birds and animals. When the emperor Nero was fleeing Rome his horse took fright at the smell of a dead body lying close to the road (Suetonius, *Nero* 48). A stray dog picked up a human hand and dropped it at the future emperor Vespasian's feet, a good omen as it turned out, since the hand was an emblem of power (Suetonius, *Vespasian* 5). Dogs also mauled a corpse during the reign of Domitian (Suetonius, *Domitian* 15). These tales of bodies and body parts may be symbolic anecdotes, but to be believable they must contain an element of truth. In times of crisis it may have been particularly difficult to enforce proper and adequate disposal. Intervention from the authorities may have been essential. In the 2nd c. AD the emperor Marcus Aurelius gave financial assistance for funerals of the poor during a plague (3.3). Rotting bodies were also emblematic of troubled times (see 4.43 and 4.45) and images of vultures and dogs consuming human remains were intended to evoke both sympathy and revulsion among readers.

4.5 Livy 41.21.5–11

History: late 1st c. BC or early 1st c. AD. Events of 174 BC, during a plague in Rome.
  For Libitina see Chapter 3. Compare Orosius 5.4.8–9.

> Slaves and their unburied bodies lay in piles along the roads and Libitina did not suffice for the funerals of free men. The corpses lay untouched by dogs and vultures and were consumed by decay, and

it was generally observed that neither in this nor in the previous year, despite the deaths of many cattle and men, had a vulture been seen anywhere.

4.6 *Martial*, Epigrams 10.5, 6–11

Poetry: late 1st c. AD.
The epigram evokes punishments for a wicked poet by imagining some of the indignities and fears of a dying homeless man.

> To him may December be long and winter wet, and a closed archway prolong his miserable cold. Let him call those happy, and acclaim those fortunate, who are carried on the litter of death. But when the threads of his last hour have been spun, and his lingering day of death has come, let him hear the wrangling of dogs and flap his rags to drive away harmful birds.

Slaves could generally rely on their masters to bury them (see below) whereas those among the free poor who were homeless and poverty stricken may have had no one, or at least no one with sufficient money, to dispose of them properly. Calculating the figures involved is difficult; it has been suggested that of an estimated 30,000 people who died in Rome each year, maybe one in twenty, that is 1,500 corpses annually, may have been unclaimed and unwanted (Bodel 2000: 129–30). Paupers' graves, which may have been mass graves, may well have been a feature of many of the cemeteries of the empire.

4.7 *Varro*, On the Latin Language 5.25

Study of language: 1st c. BC.
Varro refers to earlier writers in seeking a derivation of the word *puticuli*.

> Outside the towns there are *puticuli* 'little pits', called after *putei* 'pits', because people used to be buried there in *putei* 'pits'; unless instead, as Aelius writes, the *puticuli* are so called because the corpses which had been thrown out *putescebant* 'used to rot' there, in the public place which is beyond the Esquiline. This place Afranius in a comedy calls the *Puticuli* 'pit-lights', because from it they look up through *putei* 'pits' to the *lumen* 'light'.

In Republican Rome these open pits were probably located outside the Esquiline Gate. Excavations in this area during the nineteenth century apparently uncovered pits that had been filled with human and animal remains (Lanciani 1888; Hopkins 1983: 208–9; Bodel 1994: 40), although it can be questioned whether these were the *puticuli* (Graham 2007).

During the late Republic there were efforts to improve the unsanitary nature of the Esquiline area (see Bodel 1994). Eventually, gardens covered much of the region which allegedly had once seen bones lying on the ground (4.8). Whether the *puticuli*, or an equivalent, continued in Rome during the Imperial period is unclear. Bodel has suggested that these mass inhumation graves were replaced by mass crematoria, although Kyle has challenged this (Bodel 1994: 83; Kyle 1998: 169–70; Bodel 2000: 133).

4.8 Horace, Satire 1.8, 7–16

Satirical poetry: late 1st c. BC. The words are spoken by a wooden statue of the god Priapus located on the Esquiline, where graveyards were converted into gardens during the reign of Augustus.

Pantalabus and Nomentanus were stock characters representing the ne'er-do-goods of Roman society.

See also **6.60**.

> To here in other days a slave would pay to have carried on a cheap bier the corpses of his fellow slaves, cast out from their narrow cells. Here too was the common burial ground for poor people, for Pantalabus the parasite, and spendthrift Nomentanus. Here a pillar marked a thousand feet frontage and three hundred of depth, and stated that the graveyard should not pass to the heirs. Today one may live on the healthy Esquiline and stroll on the sunny rampart, where of late one sadly looked at whitening bones upon the ground.

Simple burials and simply marked graves suggest that at least some of the poorer elements of society did seek to attain a level of decency in death (although note that lack of memorials and modest memorials were not an automatic sign of poverty, see below and also **2.58**). At Pompeii names were scratched on to the town walls, and urns found nearby suggest that these simple inscriptions stood in place of grave markers (*CIL* X 8349–61; Senatore 1999). In the busy suburban environment modest burials, easily disturbed and lost, may have been slotted into available spaces between, in front of and behind more grandiose monuments (see for example, Tranoy 2000; Graham 2007). At the Isola Sacra necropolis, near Portus, small tombs, simple graves and cremations in pottery amphorae were interspersed with the larger monuments. Nevertheless it is still easy to imagine that many people struggled with the associated costs of even the most simple funeral, cremation and interment. The burial allowance introduced by Nerva (see Chapter 3) suggests that burial, its cost and how to dispose of the bodies of the poor, was a continuing issue, although the allowance was short-lived and may have applied to only limited groups of people.

4.9 Figures 7 and 8: Modest burials at the Isola Sacra necropolis

Cemetery: early to mid 2nd c. AD.

The so-called Isola Sacra necropolis served the harbour town of Portus (Italy). Large house tombs fronted the road (**Figures 7, 15** and **17**) and in between, behind and in front of these were dotted more modest tombs and burials. Figure 7 shows Tomb 51, a small square brick-built tomb that lies in a vacant space beside and behind the barrel-vaulted house tombs, including Tomb 55 which sits behind Tomb 51 in the figure. Tomb 51 was set up to Bassus by his brother, Myron. The legal status of the deceased is not explicitly mentioned in the epitaph, but the single names of Bassus and his brother may suggest that they were slaves. Behind Tomb 51 an amphora which marked a burial protrudes from the ground. More of these amphorae burials, with the necks now broken, are shown in Figure 8. This group of amphorae burials lay behind the main row of house tombs, some distance from the road, adjacent to Tomb 62 (to the left of the figure), a so-called 'cassone' tomb. The latter were brick-built chests, holding cremation burials, covered with semi-cylindrical roofs that recall the barrel vaults of the grander house tombs.

Figure 7
Tomb 51 of the Isola Sacra necropolis, Portus.

Figure 8 Amphorae burials at the Isola Sacra necropolis, Portus.

Cemetery development

In the towns and cities of the empire the cemeteries were generally located beyond the town walls and the sacred boundary known as the *pomerium*. In some areas of the eastern empire monumental tombs were found within the city. This represented the continuation of a local tradition of honouring exceptional and well-deserving citizens with special burial (see for example, Cormack 2004: 37–49). This tradition did have some impact on the western empire, but here burial within the town remained extremely rare.

4.10 *Cicero*, On the Laws 2.23.58

Dialogue on law: *c.* 43 BC.

Publius Valerius Poplicola was reputed to have held the consulship several times between 509–4 BC and to have been involved in the overthrow of Tarquinius Superbus; Publius Postumius Tubertus was his colleague in the consulship in 505 and 503 BC. Gaius Fabricius was consul and censor in the late 3rd c. BC.

Plutarch also refers to the burial of distinguished men within the city and a token symbolic burial of triumphators in the Roman Forum, a practice not otherwise attested: Plutarch, *Publicola* 23; Plutarch, *Roman Questions* 79.

ATTICUS: What about the burial of famous men inside the city since the time of the Twelve Tables?

MARCUS: I suppose, Titus, that there were men to whom this honour had been granted because of their merit before this law was enacted, such as Poplicola and Tubertus, and that this privilege was legally retained by their descendants, or else that there were those who, like Gaius Fabricius, were made exempt from the law on account of their merit.

During the late Republic distinguished individuals were often buried on Rome's Campus Martius by special decree of the Senate, an honour that was often associated with the granting of a public funeral (see Chapter 3). Sulla's grave was located here (Plutarch, *Sulla* 38; and see **3.61**) and this was the site selected for the Mausoleum of Augustus (**4.20** and **4.21**). Another favoured location for burial at public expense was the Campus Esquilinus, the location proposed by Cicero for honouring a certain Servius Sulpicius Rufus (**3.60**). In the towns of the empire permission to be buried in the *pomerium* was a rare honour bestowed on distinguished people. Alternatively the local council could give other prominent burial sites as a reward to leading citizens and members of their families.

4.11 AE 1911, 71 and Figure 9

Tomb: mid 1st c. AD. Pompeii (near the Nolan Gate). A seat or bench tomb.

The tomb consists of a semi-circular seating area built of stone. In the middle of the back of the seat is a column, supporting on its ionic capital a marble vase. The epitaph is contained in a panel at the base of the column. These distinctive seat tombs, which were all located near Pompeii's gates, were only awarded to leading citizens and members of their families (Kockel 1983: 18–22).

For funerals at public expense see 3.62–64. For further seating at tombs see **Figure 17**.

> Numerius Herennius Celsus, son of Numerius, of the Menenian voting tribe, *duumvir* with judicial power twice, staff officer, to Aesquillia Polla, daughter of Gaius, his wife. She lived 22 years; a burial place was given publicly by decree of the *decuriones*.

4.12 CIL X 1019

Epitaph: mid 1st c. AD. Inscription panel from a grave enclosure, Pompeii (Herculaneum Gate Necropolis).

= Kockel 1983: 115–17.

Figure 9 A bench tomb at the Nolan Gate, Pompeii.

To Titus Terentius Felix Maior, son of Titus, of the Menenian tribe, *aedile*. To him a place for burial was given publicly and 2,000 sesterces. Fabia Sabina, daughter of Probus, his wife.

How most people acquired land for burial is unclear. Those who owned rural property might choose to be buried there (see below). For those who did not own land a grave site had to be purchased or they were dependent on the generosity of others. A few epitaphs record the purchasing of land or tombs (*CIL* VI 10240, 10241, 10247). Once it was secured, the land was a valuable commodity which could be used singly by the owner or take on a more communal role. Many owners, especially from the early 1st c. AD onwards, built family tombs or grave enclosures to house the remains of relatives, slaves and freed slaves. These individuals acted as patrons caring for the living and the dead; 'while living I maintained a life of good repute; with concern I looked after many people and also provided a final resting place for many' (*CIL* IX 4796, 15–16). In such communal settings many graves or urns may not have been marked in a permanent manner; the deceased person was part of a group commemoration, but individually anonymous (Eck 1987; Hope 1997b; Sigismund Nielsen 1996). Within such communal tombs and enclosures people might make a formal gift of a burial space to a friend or even sell on spaces.

4.13 IA 601

Epitaph: 2nd c. AD. Inscribed funerary altar, Aquileia (North Italy). Found in a walled enclosure; see **Figure 14**.

For gifts of burial spaces see also **2.3**, **2.8** and **4.31**.

> Fabricia Severina, aged 16 years and 10 months. Hermes, the treasurer of the *augustales* and *seviri*, and Sentia Severa set this up. The place for burial was given by the Statii.

4.14 Isola Sacra, Tomb 94

Epitaphs: 2nd c. AD. These epitaphs were found in Tomb 94 of the Isola Sacra necropolis near Portus (Italy). The house tomb had an enclosure to the front and was built originally by Valeria Trophime.

= Thylander 1952: A96, A124, A251.

For the Isola Sacra see **Figures 7, 8, 15** and **17**.

> To the spirits of the departed. Euhodus, an imperial slave, and Vennonia Apphis, bought a burial space from Valeria Trophime, and built this for themselves, their freedmen, their freedwomen and their descendants.

> To the spirits of the departed. Caius Galgestius Helius bought a vacant burial space from Valeria Trophime and made for himself and for his family a tomb chamber joined to the wall on the right of the entry, in which are 14 urns; apart from one urn which Trophime gave to Galgestius Vitalis. Caius Galgestius Helius gave one urn to Pomponius Chrysopolis.

> To the spirits of the departed. Trophimus, an imperial slave, and Claudia Tyche, built this tomb for Claudia Saturnina, their loving daughter, who lived 15 years, 6 months and 13 days, and for their freedmen, freedwomen and their descendants. They bought as a burial place a quarter of this monument from Valeria Trophime.

In some settlements generous benefactors may have given land for the burial of the local inhabitants (**4.15**). This is rarely attested and raises issues as to how and by whom the land would have been administered and for how long the benefaction lasted.

4.15 CIL XI 6528

Inscription: 1st c. BC. Sassina (Sarsina, Italy).

= *ILS* 7846.

Horatius Balbus gave to his fellow citizens and inhabitants a place for burial from his own money. Excluded are contract gladiators, those who hanged themselves, those who made a dirty living. Each grave is to be 10 feet by 10 feet, between the bridge of Sapis and the next inscription which is at the edge of the Fangonian farm. In these places no one will be buried who wishes to build a monument for himself while alive. In these places will be buried those [sense unclear], and it will be permitted for his successors to have a monument made.

Alternatively, people could pool their resources and form burial clubs (*collegia*). By paying regular contributions people could then draw an allowance for their own funeral and commemoration (**3.2**). The columbaria of Rome, dating to the early empire, were often associated with burial clubs or large slave households. These vast constructions accommodated large numbers of urns holding cremated remains that were placed in niches that lined the walls of the structure.

4.16 *Figure 10: Vigna Codini, Columbarium III*

Tomb: early 1st c. AD. Rome, between the via Appia and via Latina.

The subterranean structure has walls lined with niches, into which were sunk urns containing the ashes of the deceased. Columbaria often had the

Figure 10
Vigna Codini,
Columbarium III.

capacity to house hundreds of such cremation burials. Inscribed panels could be placed beneath the niches. In this columbarium many of the epitaphs named freed slaves of the Julio-Claudian dynasty. The projecting blocks of stone may have supported wooden galleries for reaching the upper niches. The vaulted ceiling was adorned with painted décor.

Entrepreneurs probably also played their part in cemetery development, selling off land to those who could afford to purchase their own grave plot. The standardization in size of some burial plots and the fact that those setting up memorials could be eager to emphasize the exact dimensions of their plot (or tomb) indicate such transactions. The recording of plot size was not universal across the empire, being most common in Italy and Gaul, which may suggest localized epigraphic traditions, but may also indicate different purchasing practices and levels of demand for land. The need to state the plot size also suggests that tombs could easily be encroached upon, graves abused and bodies buried where they shouldn't be (see below). When given, the dimensions recorded are normally the road frontage and the depth into the field. These could be inscribed at the end of the titular epitaph or on a separate marker. Most recorded dimensions are modest, between 10 and 15 Roman feet (Eck 1987; Reusser 1987).

4.17 CIL V 1419

Epitaph: 1st c. AD. Aquileia (Italy).
=*IA* 1560.
For further examples of dimensions see **2.14**, **4.32**, **4.34** and **6.18**. Note as well the substantial dimensions of Trimalchio's tomb plot (**2.56**); some of this ground may have been intended for gardens.

> Caius Trosius Azbestus, the freed slave of a woman, and his wife Trosia Nymphinia, the freed slave of a woman, made this for their son Flaccus, aged 22 years. This monument is 16 feet in front and 32 feet into the field.

How closely cemetery development was regulated is unclear. The law sought to protect the inhabitants of a town from the risks of fire and pollution, whether physical or spiritual, that the dead presented. But within areas deemed as suitable for burial the existence of additional laws indicates that disputes could arise between those wishing to bury and commemorate the dead and other land owners. Cemeteries were not confined to strictly demarcated areas and a town's suburbs were not limited to the burial of the dead. Tombs there could vie for space with houses, villas, gardens, farms, shops and other small businesses (Purcell 1987; Patterson 2000b). A tomb occupied land, land was property and property was money.

4.18 Digest (Ulpian) 11.7.10

Legal text: 6th c. AD (2nd c. AD).

If the seller of a farm specifies that a place for burial should be kept for him and his descendants to be buried there, if he is denied access for the purpose of burying someone, then he can bring an action. For the agreement between the purchaser and the seller guarantees the right of way through the farm for the purpose of performing a burial.

4.19 Digest (Pomponius) 11.8.3

Legal text: 6th c. AD (2nd c. AD).

If someone is building a tomb too close to your house, you can notify him that he should not continue with the new tomb; but once the building is finished the only action available to you is one against force or stealth. If a dead man has been buried too close to someone else's building within the minimum distance laid down by statute, the owner of the building cannot afterwards prevent the same person from burying another body or building a monument there, if that person acted with the owner's knowledge in the first place.

Monuments in the cemetery

Those with sufficient funds and inclination could choose to mark graves with tombstones and monuments. Cemeteries frequently followed the line of the road and thus these markers and structures were strung out along the highways, greeting those who entered the city and providing a last farewell to those who left. The street of tombs was designed to speak to the living both visually and verbally (Koortbojian 1996). Monuments were frequently designed to catch the eye of the passer-by: scale, decoration, words and images all combined to provide a final snapshot of the deceased. Tombs entailed the art of presentation; the person who commissioned the tomb, whether for themselves or others, made considered choices, in terms of size, pictures and text, about preserving and constructing memory and identity (see Chapter 2). These factors and their powerful effects were epitomized in the tomb of the first emperor Augustus.

4.20 Strabo, 5.3.8

Geography: early 1st c. AD. Strabo is describing the sights of Rome and here focuses on the Campus Martius.

For the Mausoleum in use see **2.11**, **2.63**, **3.24**, **3.41** and **3.69**.

Believing this place the most sacred they have erected funeral monuments there to the most distinguished men and women. The most noteworthy is the tomb called the 'Mausoleum' [of Augustus] which, situated near the river, consists of a great mound of earth raised upon a high foundation of white marble, and covered to the top with evergreen trees. Upon the summit is a bronze statue of Augustus Caesar, and beneath the mound are the funeral urns of himself, his relatives, and his friends. Behind the mound is a large precinct containing wonderful promenades. In the centre of the plain [the Campus Martius] is the place of cremation which is surrounded by a marble wall and an iron fence, and planted with poplars inside.

4.21 Figure 11: The mausoleum of Augustus

Tomb: late 1st c. BC. Rome (Campus Martius).

The mausoleum of Augustus, located within sight of the Tiber, survives as a circular ruin of concrete now planted with cypresses. The outer diameter measured 89 metres and the outermost wall was 12 metres high. It was faced originally in travertine (white limestone). The form and profile of the mound and the nature of its planting remain uncertain. What is not in doubt is that this was the largest tomb in the Roman world and would come to house the remains of several emperors and many members of the Julio-Claudian imperial family. The tomb was completed in 28 BC and it symbolized Augustus' attachment and loyalty to the city of Rome, contrasting in particular with Marc Antony's eastern leanings; the mausoleum served as both tomb and war trophy (Davies 2000). The mausoleum was part of Augustus' regeneration and adornment of the Campus Martius which included a huge sundial and the *ara pacis* (altar of peace). At his death in AD 14 Augustus had a record of his achievements (*Res Gestae*), inscribed in bronze, placed adjacent to the entrance of the tomb.

Monuments jostled for frontage along the roads that led in and out of Roman towns and could compete to gain attention, with epitaphs that addressed the passer-by (**1.49**, **2.8**, **2.57** and **6.32**), or amenities such as seating (**Figures 9** and **17**) and sun-dials (**2.56**). Monuments were of varied designs, shapes and scale. They ranged from humble markers of wood and pottery (**Figure 8**) to imposing architectural flights of fancy. For those with money the possibilities were near endless: tombs in the shape of pyramids (**Figure 1**), houses (**Figure 15**), temples (**Figure 2**) and benches (**Figure 9**), or round tombs (**Figure 11**), square tombs (**Figure 13**) and tower tombs (**Figure 16**). Sculptural and stuccoed décor could also be varied, representing scenes from daily life, the occupation of the deceased (**Figure 18**), the highlights of a career (**Figure 12**) or familial bliss (**Figure 11**); alternatively, images might draw upon Rome's rich mythological traditions. Accompanying epitaphs could also be lengthy, recounting the life story of the deceased, telling of great careers or familial

Figure 11 The mausoleum of Augustus, Rome.

devotion or espousing views on the life hereafter. Most monuments, however, were modest in nature. Many were stelae (**Figures 18** and **20**) – slabs of stone that stood upright in the ground – or altars (**Figure 14**) that marked or held the remains (ossuary altars). These memorials were often decorated simply with floral patterns and were inscribed with brief epitaphs that stated the name of the deceased, the name of the commemorator and the relationship between the two. Further personal details could be added to the inscription or sculpture, such as the career of the deceased, their age or additional familial connections, but extra information was far from standard. Many monuments were probably bought from stock or pattern books. The purchaser's scope to individualize may have been limited and what to depict, what to say and how to say it governed by convention.

4.22 CIL X 1026 and Figure 12

Tomb: early 1st c. AD. Pompeii (Herculaneum Gate necropolis).
   = *ILS* 6372; Kockel 1983: 90–7.
   The monument, in the shape of an altar, was raised on a high-stepped base at the centre of an enclosure, which faced the road (see **Figure 13**). The marble altar was ornately decorated. Beneath the epitaph is depicted a large bench. This double seat (*bisellium*), used in the theatre, was an honour awarded to

distinguished citizens. Each side of the altar has an oak wreath with ribbons, a symbol of honour. The epitaph notes that the commemorated man was an *augustalis*, a priest involved in the worship of the emperor. This was one of the few offices open to ex-slaves and, although this man is not specifically described as a freedman, he may have been of servile origin (see **2.57**). The monument employs a range of communicative media, words, images, scale and location, to commemorate the deceased. It highlights certain aspects of his life, especially the public honours received and title achieved, but other aspects of his identity, such as his exact legal status, age at death (he was probably still alive), familial connections and the nature of his generosity to Pompeii are not mentioned. A funerary monument could be a limited and selective means of communication, but overall this example still effectively establishes that the commemorated man was a distinguished individual.

> To Caius Calventius Quietus, an *augustalis*. Honoured with a *bisellium* [double seat] for his generosity by decree of the *decuriones* and by consent of the people.

Unfortunately few cemeteries survive sufficiently well to give us a detailed impression of how the memorials, and thus the cemetery overall, appeared and functioned. Some insights are provided by a handful of well-preserved cemeteries or areas of cemeteries. We need to be cautious, however, of

Figure 12 Tomb of Caius Calventius Quietus, Pompeii.

becoming over-dependent on these limited examples. The cemeteries of Pompeii, for example, are evocative, but relate to a particular chronological period and geographic region. The cemeteries of the Roman empire may have been united by extramural burial and burial rites (for example, cremation), but could retain distinctive features. Different areas of the empire could employ different shapes of monument or decorative motifs or materials; for example, the rock-cut tombs of Asia Minor or the earth barrows from Britain and the north-west provinces (Toynbee 1971: 179–99; compare von Hesberg 1992: 102–11) or the barrel-shaped tombstones of Roman Spain (Tupman 2005). Not all provincial burial grounds and places would have conformed exactly to the Italian prototype with large stone monuments stretched out along suburban roads. The adoption or indeed rejection of 'Roman' style memorials was not simply a gauge of the success or failure of Romanization. In Britain, for example, the number of surviving stone grave markers and tombs of the Roman period is comparatively low. This may reflect a lack of suitable stone for carving, but is also suggestive of the localized ways in which 'Roman' customs were adopted and adapted (Mann 1985; Hope 1997a). The dialogue between Rome and indigenous cultures could be reflected in the funerary sphere (Hitchner 1995).

4.23 *Figure 13: Herculaneum Gate Necropolis, Pompeii*

Cemetery: mid 1st c. AD. Pompeii (Italy).
= Kockel 1983.
The figure shows a section of a cemetery situated a short distance from the Herculaneum Gate of Pompeii. The tombs, in various states of preservation, flank the sides of the road. Most of the tombs in this section of the necropolis are shaped as altars, some raised up on steps and placed in walled enclosures. The well-preserved and ornately decorated tomb of Caius Calventius Quietus is visible; for this see **Figure 12**.
For further tombs from Pompeii see **Figures 2** and **9**.

4.24 *Figure 14: Via Annia Necropolis, Aquileia*

Cemetery: late 1st or early 2nd c. AD. Aquileia (Italy).
= Brusin 1941; Toynbee 1971: 79–82.
This section of cemetery consisted of low-walled enclosures. The enclosures share a common depth (30 Roman feet) and a rear wall, but vary in width. This may suggest that the burial area was marked out by a developer and then the plots sold on to individuals. Each enclosure had a central altar raised on a low base, and these were surrounded by burials, mainly cremations sunk into the ground, most of which appear to have been unmarked. The easternmost tomb (right of the figure) has been assigned to the Statii family; here was found, on a subsidiary altar, the epitaph to Fabricia Severina (**4.13**). Some of the enclosures continued in use or were reused as

Figure 13 The Herculaneum Gate necropolis, Pompeii.

late as the 5th c. AD, and the cemetery exhibits the shift to inhumation with the presence of sarcophagi in several enclosures.

Differences in the design and appearance of memorials occurred within the same province as well as across the empire. Italy itself exhibited a range of tomb options, and the cemeteries of towns such as Pompeii, Ostia, Portus and Aquileia were not all identical. Some differences in appearance and function of cemeteries are admittedly explained by time. So for example, the Isola Sacra necropolis (**Figure 15**) with its house tombs differs in appearance to the Herculaneum Gate necropolis of Pompeii (**Figure 13**). This difference may be largely explained by a shift in the early imperial period away from grand tombs (**Figures 1** and **11**) focused primarily on the individual toward tombs of a more communal nature with internalized display (von Hesberg 1992). In short, when the Isola Sacra cemetery began Pompeii had already been dead and buried for many years; the cemeteries of the two towns represent different eras and fashions. Indeed with time the tombs of the Isola Sacra also saw changes, many being adapted to inhumation burial. A range of factors could impact upon how a cemetery developed and was monumentalized (or not); time, geography, stone supplies, local traditions, fashion, economics and status would all have played their part. There was no blueprint for a Roman cemetery.

146

Figure 14 The via Annia necropolis, Aquileia.

4.25 Figure 15: The Isola Sacra necropolis

Cemetery: early to mid 2nd c. AD. Portus (Italy).
= Baldassere 1996; Calza 1940.

The so-called Isola Sacra necropolis served the harbour town of Portus. The tombs lie on either side of the road connecting Portus with Ostia. The tombs date to the 2nd and 3rd c. AD, with the later tombs placed in front of the earlier examples. The figure shows tombs 93 to 85 which date to the early and mid 2nd c. AD. The tombs are built of brick and some were barrel vaulted. The tomb facades have a doorway, above which was located a marble panel for the inscription, many of which are now lost. Slit windows flank the inscription on some of the tombs. The interior walls of the tombs are filled with niches for cremation burials; some tombs were also adapted for inhumation burial. Unroofed enclosures or precincts could be built in front of the tomb, with the walls lined with niches for urns containing cremated remains.

For epitaphs and tombs from the Isola Sacra see **4.9, 4.14, 4.32** and **4.36**.

Figure 15 The Isola Sacra necropolis, Portus.

Monuments in the landscape

The landscape of the Roman empire was peppered with cemeteries and funerary monuments. Some of the most impressive monuments were not in the urban centres, but located in the countryside. These could take advantage of the natural terrain such as mountainsides or the coastline to create an eye-catching spectacle. Impressive rural monuments had their origins in the fact that the wealth of the élite was invested in land. In Republican Rome aristocratic families had their own traditional burial places. Some of these were clustered together between the via Appia and the via Latina (for example, the tombs of the Claudii Marcelli, the Servillii, the Metelli and the Scipios) suggesting competition for prime spots (Cicero, *Tusculan Disputations* 1.7.13), but others were buried where the family owned substantial tracts of land. Indeed, the land-owning élite could choose to be buried not in Rome or other urban centres, but on their country estates.

4.26 Livy 38.53.8

History: late 1st c. BC or early 1st c. AD.
  Scipio Africanus (236–184 BC), a prominent general in the Punic War, was an early example of a leading politician requesting burial away from Rome.

The decision was no doubt politically motivated since in his final years Scipio had withdrawn to his villa, embittered by political disputes in Rome. Elsewhere Livy expresses uncertainty as to where Scipio was actually buried (38.56.3–4); see also Seneca, *Epistles* 86.

> Scipio spent his life at Liternum, with no desire to return to the city; when dying they say that he gave instructions that he should be buried in that same place in the country and that his monument should be built there, so that his funeral might not be held in an ungrateful homeland.

In Rome of the late Republic there was a struggle to curb the competitive ethos of the élite which was expressed, amongst other things, through extravagant funerals and grandiose tomb buildings; then, with the advent of the principate, the emperor began to dominate display in the capital (see Chapter 3 and above). Away from Rome there was more scope for personal or extravagant expression. Houses were traditionally of great familial, emotional and symbolic importance; they were part of how the élite communicated their success and standing to the wider community (see for example Treggiari 1999; Hales 2003). Villa estates, including the tombs of the owners, became part of this process; villa and tomb became monuments to their creators (Bodel 1997). We can note Pliny's description of the tomb of Verginius Rufus, a great man commemorated away from Rome (**2.38**). Individual rural memorials also survive from across the provinces, reflecting the success of local dignitaries, the importance of non-urban display and the impact of monuments upon the landscape and indeed vice versa.

4.27 *Figure 16: Igel Saul*

Tomb: early 3rd c. AD. Igel (to the south-west of Trier).
= Dragendorf and Krüger 1924.
Visible from both road and river, the sandstone tower tomb stands approximately 23 metres high. It was adorned with sculpture depicting mythological themes and scenes from daily life (no longer fully visible). The damaged epitaph names the Secundinii family and the sculpted images suggest that they were involved in the production and sale of cloth.

Of relevance here also is Cicero's attempt to console himself by planning a memorial shrine for his daughter. This was not to be a tomb, as Cicero is keen to stress, but his correspondence with Atticus on the matter does suggest the memory function of villas (estates), the importance of a good visible location for a monument and the challenge and expense of obtaining suitable land. Cicero does not discuss the appearance or exact purpose of the shrine in detail with Atticus, instead giving much attention to finding the right spot. The shrine does not appear to have been built, disappearing from

Figure 16
The Igel Saul, near Trier.

the correspondence when purchasing a building plot was still under discussion. Perhaps the scheme, and obtaining an appropriate location, became too complex or maybe Cicero decided that the project was a hindrance rather than a help in the search for a cure to his grief (see **5.45–5.50**).

4.28 Cicero to Atticus 12.18.1 (254); 12.19.1 (257); 12.23.3 (262); 12.36.1 (275)

Letters: March–May 45 BC.

In trying to escape the memories that cause me biting pain, I have reason to send you a reminder. I hope that you forgive me, whatever you think. I can indeed refer to several of the authors whom I am reading just now as recommending the project about which I have often talked to you and for which I want your approval. I refer to that shrine. Do give it consideration in proportion to the affection in which you hold me. I have no doubts about the form of the shrine (I like Cluatius' plan), nor about the idea (for it is settled); but I have some doubts about the place. Therefore I'd like you to think it over. As far as is possible in this time of learning, I shall naturally honour her with every kind of memorial which Greek and Latin genius can

150

provide. Perhaps it will reopen my wound. But I consider myself as virtually held by a vow and promise, and the long time I will not be moves me more than this small span, which seems to me too long. There is nothing I have not tried and still found no comfort.

This is a pleasant spot, and in the sea; it can be seen both from Antium and Circeii. But I have to consider how to make sure it can stay as it were consecrated through the innumerable changes in ownership which may occur in the infinite future, if our society survives. For myself I no longer need incomes, and I can be content with little. I sometimes think of buying a suburban property across the Tiber, mainly on account of this, and I can't think of any place which could be so much in the public view. But what property we must discuss together, but the shrine must be completed this summer.

If nothing across the Tiber can be settled, Cotta has something near Ostia in a well-frequented place, with very little ground, but enough, even more than enough, for this purpose. I'd like you to think of it. However don't let these prices of suburban estates perturb you. I don't want silver or expensive clothes anymore or the pleasant places I used to care for; this is what I want.

I want it to be a shrine and from this there's no persuading me. I am anxious to avoid the appearance of a tomb, not on account of the fine but in order to achieve apotheosis, as far as is possible. This I could do if I built within a villa, but as we have often said, there would be changes in ownership. On open land, wherever I put it, I think I can ensure that its religious nature is respected by posterity. You must bear with this foolishness of mine (for I admit it), for there's no one, not even myself, to whom I can speak so plainly as to you.

There existed a degree of emotional and sentimental attachment to the land (wherever it was located) and the family tombs that it held (Martial 1.114). These were idealized sentiments; few people owned houses, villas and land, and those that did may not have retained these holdings across the generations. Many who lived in rural areas would have been peasants and slaves who may have been buried in the fields in which they worked (see, for example, Collis 1977), their simple graves often rapidly blending into the landscape, to the point that they might be easily confused with other things.

4.29 *Siculus Flaccus,* On the Conditions of Land 49

On land surveying: date uncertain.
  For a rural cemetery see **4.56.**

Here is another thing to watch out for: the custom of making graves and putting up funerary markers at the edge of fields which can be taken in error as boundary markers; for on ground that is stony and barren, tombs are made from the same material as ownership markers.

Maintaining the cemetery

Self-presentation and the promotion of memory were a key element of monument design. Many people gave thought to how they wished to be remembered and the nature and form of their memorial. Wills might contain quite elaborate details as to what the testator desired (2.33–2.35, 2.37 and 2.38). An alternative was to build a tomb before death, which was one way of ensuring that you got what you wanted (2.54–2.57). But whether it was built by others or oneself there must have been knowledge that memory was fickle. Cicero worried about ensuring the sanctity of the site of his daughter's memorial after future changes of ownership (4.28). Pliny the Younger complained that Verginius Rufus' memorial was unfinished some years after his death (2.38). People were unreliable and the dead were soon forgotten, and tombs declined and decayed (see below). To survive, a tomb needed the living more than the dead. People looked for ways by which to protect and maintain their graves. One way was to give the living a vested interest in a tomb; one day it would be their resting place too. The ideal was for a family tomb, perhaps best epitomized by that of the Scipios which was used from the 3rd c. BC to the 1st c. AD (Hopkins 1983: 206; for epitaphs see Courtney 1995: n. 9–13). However, the reality was that tombs rarely stayed in use for long. Families died out, people moved away, new generations wished to build their own memorials. Yet this reality did not remove the hope and expectation of continuity, even if people looked to their freed slaves and the descendants of freed slaves, who would carry the family name, as much as to their own blood relatives. A common formula in epitaphs was *libertis libertabusque posterisque eorum* meaning 'for their freedmen and freedwomen and their descendants' (4.14, 4.32, 4.33, 4.34, 5.38 and 6.32). This was an effective way of tying dependants to the tomb and thus promoting its maintenance and the memory of its founders. The freed slaves gained a place for burial and their economic circumstances may have rendered them more reliable than an independent heir. Any freed slave who had offended their patron could, however, find themselves excluded (4.31).

4.30 Digest (Ulpian) 11.7.6

Legal text: 6th c. AD (3rd c. AD).

> Those disinherited are allowed, on the grounds of compassion, to be buried themselves unless the testator, acting out of reasonable ill-

feeling, has specifically forbidden it. However they may not bury anyone other than their own descendants. Freedmen cannot be buried or bury others, unless they are heirs to their patron, although some people have inscribed on their tomb that they have built it for themselves and their freedmen.

4.31 CIL VI 7470

Epitaph: 2nd c. AD. Rome.
= *ILS* 8286.
See also **6.32**.

> Publius Aelius Callistus, from the grant made to him by Marcus Aurelius Epagathus, granted [space] to Aelia Primenia and Licinia Antesphoris and their freedmen. My other freedmen did not deserve it, nor my daughter.

Some founders of communal tombs had concerns about their heirs and what might happen to the tomb if it was inherited by others. The formula HMHNS (*hoc monumentum heredes non sequetur*; this monument does not go to the heirs) is found on some epitaphs, especially in Italy and southern Gaul, in an attempt to stop the tomb passing to the heirs who might sell, subdivide or abandon it.

4.32 Isola Sacra, Tomb 79

Epitaph: 2nd c. AD. Inscribed on a marble slab located over the entrance to the tomb.
= Thylander 1952: A25.

> To the spirits of the departed. Quintus Appius Saturninus, son of Quintus, built this for himself and Annia Donata, his well-deserving wife, and for their children and their freedmen and freedwomen and their descendants. This tomb does not go to the heir, and may the right of sale not be allowed either to those to whom I have left it, or to Donata. In front 10 feet, into the field 12 feet.

Testators and tomb founders could leave money for guards to protect their tomb (**2.20** and **2.56**) and money in trust for its maintenance. Property such as gardens could be attached to the tomb, providing a pleasant environment for those visiting the tomb, and the produce from such a garden tomb (*cepotaphium*) could be used in tomb cult or sold to help maintain the tomb (Jashemski 1979: 141–53; Heulsen 1890; Toynbee 1971: 94–100). The testator from Langres provided money for the repair of his tomb and the upkeep of the gardens, including employing three gardeners and their apprentices (2.37). Basically the testator or tomb founder could use his or her earthly wealth to provide not just a suitable tomb, but ensure that it was well provided for, and even self-sufficient.

4.33 CIL VI 13244/5

Epitaph: 2nd or 3rd c. AD. Rome (Porta Maggiore). The inscription was found inside a tomb.
See also *CIL* VI 13040, 21020 and *CIL* X 2066.

> To the spirits of the departed. Marcus Aurelius Syntomus and Aurelia Marciane built this with a *cepotaphium* and made it for their memory only, and for their children Aurelius Leontinus and Aurelia Fructuosa, and for their freedmen, freedwomen and their descendants.

4.34 CIL VI 1319

Epitaph: late 1st c. BC. Rome.

> Caius Hostius Pamphilus, freedman of Caius, a doctor bought this monument for himself and Nelpia Hymnis, freedwoman of Marcus, and for all their freedmen, freedwomen and their descendants. This is our eternal home; this is our farm; these are our gardens; this is our monument. In front 13 feet, into the field 24 feet.

4.35 CIL XII 1657

Epitaph: 2nd or 3rd c. AD. Lucus Augusti (Luc-en-Dois, France).
For plants that may have been found in a tomb garden see Virgil, *Culex* 398–407.

> To the spirits of the departed children and wife of Publicius Calistus, who for himself consecrated a vineyard two thirds of half an acre in area, from whose yield he wishes libations of no less than 15 measures of wine to be poured for him each year.

An additional way of perpetuating memory was to encourage people to visit the memorial by leaving money to fund feasts and celebrations, or even paying people directly to celebrate annual rites (2.43). Tomb founders might provide facilities specifically for tomb cult. The testator of Langres richly furnished his tomb with items that were aimed at the comfort of the living more than the dead (2.37). An imperial freedman Marcus Ulpius Hermadio built a tomb for his wife that included an atrium (hall), a *triclinium* (dining room), a *solarium* (sun room) and a portico (*AE* 1977: n.31); this amounted to 'all the comforts of home' (Champlin 1991: 174). Other epitaphs make reference to more limited facilities such as dining rooms (*CIL* IX 1938) and sun terraces (*CIL* XI 3895). Wells, ovens, seating areas and dining rooms are attested archaeologically. At the Isola Sacra necropolis tombs often had wells and areas for the preparation and cooking of food (Graham 2005a, 2005b). Some tombs had second storeys which could be used as sun terraces or dining spaces, while other tombs had *biclinia* or dining couches flanking the entrance of the tomb.

4.36 *Figure 17: Isola Sacra, Tomb 15*

Tomb: 2nd c. AD.

The façade of the house tomb incorporated a doorway above which was set a marble panel, with slit windows, for the inscription. The epitaph above the door records Verria Zosime and her husband, but this epitaph may not be the original. Outside the door were two stone benches presumably to seat visitors to the tomb.

Military cemeteries and burials

Not everyone was able to make elaborate provisions for a tomb and its upkeep. Individuals found their actions restricted not just by financial

Figure 17 Tomb 15 of the Isola Sacra necropolis, Portus.

circumstances, but by social position or the circumstances of their death. A striking social group is soldiers of the Roman army. There survive, from across the Roman empire, thousands of tombstones that commemorate men who died while serving in the Roman legions and auxiliary units. Some of these men had prospered and stress their success; the honours they had won, the promotions achieved (**4.38**) or, in the case of auxiliary troops (**4.39**), a new-found identity as soldiers and would-be citizens of Rome (Hope 2000c). The majority of these military men were probably not particularly wealthy, but soldiers did have certain advantages over civilians in achieving decent burial in a marked grave (Hope 2001: 39). The soldier was in receipt of regular wages and the military unit could act as a *collegium*, with the soldier making contributions to a burial fund (Vegetius II. 20). The soldier was also surrounded by a supportive network of like-minded comrades who acted as pseudo-family. Burial and commemoration of serving soldiers was a private matter; it was not paid for or organized by the military authorities. If the soldier failed to make adequate provision for his burial he presumably went to a common grave or fellow soldiers stepped in and did the decent thing. Many military epitaphs make reference to the will of the deceased and the role of fellow soldiers as heirs, which suggests that many men planned ahead and anticipated their demise (**4.37** and **4.39**).

4.37 CIL XIII 6940

Epitaph: early 1st c. AD. Mogontiacum (Mainz, Germany). A stele with a triangular gable decorated with a single rosette.
 = Boppert 1992a: n.87; Selzer 1988: n.44.

> Caius Iulius Andiccus son of Caius, of the Voltinian voting tribe, a soldier of *legio XVI*, aged 45 years, served 21 years. He lies here. The heirs set this up.

4.38 CIL III 11213

Epitaph: 1st c. AD. Carnuntum (Petronel, Austria). A stele with a triangular gable decorated with a rosette.
 = Vorbeck 1980a: n.140.
 The epitaph tells how the deceased had been promoted through the auxiliary ranks, ultimately becoming a legionary centurion.

> Titus Calidius Severus, son of Publius, of the Camilia voting tribe, an *eques*, *optio*, and *decurio* of *cohors I Alpinorum*, and then centurion of *legio XV Apollinaris*. Aged 58 years, served 34 years. He lies here. Quintus Calidius his brother put this up.

156

4.39 CIL VII 66 and Figure 18

Tombstone: 1st c. AD. Corinium (Cirencester, England). A stele with a triangular gable.

= Collingwood and Wright 1995: n.108; Webster 1993: n.138.

Above the epitaph is a horseman and barbarian relief, a design commonly used on tombstones set up to auxiliary cavalrymen. The deceased is depicted on horseback, spear in hand, with a fallen enemy at the horse's feet. The single name of the deceased (Dannicus) suggests that he was not a Roman citizen. Dannicus came from Augusta Raurica (Augst, Switzerland).

> Dannicus, a cavalryman of the *ala Indiana*, from the troop of Albanus, who served 16 years, a tribesman of the Raurici. Fulvius Natalis and Flavius Bitucus set this up according to the will. He lies here.

4.40 CIL VIII 2961

Epitaph: 2nd or 3rd c. AD. Lambaesis (Tazoult, Algeria).

A *missicius* was a retired soldier who could still be called upon to serve. A *cornicularius* was a horn player. Note the neatly rounded numbers employed for the ages and periods of service.

Figure 18
The tombstone of Dannicus, Cirencester. Photograph: copyright Corinium Museum.

157

To the spirits of the departed Lucius Pompeius Felix who joined the army aged 20 years, he served for 25 years and afterwards was a *missicius* for 35 years. He lived 80 years. His son Lucius Pompeius Maximus, a former *cornicularius,* made this for his father.

Military cemeteries must have been marked by row upon row of tomb-stones that, through similar language and images, recalled the serried ranks of the army. This suggests a unity of identity among the soldiers and further that substantial cemeteries located outside the provincial forts would have acted as powerful symbols of a collective Roman identity and Roman pres-ence. However, it needs to be emphasized that the Roman military cemetery was the product of peacetime rather than conflict. For soldiers killed in combat all their saving and planning may have counted for naught. From the late Republic those killed on the battlefield did not receive singular burial in a marked grave, nor were their bodies returned home.

4.41 Appian, Civil Wars 1.43

History: 2nd c. AD. Events of 90 BC, after a Roman defeat in the Social War.

When the bodies of Rutilius and many other aristocrats were brought for burial to Rome, the dead bodies of the consul and so many others proved a sad sight and the resulting mourning lasted many days. After this the Senate decreed that those killed in war were to be buried where they died, so that others should not be deterred from joining the army by what they saw.

During the Empire when soldiers, now of a professional and full-time nature, were recruited from across the territories of the empire and served in diverse regions, any repatriation of remains would have been impos-sible and impractical. Exactly how the bodies of those killed in conflict were collected, treated and disposed of remains largely unclear. Decent, or at least adequate disposal, was expected (**3.40**) and mass cremation on a common pyre seems the most likely option.

4.42 Virgil, Aeneid 11, 184–202

Epic poetry: late 1st c. BC.
    This poetic account of a mythical funeral may provide some insights into Roman military funerals. Note the circling of the pyre (*decursio*), an honour reserved for military men, especially generals; compare **3.42**.

Now both Tarchon and Father Aeneas built funeral pyres on the winding shore and carried there the bodies of their dead, according to the fashion of their fathers. Fires were set beneath and the heights of heaven were plunged into gloomy darkness. Three times they ran round the blazing pyres in gleaming armour. Three times on horseback they circled the mournful fires of the dead with wails of lamentation. Tears fell upon the earth and upon their armour. The cries of men and the blare of trumpets rose to heaven as some threw into the flames spoils taken from the bodies of the Latins, their splendid swords and helmets, the bridles of horses and scorching chariot wheels; while others burned the familiar possessions of their dead, the shields and luckless spears. All around, cattle were sacrificed and offered to Death, while bristling swine and animals carried off from the fields were slaughtered over the fires. All along the shore they watched their comrades burn and guarded the dying pyres; they could not tear themselves away until dank Night turned over the heavens and the sky was studded with gleaming stars.

A battle ground needed to be cleared quickly to avoid the decomposition and desecration of corpses. There would have been little opportunity for individual identification of the dead or separate burial, although those distinguished by rank or deed may have sometimes been singled out (Appian, *Civil Wars* 2.82). The anonymity that confronted many killed in action stands in stark contrast to the fortress military cemeteries. Yet provided Rome was victorious, the bodies of the Roman dead were at least collected and disposed of, albeit in a basic manner. If on the other hand Rome lost the fight the bodies might be abandoned on the battlefield and left unburied. In literary descriptions Roman defeat is rendered more humiliating and shocking when the corpses of dead soldiers were left above ground to rot.

4.43 *Tacitus,* Annals *1.60–62*

History: early 2nd c. AD. Events of AD 15. Germanicus buries the dead massacred six years previously in the Teutoburgian Forest, when three legions under Varus were lost.

Germanicus is manipulating civil and military sympathy for the war dead for his own ends.

On the open ground were whitening bones, scattered or heaped up where men had fallen, fleeing or standing fast. Close by lay fragments of spears and horses' limbs, and also human skulls, prominently nailed to tree-trunks. In groves nearby were the savage altars at which the Germans had slaughtered the tribunes and senior centurions ... [Survivors indicate where Varus had fallen] ... And so, six years after the massacre, a Roman army present on the ground had come to bury the bones of three legions. No one knew if he was burying the remains of a stranger or a kinsman. But they all thought of all as friends and members of one family, and with rising fury against the enemy, they mourned and hated at the same time. Germanicus laid the first turf of the funeral mound, paying a heart-felt tribute to the dead and sharing in the grief of those around him.

In times of civil conflict, when both victors and defeated were Roman, the sight of unburied soldiers became particularly controversial and poignant (see **1.33**). At such times the right of the fallen to honourable burial could become problematic and debated. Cicero proposed exceptional honours including a war memorial for Republican victors, something hitherto unheard of, but he has nothing to say on how the 'enemy' dead, who were also Romans, should be treated (**4.44**). In other works (**4.45**) a moral commentary is created on the corruption of power as Roman leaders look on the 'Roman dead' and feast their eyes on the carnage (Morgan 1992; Pagán 2000).

4.44 Cicero, Philippic 14.12.31–32

Speech: 43 BC. Cicero addressed the Senate following a victory for the Republican forces against Marc Antony, suggesting a war memorial for the fallen. It was not constructed although the consuls who led the attack (Hirtius and Pansa) were awarded public funerals and tombs on the Campus Martius, see **3.9**.

> It is therefore my wish, Conscript Fathers, that to the soldiers of the legion, and to those that have fallen fighting by their side, there should be built a monument in the noblest possible form ... [Cicero notes the legion's services to the state] ... There shall be constructed a magnificently worked memorial and an inscription cut, an ever-lasting witness to your divine bravery; and in your praise, whether men see your monument or hear of it, the words expressing deep gratitude will never be silent. Thus you will have exchanged life's mortality for immortality.

4.45 Lucan, Civil War 7, 786–804

Epic poetry: mid 1st c. AD. The aftermath of the battle of Pharsalus (48 BC).
Julius Caesar is portrayed as acting tyrannically when he fails to bury the dead. Even Rome's greatest enemy, Hannibal, had acted with greater humanity.
Compare Tacitus, *Histories* 2.70.

> When daylight revealed the casualties of Pharsalus no feature of the landscape stopped him looking on the fatal field. He sees streams still running red and the heaps of corpses high like hills which are

settling down into corruption. He counts the peoples who had followed Pompey. He selects a spot from where he can study and recognize the features of the dead, and tells his men to prepare his feast; he rejoices that he cannot see the soil and that the plain which his eyes pass over is concealed by death. In bloodshed he sees his victorious Fortune and the favour of the heavens. In his madness he is reluctant to spoil the spectacle of his wickedness and he denies the wretched dead a pyre; and forces the sight of Pharsalus upon the guilty gods. When the Carthaginian [Hannibal] buried the consul [Paulus Aemilius] Cannae was lit up by Libyan torches; but that example did not influence Caesar to treat his enemies with humanity. His rage was not satisfied with the slaughter and he remembered that these citizens were his enemies. We do not ask for a single or separate pyre for each of the dead; but just one for all of them.

By the late Republic and Imperial period, in most conflicts (other than civil war) the men killed in battle were far removed, in terms of location and origin, from the capital city. The rough, provincial, poorly educated soldiers were probably perceived as expendable by the literary élite and the populace of Rome, and thus little-remembered as individuals at least. Even Cicero's proposed Republican tomb was never built and Germanicus' mound was soon destroyed by the enemy and was not restored (Tacitus, *Annals* 2.7.3–4). Rome celebrated and commemorated victories (note trophy monuments such as Trajan's column and triumphal processions) rather than the victims of war (Hope 2003; Cooley 2007). Victories promoted political stability and the prowess of the emperor, defeats and dead soldiers did not. It is easy to imagine that most anonymous mass graves on battlefields were soon forgotten. Only rarely do we find the war dead being given individuality and their memories promoted.

4.46 CIL III 14214

Inscription: late 1st or early 2nd c. AD. Adamklissi, Dacia (Romania).
= *ILS* 9107; Dorutiu 1961.

The fragmentary inscription comes from a large altar, approximately 12 metres wide and 6 metres high. The inscription began with the name of the emperor (now lost), and listed casualties, supplying perhaps as many as 3,800 names, most of which are now lost or incomplete. The altar was found 200 metres from a huge circular victory trophy, built by Trajan (AD 108/9), and those listed on the altar may have died during Trajan's first Dacian campaign. However Domitian also campaigned and endured heavy casualties in Dacia. Whatever the exact date of the altar, it is the only surviving example of a war memorial that listed the dead, although its juxtaposition with a victory monument ultimately promoted Roman success.

... in memory of the most valiant men who met death in the service of the state ... Lucius Valerius Sacer from Vienne, Lucius Gavillius Primus from Cologne, Lucius Valerius Lunaris, Caius Octavius Secundus from Fréjus ...

4.47 Cassius Dio 68. 8.2

History: late 2nd or early 3rd c. AD. Trajan, 'the soldier emperor', honours soldiers who fell in the Dacian campaigns.

It is uncertain if the altar mentioned here is the same as that found at Adamklissi (**4.46**).

Nevertheless he [Trajan] engaged the enemy, and saw many of his men wounded and killed many of his opponents. And when the bandages ran out, he is said not even to have spared his own clothing, but to have cut it up into strips. In honour of the soldiers who had died in the battle he commanded an altar to be built and funeral rites to be performed annually.

Exclusion from the cemetery

The right to burial was a fundamental one, but there were some limitations that applied to certain sections of Roman society. As noted above, soldiers killed in combat did not receive standard cemetery burial and in the extremes of defeat might not be buried at all. Others could find themselves more formally excluded from the urban cemetery. An inscription from Sarsina (**4.15**) suggests that there were groups who were deemed as 'unclean' and thus not worthy for inclusion in formal cemetery areas. Prostitutes, undertakers and gladiators were probably among those so stigmatized. All were involved in dirty jobs which could entail the legal stigma of *infamia*. In Roman eyes, these people demeaned themselves for profit and debased their bodies by providing pleasure for others or by being associated with death. The fate of the bodies of these professions is difficult to establish, especially since they were mainly drawn from slaves and the poverty-stricken whose graves were unlikely to be marked. However, the treatment of gladiators does provide some clues. The stars of the arena were often recruited from slaves and criminals, although free men, inspired by the hope of fame and fortune, could choose to become gladiators. Those who perished in gladiatorial combats were unceremoniously dragged from the arena and many may have been disposed of rapidly and basically, with some even denied burial altogether (Hope 2000b). However, the survival of tombstones that commemorate gladiators suggests that at least some gladiators were buried with a degree of respect and were remembered by others. Like other servile groups, or people who worked together, gladiators may have formed *collegia* that assisted with burial (see Chapter 3). Some gladiators were commemorated by fellow gladiators with whom they had established bonds in the same way as soldiers did with their comrades (see above). Gladiatorial tombstones have often been found grouped together which may support the existence of *collegia*, but may also indicate a degree of separation from the wider community (Hope 2000b: 99–100; Edmondson 1999: 658–9). It is possible that some gladiators were formally debarred from the cemetery (**4.15**; and Levick 1983), but at the very least we can imagine that just as these men lived on the edge of society and acceptability, so they were buried.

4.48 CIL *XII 3327, 3329 and 3332*

Epitaphs: 1st c. AD. Nemausus (Nîmes, France).

These small and undecorated stelae were found grouped together to the south of the town's amphitheatre. Note how the gladiatorial titles precede the names of the deceased in the epitaphs; this word ordering is unusual and gives added prominence to the job title. A *retiarius* fought with a net and the Thracian with a curved sword and a small shield. The legal status of the men is uncertain; Aptus may have been a slave and the other two may have been free men, but whether freed slaves or free born remains unclear. The varied geographic origins of the gladiators suggest the mobility of gladiatorial troops. Is it only coincidence that two of the men are commemorated by a wife called Optata?

See Hope 1998.

> To the retiarius Lucius Pompeius, fought 7 times, from Vienne, age 25 years. His wife Optata paid for this.

> To the Thracian Aptus from Alexandria, aged 37 years, his wife Optata made this.

> To the Thracian Quintus Vettius Gracilius of 3 victories, age 25 years, from Spain. Lucius Sestius Latinus gave this.

Other individuals could be denied burial altogether. Suicides may have been singled out. In the Lanuvium *collegium* suicides would not get their burial allowance (**3.2**). This prohibition may have been to prevent abuse of the society's funds, but it may also have had a spiritual dimension. In the Roman world suicide was viewed with ambivalence; on the one hand to take one's life could be seen as an honourable exit; on the other, the souls of suicides were viewed as existing in limbo and their right to burial could be questioned (see Chapter 1). The method of suicide appears to have been crucial to how the body of the suicide was treated. Hanging was viewed as sordid and demeaning and those choosing this method might be stigmatized. In Puteoli it was specified that the bodies of the hanged were to be removed within an hour of their being reported (**3.10**). In Sarsina those who hanged themselves were excluded from the burial ground donated by one of the town's citizens (**4.15**). In certain circumstances the corpse of a suicide may have been equated to that of a criminal (Quintilian, *Institutes of Oratory* 7.3.7). Indeed, for criminals and traitors the fate of their bodies was at best uncertain (*Digest* 48.24.1). Post mortem insult could form part of capital punishment and the display of dead bodies became a warning to the living, a warning that could take on large or spectacular dimensions (**1.38–1.40**). Suffering and degradation provided a potent image for spectators. Executions of criminals could take place at the edge of settlements and thus in or near cemeteries; the exposed bodies of the condemned must have contrasted sharply with the graves of the respectable (Kyle 1998: 53). Note the tale in Petronius about a criminal's body being displayed in or near a cemetery area (**5.44**). In Rome the bodies of lowly criminals (*noxii*) executed in the arena might be dumped in the Tiber (Kyle 1998: 218–24). The bodies of traitors, including those who had once been powerful and distinguished (Varner 2001b), might suffer a similar fate after being exposed on the Gemonian Steps or Stairs of Mourning (*Scalae Gemoniae*). These steps, in full view of the Forum, and thus at the heart rather than the edge of the city, first appear in accounts of Tiberius' reign. Tiberius was notorious for his many victims (**4.49**).

4.49 Tacitus, Annals 6.16

History: early 2nd c. AD. Events of AD 33. Sejanus, the Praetorian Prefect, was denounced and executed in AD 31.
  Compare Cassius Dio 58.11.1–6

> And as executions had whetted his appetite, the emperor now ordered the death of all those held for complicity with Sejanus. The vast number of victims of the massacre lay on the ground; either sex, all ages, the famous, the obscure; their bodies scattered or heaped together. Relatives or friends were not allowed to stand by or to weep over them, or even look for too long. Guards surrounded them, watching their sorrow, and escorted the rotting bodies that were dragged to the Tiber. There they floated away or grounded, with no one to cremate or touch them. Terror had dissolved the ties of humanity and the growing cruelty drove compassion away.

Indeed, the fear of both public execution and subsequent corpse abuse led some individuals to commit suicide and to urge others to dispose of their bodies rapidly (**1.57** and **1.58**). Decapitation of the corpse was a common act of mutilation. With its easily recognizable features the head was particularly suited to display and abuse (Voisin 1984; Richlin 1999). The heads of those declared public enemies might be placed on the *rostra* in the Roman Forum. Cicero's head and right hand were displayed there after his assassination in 43 BC (**4.50**). The fate of the emperor Galba's head also illustrates the extensive abuse of body parts, although Galba did at last receive proper burial

(**4.51**). Not all bodies were honoured in death or found their way peacefully and intact to the cemetery.

4.50 *Plutarch,* Antony 20

Biography: early 2nd c. AD. Events of 43 BC.
  See also Plutarch, *Cicero* 49; and **2.62**.

> Three hundred men were put to death by proscription. Antony gave orders to those who killed Cicero to cut off his head and right hand, the hand with which Cicero had written his speeches against him; and, when they were brought before Antony, he gazed upon them joyfully, actually laughing out loud several times. When Antony had satiated himself with the sight of them, he ordered them to be placed on the rostra in the Forum, as though he was insulting the dead rather than displaying his own insolence and abuse of the power that Fortune had given him.

4.51 *Suetonius,* Galba 20

Biography: early 2nd c. AD. Events of AD 69.
  For Galba's final moments see **1.53**.

> Galba was killed beside the Lake of Curtius [in the Roman Forum], and was left lying just as he fell. A common soldier returning from the grain distribution put down his load and cut off the head. Then, since there was no hair by which to carry it, he placed it under his cloak and later thrust his thumb into the mouth, and so took it to Otho. Otho handed it over to a crowd of servants and camp-followers, who stuck it on a spear and paraded it round the camp ... [while singing insults] ... A freedman of Patrobius Neronianus bought the head for 100 gold pieces and threw it down at the place where Patrobius had been executed at Galba's orders. At last Galba's steward Argivius took it, with the rest of the body, to the tomb in Galba's private gardens on the Aurelian Way.

Abuse of the cemetery

For all its desired grandeur the cemetery was a fickle place (Hope 2000a). Memories rarely lasted. Tombs fell into disrepair, were reused, plundered or demolished. As was noted above, people sought to protect their tombs with guardians and left money for their maintenance, but ultimately such provisions could not last. Once personal interest fell away who would protect a tomb? In theory tombs were sacred; they were religious places protected by the law and thus the law came to punish grave-violation as sacrilege.

4.52 Digest (Paul) 47.12.11

Legal text: 6th c. AD (3rd c. AD).

> Those guilty of violating tombs, if they remove the bodies or scatter the bones, will suffer the ultimate penalty if they are of the lower orders [*humiliores*]; if they are more reputable [*honestiores*], they will be deported to an island. Otherwise the latter will be relegated and the former condemned to the mines.

The punishments that faced a tomb violator, at least during the mid to late Empire, were great, but the law must have been difficult to enforce when the forgotten dead had few to champion their cause. It is not surprising that people sought to reinforce the law by providing their own sanctions and threats against would-be violators in epitaphs (Strubbe 1991). These penalties took several forms: fines to be paid to the town council in an attempt to engage the protective interest of the authorities through financial gain (4.53); spiritual or emotional threats that emphasized man's common fate and capacity for suffering (1.4); and curses that evoked the gods and threatened physical and spiritual suffering (4.54).

4.53 CIL V 952

Epitaph: 2nd c. AD. Aquileia (Italy). Funerary altar.
  = *IA* 2830.

> Marcus Vocusius Crescens, freedman of Marcus, built this while living for himself and Vocusia Veneria, his very good wife, and Petronius Vocusianus, his son, soldier of the Third Praetorian Cohort, aged 18 years, 3 months, 18 days. If anyone tries to sell, buy or break open this altar, then he shall pay a penalty of 20,000 sesterces to the municipality of Aquileia, and the informer shall receive one fourth.

4.54 CIL VI 36467

Epitaph: 1st or 2nd c. AD. Rome (via Ostiensis).
  = *ILS* 8184.

> Gaius Tullius Hesper had this tomb built for himself, as a place where his bones will be laid. If anyone damages them or removes them from here, I wish for him that he will live in physical pain for a long time and that the gods of the underworld will not accept him when he dies.

From the 2nd c. AD the phrase *sub ascia dedicavit* (dedicated while under the hammer) became common in epitaphs in parts of Gaul and Italy. In addition or instead of this a hammer was carved onto the tombstone. This may have been intended to signify symbolically that the grave was a religious place and to emphasize that the tomb was protected and only intended for those named (Hatt 1951: 85–107). However, despite the best efforts of the law, testators and tomb-founder, graves could soon become neglected and tombs fall into a state of disrepair. In an area of cemetery preserved near the Vatican a landslide appears to have toppled some tombstones not long after they were set up; they were not repaired (4.55). At Pompeii, election notices and advertisements were painted onto the exterior walls of tombs (Jashemski 1979: 142). In the longer term, cemeteries were plundered for building materials. The late defensive walls of Roman Chester contained many old tombstones (Wright and Richmond 1956: 5) and in Ostia a tombstone was even reused as a toilet seat in the public latrines (Meiggs 1973: 143). Grave sites marked by earth mounds or perishable or temporary markers may have been easily disturbed (4.56), as the cross-cutting of graves in many excavated inhumation cemeteries so well illustrates.

4.55 Figure 19: Tombs under the Vatican car park

Cemetery memorials: 1st c. AD. Rome (via Triumphalis).
= Steinby 1987; Väänänen 1973.
A section of a cemetery, originally aligned with the via Triumphalis, was excavated in the 1950s during the construction of a car park in the Vatican. The cemetery has a mixture of monument types; modest house tombs and funerary enclosures are interspersed with stelae, altars and amphorae burials. The figure shows at the centre a stele, adorned with two portrait busts, which commemorated a slave of the emperor Nero. The pipe at the base of the stelae would have been used for libations. The partially buried amphorae, with necks protruding, were used for burials, although it is not certain whether these were associated with the stele. Two adjacent stelae, the rightmost of which is obscured by the wall of a later enclosure tomb, commemorated members of the Aufidii family. The cemetery was later affected by a landslide after which many of the more modest tombstones and graves were not repaired.

4.56 Sidonius Apollinaris, Letters 3.12.1–2

Letter: 5th c. AD.
Sidonius is writing to his nephew about the grave of his grandfather who had been Praetorian Prefect of Gaul in AD 408. The letter concludes with a request that the grave be restored and a new epitaph inscribed. The letter may be a literary set-piece for the composition of this epitaph, but it is still

Figure 19 Tombs under the Vatican car park, Rome.

suggestive of a rural cemetery and how graves might be rapidly forgotten or deliberately disturbed.

> Yesterday profane hands almost violated the grave where my grand-father and your great-grandfather lies, but God helped and stopped this impious act. The cemetery had for years been overcrowded with cremation burials and buried bodies and interment there had long finished. But snow and heavy rainfall had caused the mounds to settle; the raised earth had been spread out, and the ground had resumed its former flat surface. And this was why some undertaker's men dared to desecrate the spot with their grave-digging tools, believing that it was unoccupied by bodies. Must I tell what happened? They had already removed the turf, so that the soil showed black, and were piling the fresh clods upon the old grave. By chance I happened to be passing on my way to Clermont, and saw this public outrage from the top of a nearby hill. I gave the reins to my horse, and galloped at full speed over the steep and level ground so impatient was I to get there. Before I reached the spot I stopped the crime by shouting out.

168

Outside the city the cemetery was in many ways a marginal zone, the haunt of undesirables such as tramps (**4.57**), thieves (**4.58**) and prostitutes. Martial referred to whores as 'tomb-frequenting' and noted how they used tombs as hiding places (Martial 3.93.15; 1.34.8). The cemetery could be a focal point for superstition and superstitious activities. Petronius sets a story of a werewolf in a cemetery (*Satyricon* 62). Horace has witches frequenting the Esquiline (**6.60**) and gathering harmful herbs from tombs (*Epode* 5; see also Tibullus 1.2, 41–5; 1.5, 51–2). The witches of Thessaly (north-east Greece) were particularly infamous (Phillips 2002), and Lucan's Thessalian witch Erictho was a frequenter of cemeteries, living in a tomb and seizing corpses (*Civil War* 6, 511–2; and **6.61**).

4.57 Digest (Ulpian) 47.12.3

Legal text: 6th c. AD (3rd c. AD)
  See also *Digest* 47.12.6 and 47.12.11.

> And if anyone deceitfully lives in a tomb or sets up some other estab-lishment in what was built as a tomb, I will give an action against him for two hundred gold pieces to anyone who wishes to proceed against him on that account.

4.58 Apuleius, Metamorphoses 2.21 and 4.18

Satirical Novel: 2nd c. AD.
  The witch story is told at a dinner party by a certain Thelyphron who agreed to guard a corpse in Thessaly. Later the corpse (revived to accuse his wife of murder), tells that the witches took the nose and ears of Thelyphron when he was sleeping. For necromancy see Chapter 6.

> My money was running out, so I was looking around for a means of solving my poverty, when I saw a tall old man in the public square. He was standing on a stone and saying loudly that if anybody was willing to guard a corpse, he would negotiate a price. I asked a passer-by, 'What's this? Do corpses here run away?' 'No, no,' he said, 'A young man and stranger like yourself obviously doesn't understand that this is Thessaly, where witches regularly chew pieces off the faces of the dead to get supplies for their magic art.'

> After coming through the city gate, we saw a large tomb in a remote and hidden spot some distance from the road. In it we found some coffins, with their old lids only half-closed, filled with the dust and ashes of men long dead. We opened up some of these to act as a hiding place for the loot we were expecting.

For some people the cemetery may have held a real fascination and the bodies (and spirits) of the dead special powers. Curse tablets (*defixiones*), which sought to harness the powers of the dead to perform special tasks for the living, have been found in graves (**6.59**). Some individuals may have felt that bodies or body parts were imbued with healing or magical properties. Pliny the Elder lists, in a sceptical fashion, some of the cures which were purportedly to be obtained from corpses. This suggests that violent and premature death could imbue these dead with special powers. The bodies of the unclaimed and the exposed bodies of criminals may have been particularly susceptible to those who sought souvenirs, amulets and cures.

4.59 Pliny, Natural History 28.2.4–5 and 28.11.45–6

Natural history: 1st c. AD.

The blood of gladiators is drunk by epileptics as though it were a draught of life, though it is a horror to see wild animals do this in the same arena. But, by the gods, the patients think it most effective to suck from a man himself warm, living blood, and they put their lips to the wound to drain the very life, even though it is not the human custom to apply their mouths to the wounds of wild beasts. Others seek out leg bone-marrow and the brains of infants. Some among the Greeks have even spoken of the taste of each organ and limb, going into all the details, not excluding nail clippings; just as though it could be thought healthy for a man to act as a beast, and in seeking a cure to risk more disease as punishment. And, by the gods, it would serve them right if these remedies were ineffectual. To look at human entrails is thought a sin.

We are assured that the hand of the prematurely dead cures with a touch glandular sores, diseased parotid glands, and throat infections; some however say that the back of any dead person's left hand will do this if the patient is of the same sex. A remedy for the pain of toothache is to bite off a piece of some wood that has been struck by lightning, with hands thrown behind your back. Some prescribe fumigation of the tooth with a human tooth from someone of the same sex, and to use a canine tooth taken from an unburied corpse as a charm. Earth taken from a skull acts, so it is said, as hair remover for the eyelashes, while any plant that has grown in the skull makes the teeth fall out when chewed and ulcers marked round with human bone do not spread.

Some graves were interfered with not for malicious or superstitious reasons, but for political and symbolic ones. The political value of human remains could increase when power changed hands. Caligula gathered up and reburied the remains of his mother and brother, victims of Tiberius (**2.63**). The emperor Augustus visited the tomb of Alexander (**4.60**) and even viewed the body (mummy); Caligula on the other hand stole an armour breastplate from the same tomb (Suetonius, *Caligula* 52). These actions reflected the continuing potency of Alexander as enshrined in his remains, and Augustus' respect and Caligula's disrespect. Across the empire the living and the dead interacted; their worlds were not clearly demarcated or separated. The cemetery might be on the margins of the city, but the suburb, including tombs, could be an extension of the town (Purcell 1987; Patterson 2000b). With its villas, gardens, baths, businesses and travellers the suburb could be a busy and bustling place. The tombs of the cemetery may have aspired to dignity and grandeur, but the liminal context of the cemetery meant that its inhabitants may have rarely rested in peace.

4.60 *Suetonius*, Augustus 18

Biography: 2nd c. AD. Events of 30 BC, when Augustus was in Egypt, following the Battle of Actium.

For the precinct at Alexandria containing the tombs of Alexander and other kings see Strabo 17.1.8.

> About this time he had the sarcophagus and body of Alexander the Great removed from its shrine. After looking at it he showed his respect by placing a golden crown upon it and scattering flowers. When asked if he wished to see the tomb of Ptolemies as well, he replied, 'My wish was to see a king, not corpses'.

5

GRIEF

Introduction

Grief is a reaction to loss; grief is pain and suffering; grief is raw emotion. Mourning is a time when grief is made visible; mourning is the process of coping with loss and giving that loss social expression. Reconstructing the emotional responses of individual members of past societies is a historical conundrum. It is dangerous and misleading to assume that we know what people must have experienced in a given situation, to infer that their grief was the same as ours. Death is a universal, but how the bereaved articulate their sense of loss is not. Mourning, its practices, rituals and processes, is often more accessible than grief. Yet mourning does not necessarily reveal how people feel (see, for example Hockey 2001: 198); public behaviour may not illuminate private loss.

In the Roman world death was undoubtedly a time of heightened emotions both for the dying and the bereaved, but how people experienced and how they expressed emotion is difficult to judge from the surviving sources, which are often formal and formulaic and intended for public rather than private consumption. We do gain a strong impression of what was expected and idealized. On the one hand loss should be taken bravely (especially by men), with minimal displays of emotion and a 'stiff upper lip'. On the other hand a death was a time for outbursts of weeping and wailing (especially by women) and other public demonstrations of loss. Beyond these conventions and ideals there is also substantial evidence of a more emotive kind. Bereavement was a great source of artistic inspiration and words and images inspired by grief still pull at the heartstrings, encouraging us to empathize with their creators. But, as Hopkins has put it, 'a poet writing odes, however evocative, is not necessarily heartbroken, while she who mourns silently or expresses her grief conventionally on a tombstone may nevertheless be truly grief-stricken' (1983: 221). It may remain impossible to reconstruct the true level of emotion that lay behind a poem, a letter or a tombstone, or to view these as little more than romanticized sentimentalizing over the dead, but the very production of these items suggests a public acknowledgement of grief, that people felt loss and gave expression to it. In addition, the fact that some individuals sort to codify grief and to set a limit to its expression indicates that others deviated from these codes and limits. In other words, in their grief people could and did defy what was deemed acceptable.

Modern studies of grief are increasingly acknowledging that people's reactions to death can vary greatly. After years of pigeonholing people's experiences into a neatly schematized 'grieving process' there is now a growing awareness that people do grieve and cope with their grief in a variety of ways (Walter 1999). Grief has been seen as an illness (Small 2001; compare **5.49**); however, the pain of grief is not simply 'cured' in the same way or in the same time for everyone. For some bereaved people there may be no end to grief since they maintain continuing bonds with the dead. This is not to argue that we can make simple comparisons between modern western experiences of bereavement and those of a 'Roman', but nor should we view all the inhabitants of the Roman world as having the same reaction to loss. It is challenging to get beyond the ideals and stereotypes created in literature, but we should be careful not to dismiss all the inhabitants of the Roman world as unfeeling (for example, on the strength of Seneca) or view all emotions expressed (for example, in epitaphs) as the contrived products of convention.

This chapter explores some of the conventions and societal expectations which structured and guided the expression of grief, but that did not necessarily suppress it. It also considers texts that took the consolation of the bereaved as their central theme. Issues of genre, context and purpose of these sources are key to understanding the portrayal and characterization of Roman grief. In the ancient world it was understood that people did react to the death of others in different ways, and these different responses find voice in varied genres. There were discussions as to whether grief was a natural response or a product of society's expectations, and there were also attempts to evaluate the impact of the gender, age and social status of both the dead and the bereaved upon the reactions of the survivors. Admittedly these debates were largely the preserve of the intellectual minority and probably of little interest or relevance to many people. How most people reacted to death in the Roman world was inevitably a mixture of both raw emotion and expected behaviour.

Guidelines for mourning

In the Roman world the bereaved were marked out and thus in some sense separated from the wider community. A cypress branch was placed outside the house of the deceased; the mourners wore dark clothing and might have a dishevelled appearance (see Chapter 3). This exterior appearance was intended to reflect internal feelings of sadness and loss. It also allowed others to respect the grief of the bereaved, and may have been connected to religious and spiritual ideas of the pollution brought by death (Lindsay 2000). The family of the deceased, and those who came into contact with the dead, such as undertakers, could be perceived as impure (**3.10**). On the ninth day after the funeral the house and family were purified and the bereaved could resume their normal roles within the community (see Chapter Three). However, mourning could be extended, and for female mourners in particular, was expected to continue. In theory the length of time and the extent to which one mourned (in public at least) was socially and to some extent legally regulated. To mourn for too long or too ostentatiously was not acceptable. Mourning was supposed to be in proportion to the age and status of the deceased.

5.1 Plutarch, Numa 12

Biography: early 2nd c. AD.
Pompilius Numa was the legendary second king of Rome (*c.* 715–673 BC) who was credited with creating the basic framework of Roman public religion.

> Numa himself also set out rules for the periods of mourning according to age and time. So, for example, there was to be no mourning at all for a child of less than 1 year; for a child older than that, up to 10 years old, the mourning was not to last more months than it had lived years; and the longest time of mourning for any person was not to exceed 10 months. This was also the time set for widowhood for women who had lost their husbands, and any woman who took another husband before this time was out was obliged by the laws of Numa to sacrifice a cow with calf.

5.2 Paulus, Opinions 1.21.2–5

Legal text: late 2nd c. or early 3rd c. AD.
See also Cicero on the Twelve Tables (**3.67**) and Seneca (**5.8**).

> Parents and children over 6 years of age can be mourned for a year, children under 6 for a month. A husband can be mourned for 10 months, close blood relatives for 8 months. Anyone who acts contrary to the restrictions is placed in public disgrace. Anyone in mourning ought to refrain from dinner parties, jewellery and other adornments, and purple and white clothing.

Moderation in grief, with minimal and controlled displays of emotion, was part of the constructed ideal. It was best to bear one's losses with restraint and dignity, at least in public. In the formal male world to lay bare emotion was to risk criticism for unmanly overindulgence or false and exaggerated displays of grief. The behaviour of those who prioritized public duty over private loss was often praised and idealized. Leading politicians were expected to put the state before their own sorrows. To show excess emotion was incompatible with public position. However, we should not overlook the possibility that comfort and distraction could be found in public duty (**5.47** and **5.48**).

5.3 Scriptores Historiae Augustae: Marcus Aurelius, 21.1

Biography: 4th c. AD. Events of AD 172.

> Just before the day of his [Marcus Aurelius'] departure, while living in retreat at Praeneste, he lost his 7-year-old son, Verus Caesar by name, after an operation on a tumour under his ear. He mourned him for no more than 5 days, and after comforting the doctors returned to public affairs.

It was a positive example to demonstrate resolve, that shows of grief and excessive lamenting benefited no one. Philosophical debates on the nature of grief which explored whether it was a natural response, an expected parade or a matter of belief, reinforced this. The philosophical viewpoint was that death in itself was not an evil (see Chapter 2) and therefore grief was of little benefit.

5.4 Cicero, Tusculan Disputations 3.28

Philosophical dialogue: 45 BC.
   Compare **5.49**.

> What, however, has more impact in putting grief aside than knowledge of the fact that it gives no benefit and that indulgence in it is useless? If, therefore, it can be set aside, it is also possible not to indulge in it. It then must be admitted that such distress is an indulgence through an act of will and judgement.

In consolation letters and literature (for these genres see below) emphasis was often placed on well-known people who bore their grief well, with bravery and resignation (**5.5**). These lists of moral examples were intended both to inspire and comfort the bereaved. Composed behaviour may have been the ideal, but over-zealous restraint in the expression of grief could backfire (**5.6**). It was essential to exhibit humanity not callousness. Indeed the male élite code of conduct may not have been understood or admired by all, and was open to misinterpretation.

5.5 *Seneca,* Consolation to Marcia 3.2

Philosophical consolation: AD 39/40.

Marcia is consoled for the death of her son by reference to Livia, wife of the emperor Augustus, whose son Drusus died on campaign in Germany (9 BC). Tiberius was the brother of Drusus and became emperor on Augustus' death.

Compare **5.60.**

> Throughout Italy, crowds poured out from the towns and colonies and, escorting the funeral procession all the way to the city, made it seem more like a triumph. His mother had not been allowed to receive her son's last kisses and hear the kind words of his dying mouth. On the long journey, while she accompanied the remains of Drusus, she was cut to the heart by the countless pyres that burned throughout all Italy, for on each it was as if she lost her son again. Yet once she had placed him in the tomb, she laid away her sorrow along with her son, and grieved no more than was respectful to Caesar [Augustus] or fair to Tiberius, seeing that they were alive.

5.6 *Tacitus,* Annals 3.2–3

History: early 2nd c. AD. Events of AD 19, following the death of Germanicus, the nephew of Tiberius and son of Drusus (see **5.5**).

Note Tacitus' negative interpretation of the emperor's behaviour.

For the honours bestowed on the dead Germanicus see **2.60.**

> The consuls, the Senate and a great part of the population filled the roadside, standing in scattered groups and weeping as they pleased. There was no adulation of the emperor in this since everyone knew that Tiberius was struggling to conceal his joy at the death of Germanicus. He and the Augusta [Livia] made no appearance in public. Either they considered it beneath their dignity to mourn openly, or feared that if all eyes studied their looks they would discern hypocrisy.

Getting grief right, or more accurately, mourning in public in the correct way, was part of the self-definition of the élite. Grief and the display of grief were considered to be determined by gender, culture and education (**5.7**). The ability to control emotion was part of the Graeco-Roman moral tradition; the suppression of grief was an aspect of what distinguished the educated élite male from the other sex, other social groups and other cultures. Restrictions on mourning were aimed particularly at women, who were perceived as having a lack of self-control and decorum in such matters, when compared to men. To mourn openly and in excess was characterized as womanly (*muliebris*) and behaviour best suited to a bereft mother (Cicero, *Letters to his Friends* 9.20.3; Seneca, *Consolation to Marcia* 2.3.4; Plutarch, *Consolation to his Wife* 4). Even for grieving women there was a time and a place for tears, after which excessive indulgence in grief was no longer tolerable (**5.8**). These male philosophical dictates may seem harsh to a modern viewer, but seek to address common truths that prolonged overt grief can create social awkwardness for both the bereaved and the non-bereaved. After a time people were expected to get on with their lives, or sympathy began to diminish.

5.7 Plutarch, Letter to Apollonius 22

Philosophical consolation: early 2nd c. AD.
= *Moralia* 113.
Lycia was in south-west Asia Minor.

> They say that the lawgiver of the Lycians ordered his citizens to put on women's clothes whenever they mourned. He wished to make it clear that mourning is womanish and ill-suited to decent men who can claim to be educated and free-born. Mourning is feminine, weak and dishonourable, since women are more given to it than men, and barbarians more than Greeks, and inferior men more than better men.

5.8 Seneca, Letters 63.13

Philosophical letter: mid 1st c. AD. Seneca is writing to Lucilius on the death of his friend Flaccus.
Compare Seneca, *To Helvia* 16.1–2. For further extracts from this letter see **5.54** and **6.33**.

> Our ancestors have decreed a year of mourning for women; not that they needed to mourn for so long, but that they should mourn for no longer. For men, no time was set, because it is not honourable to mourn. However, what woman can you show me, of all the sad examples that couldn't be dragged away from the pyre or removed from the corpse, whose tears have lasted a whole month? Nothing else becomes offensive as quickly as grief; when it is new it finds someone to console it and attracts one or another to itself; but if it becomes established, it is derided, and rightly so. For it is either false or foolish.

Women played a role in public mourning in ways that were not viewed as acceptable for men; their bodies, actions and behaviour gave visual and audible expression to the community's grief. The display of female loss and pain could dramatically symbolize and summarize the overall losses of society, sometimes to a dangerous, almost crippling extent. Livy captures the devastation that hit Rome following the battle of Cannae (216 BC) by picturing a city almost paralysed by wailing and grieving women (Livy 22.55.3 and 22.56.4–5.) Equally, a lack of female mourning could be a sign of disrespect, hence the prohibitions found in *damnationes memoriae* against women mourning in public (see Chapter 2). In general women were more readily associated with death and the dead than were men. It was women who would often give the last kiss, wash the body, wail at the graveside and receive the ashes, and it was women who would subsequently signal their bereavement for a year by covering the head (with a *ricinium*) and dressing simply (no jewels or colourful clothing). Death was women's work but men still sought to control it (Mustakallio 2005). Grief could be perceived as dangerous and the use of undertakers, hired mourners and restrictions on mourning times served, with time, to lessen the link between bereaved women and the symbols of grief. By the late Republic overly melodramatic displays were not seen as the norm or ideal for a Roman lady. Cleopatra's reaction to Antony's death, the extent of personal injury and her subsequent suicide, is deliberately created as something exotic, foreign and non-Roman.

5.9 *Plutarch*, Antony 77

Biography: early 2nd c. AD. Events of 30 BC, Antony commits suicide at Alexandria.

Plutarch (*Antony* 82) later speaks of Cleopatra suffering a subsequent illness caused by the self-inflicted lacerations.

Compare **5.34** and **5.58**.

> When she had got him in and laid him down, she tore her clothes over him, beat and lacerated her breasts, and wiped the blood from his wounds on her face. She called him her master, husband and emperor, and almost forgot her own misfortunes in pity for his.

Bereaved women, especially those of high status, could find themselves in a contradictory position, being expected to conform to both female and male expectations; to both express and suppress grief. All this underlines that people in mourning (both men and women) often behaved in certain ways which could serve deliberately to mask genuine emotion. Meeting social expectations and behaving as one should, in public at least, did not necessarily reflect the depth of people's feelings.

5.10 Cicero, Tusculan Disputations 3.27

Philosophical dialogue: 45 BC.

> They do all these things in their grief, from the belief that such
> things are right and proper and mandatory. The chief proof that
> they act from some sort of belief in duty is shown by the fact that,
> if anyone who thinks he should be sorrowful acts by chance more
> humanly or speaks more cheerfully, he must resume a gloomy
> appearance and blame himself for this interruption to his grief.
> Indeed, if during family sorrow children are unsuitably cheerful
> in actions or speech, mothers and teachers are used to punishing
> them, and not only with words but even with a beating they make
> the children cry.

It was relatively easy to write about how one should behave from a philosophical and idealizing standpoint, but it was another to live up to this
expectation. Not everyone had a philosophical outlet for their grief. The
opinions of people such as Cicero and Seneca, and nominal legal restrictions, may have meant little to many people facing bereavement (for
Cicero's own reactions to his daughter's death see 5.46–5.49). The antithesis of the school of thought that grief and emotion should be suppressed
was that grief should be indulged in. The extent of people's weeping and
wailing and withdrawal from society could symbolize the extent of their
loss and love. The ultimate expression of grief, to refuse to live without a
loved one and to commit suicide, was rare (see Chapter 1). Occasionally
we hear of suicides prompted by the death of an important individual;
Suetonius claims that at Germanicus' death people cast out their newly
born children (*Gaius* 5) and that at Otho's death many soldiers killed themselves (**1.58**). These may have been acts of devotion, intended as a compli-
ment to the deceased, but also served to symbolize uncertain political times
and a sense of disillusion and desperation (Versnel 1980). Such self-sacrifice was not the norm, but could provide a powerful contrast with the élite
ideal. Indeed for those without power and reputation, even if suicide was
rare, behaving with the restraint and decorum of a gentleman would have
been of little relevance. Popular tastes may have been very different to
philosophically driven 'educated' tastes. Whereas philosophy might advocate the importance of public restraint other literary genres, poetry in
particular, might prioritize the emotion and the sentiments of the private
sphere. Poetry can provide a counterpoint to other genres which seem to
reject grief, but can we ever access the true sentiments that lie beneath such
artistic constructs?

5.11 *Statius,* Silvae 5.5, 56–64

Poetry: late 1st c. AD. A lament to the adopted son of Statius.

> Am I called perhaps too immoderate and too eager for sorrow, and
> too excessive in my weeping? But who are you to blame my groans
> and tears? Oh, he is too happy, and cruel, and ignorant of the laws
> of Fortune who dares to control mourning or set a limit to grief.
> Alas! Mourning incites mourning. You will sooner stop the rivers
> that break their banks or extinguish devouring fire than forbid the
> sorrowful to grieve.

It can be difficult to square ideal exhortations to mourn in moderation with
expressions of extreme pain and loss. We need to remember that we are
looking at grieving Romans through evidence shaped by convention and
genre. The extracts contained in this chapter often reveal a tension between
different genres such as philosophy, poetry and rhetoric and how these characterize the bereaved and the emotion of grief. Literature may present us with
ideals, counter-ideals and stereotypes, but these at least suggest that there were
different ways to grieve and manage the dynamic between public and private.

5.12 *Tacitus,* Agricola 29.1

Biography: AD 98. Agricola's son died while Agricola was in Britain, AD 84.
    Tacitus hints at the different perspectives on grief, and the tendency to
polarize people's behaviour.
    Compare Juvenal's ironic comments about the consolatory roles of philos-
ophy; the implication being that most people were educated in the school of
life and hard-knocks, not by philosophers (*Satire* 13, 19–22, 120–34).

> Early next summer Agricola suffered a severe personal blow in the
> death of a son who had been born a year before. He accepted this
> loss without displaying the ostentatious fortitude of many men or
> giving way to tears and grief like a woman.

Parents and children

The need to control mourning is most profoundly expressed in the expectations concerning the death of children. Small babies were not given full funeral
rites and those who had not teethed were not cremated (Pliny, *Natural History*
7.16.72; see also Fulgentius, *Exposito sermonum antiquorum* 7). Children's
burials could be performed at night by torchlight (**3.22–3.24**). This suggests
that children were not always treated as full members of the community
(**5.13**); simple rites reflected the brevity of their life, although this very fact
could still evoke a natural emotional response (**5.14**).

5.13 *Plutarch,* Consolation to his Wife *11*

Philosophical consolation: late 1st c. AD.

= *Moralia* 612.

Note the Greek context and that Plutarch was influenced by Platonic philosophy that believed in the continuity of the soul (see Chapter 6).

See also **5.56.**

> For our people do not bring offerings to any of their children who die in infancy, and in their case they do not observe any of the other rites that the living are expected to perform for the dead, since these children have no part in earth or earthly things. The mourners do not stay at the graves where the burial is celebrated or at the laying out of the dead, and sit by the bodies. For the laws forbid us to mourn for infants, holding it an impiety to mourn for those who have been exempted from life and gone to a place that is better and more divine.

5.14 *Juvenal,* Satire 15, 138–40

Satirical poetry: early 2nd c. AD.

> It's at nature's command that we weep when we meet the funeral procession of a full-grown virgin, or when the earth covers over an infant too young for the pyre.

The perfunctory treatment of the bodies of the young, coupled with factors such as infant exposure (**1.7** and **1.8**), has led some scholars to suggest that Roman parents were distanced from their children. High infant mortality rates may have discouraged people from becoming too emotionally involved with their very young offspring. For the wealthy, at least, the employment of servile wet nurses and other carers may have provided a cushion against repeated bereavements (Bradley 1991: 28). The view existed that the loss of a baby was less upsetting than the loss of others (**5.15**); that more tears should be shed for older children and adults, in whom more time and emotion had been invested.

5.15 *Cicero,* Tusculan Disputations *1.39*

Philosophical dialogue: 45 BC.

Compare Plutarch, *Letter to Apollonius* 23.

> The same people think that if a small child dies, the loss must be taken calmly; if a baby in the cradle, there must not even be a

lament. And yet it is from the latter that nature has more cruelly demanded back the gift she has given.

Philosophical literature advocated an accepting attitude at the death of a young child, but to note what was expected and what was criticized is not to suggest that people did not grieve for a baby (Golden 1988). Many parents did not conform to the expectation and, although some others may have condemned their lack of self-control (5.16), these parents could not disguise their sense of loss (5.17). Belief in the immortality of the soul and well-worn philosophical arguments such as 'the good die young' may have been of little real comfort to bereaved parents (5.18).

5.16 Seneca, Letters 99. 2–3

Philosophical letter: mid 1st c. AD.
    Seneca is quoting from a letter he wrote to Marullus on the death of his infant son. Seneca goes on to state that the infant child must have been better known to his nurse than his father (99.14)! For the purpose of the letter see below and 5.53.

> Is it solace that you expect? Accept reproach instead. You are like a woman in the way you take your son's death; what would you do if you had lost a close friend? A son, a little child of uncertain promise, is dead; a fragment of time has perished.

5.17 Tacitus, Annals 15.23

History: early 2nd c. AD. Birth and death of Nero's daughter, AD 63.
    Tacitus suggests that Nero's lack of self-control is an indication of his failings as both man and emperor.
    Compare Pliny's account of Regulus' mourning, Letters 4.2 (3.48) and 4.7.

> Within less than four months the baby was dead. Then new forms of adulation appeared. She was voted the honour of deification, a place on the gods' ceremonial platform, a temple and a priest. The emperor's delight [at the birth] had been immoderate; so was his sorrow.

5.18 Fronto, To Antoninus Augustus ii.5

Letter: AD 165. On the death of Fronto's 3-year-old grandson.
    See also 1.2.

However all this, true as it is, makes little difference to us who long for our lost ones, nor does the immortality of the souls bring us any consolation, since while we live we are without those we love best. We miss the well-known stance, the voice, the features, the free air; we mourn over the pitiable face of the dead, the silent lips, the averted eyes, and the fleeing of the colour of life. Even if the immortality of the soul is well established, it will remain a theme for the discussion of philosophers, and will never heal the yearning of a parent.

In the epigraphic record babies and young children are under-represented, especially when we consider how many must have died (Garnsey 1991: 51–2; Rawson 2003: 344). This suggests that it was not common for an infant to have their grave marked by a permanent tombstone. However, this does not mean that their bodies were treated with disrespect and that their deaths were unmourned. Infant skeletons and remains are less likely to survive compared to those of adults; nevertheless, infant burials are reasonably well attested in Roman cemeteries and are associated with considered and diverse burial rites (Pearce 2001). The symbolic disposal of some infants in new buildings or at the decommissioning of old ones may suggest a certain marginality for the young, but these were careful and considered rather than casual choices (Scott 1990, 1999: 109–23). In epitaphs to babies and young children the language employed may appear conventional and sentimental, but it can give public acknowledgement to a grief that many must have experienced and others could at the very least empathize with (**1.3–1.6**). The emotional dimension to children's epitaphs and delight in childish characteristics is also exploited and echoed in poetry.

5.19 *Martial,* Epigrams 5.34

Poetry: late 1st c. AD. A poetic epitaph to a slave child.
  See also Martial 10.61 and 7.96.

> To you father Fronto and mother Flacilla, I commend this girl my darling and delight. Little Erotion must not fear the dark shades and the unnatural mouths of Tartarus' hound. She would have completed her sixth cold winter, if she had lived but a few days more. Let her now play happily with her old patrons and chatter my name with a lisp. Do not be inflexible, the turf that covers her soft bones, do not be heavy upon her, earth; she was not heavy upon you.

5.20 *Ausonius,* Parentalia 10

Poetry: 4th c. AD. A poem in memory of the author's son.

183

I will not leave you unlamented, my son, nor deny you the complaint due to your memory, you my first born child and my namesake. Just as you were beginning to turn your baby talk into the first words of childhood and you were full of natural gifts we had to mourn for your death. You lie on your great grandfather's breast sharing one common grave so that you will not suffer a solitary grave.

In contrast to the relatively small numbers of epitaphs that recall babies and toddlers, many epitaphs do record the deaths of older children emphasizing that parents marked their graves and their loss. Graves of older children may have been more readily integrated into the cemetery than those of infants and furnished more richly (Gowland 2001). The epitaphs, however, do not represent all social groups and all children. More boys, for example, are commemorated than girls, suggesting the greater valuation of the male that pervaded society. The epitaphs thus cannot be used for creating demographic statistics on areas such as life expectancy since they are a product of expected and accepted commemorative conventions (Hopkins 1966). The language employed is also formulaic; many epitaphs are short, containing little more than poignant basic details. More elaborate examples use stock phrases and commonplace expressions of grief. Young teenagers were often referred to as devoted (*pientissimus*), emphasizing the frustrated hopes of the parents who had looked forward to the filial duty (*pietas*) expected from children (Sigismund Nielsen 1997: 197–8). Nevertheless the epitaphs do evoke the dashed expectations of parents, genuine fondness for childish characteristics and the pain of bereavement. Convention may hinder our ability to isolate the true feelings of the creators of the epitaphs, but equally we cannot assume that the emotions expressed are all artificial and false (King 2000).

5.21 CIL XIII 7123

Epitaph: 1st c. AD. Mogontiacum (Mainz, Germany). A stele; above the inscription panel the boy is represented standing between two foals.
    = Boppert 1992b: n.13; Selzer 1988: n.111.

> Quintus Voltius Viator, son of Quintus, aged 16 years, lies here. His mother and father piously set this up.

5.22 CIL XIII 842

Epitaph: 2nd c. AD. Burdigala (Bordeaux, France).

> To the spirits of the departed Secundinus, son of Caius, aged 12 years. His mother Secundina put this up.

GRIEF

5.23 CIL XII 807

Epitaph: 2nd or 3rd c. AD. Arelate (Arles, France). Marble tablet.

To the spirits of the departed Flavia Daphne. Her mother Maria Fronime for an incomparable daughter who lived 7 years, 9 months and 15 days.

The acute sense of loss following the death of a child is often articulated in literature, creating a contrast to the stern exhortations driven by philosophy (**5.24**). Poetic licence could express the distress, tears and despair of the surviving adults.

5.24 *Statius*, Silvae 5.5, 38–45

Poetry: late 1st c. AD. Lament to the adopted son of Statius.
Compare Catullus 65 and 68, 15–140, where the poet struggles to write after the death of his brother,

Yet I am he who was able so many times to ease with soothing words the pain of mothers and fathers, and the sorrow of bereavement. I, the gentle consoler of the bereaved, who was heard at untimely deaths by departing spirits, I am now at a loss, and seek healing hands and the most powerful remedies for my wounds. Now is the time, my friends, whose streaming eyes and wounded hearts I helped; bring me support, pay your debt of frenzied thanks.

Admittedly much literary angst was reserved for those children who, having passed the dangerous years of infancy, were beginning to show their potential as adults. Even the very young could become imbued with adult-like qualities and a maturity beyond their years, in order to justify the extent of the parents' sense of loss (**5.25**). Hopes and expectations could be enshrined in children and their absence could leave a vacuum that stretched into the future.

5.25 *Quintilian, 6, Prologue 7–9 and 11–12*

Treatise on oratory: late 1st c. AD.
Quintilian, having lost his young wife, tells here of the deaths of his two sons aged 5 and 9. For Quintilian there must have been an irony that his great literary work, aimed at educating young men, would never be an inspiration to his own sons.

My younger son, who was barely five, was the first of the two to die, taking from me as it were the sight of one of my two eyes. I have no desire to be ostentatious in my sorrow or to exaggerate the cause I have for tears; I wish that I had some means of lessening them! But how can I forget the beauty of his face, the sweetness of his speech, his first signs of promise and his actual possession of a calm and, incredible though it may seem in one so young, a powerful mind. Such a child would have won my love, even if he had been the son of a stranger.

He [the elder boy] had greater qualities, courage and dignity, and the strength to resist both fear and pain. What fortitude he showed during an illness of eighth months, gaining the admiration of his doctors! How he consoled me during his last moments. How, even when he was losing his senses and unable to recognize me, did his thoughts return to his lessons and his literary studies. Child of my disappointed hopes, how did I endure to see your eyes sinking in death and your breath taking its last flight? How could I, after embracing your cold and lifeless body and receiving your last breath, continue to breathe the common air? It is just that I now endure my agony and the thoughts that torment me.

The idea of children dying before their time and being given maturity beyond their years is sometimes termed the *puer senex* motif (Carp 1980; Dixon 1992a: 105). It is seen in funerary art where children can be depicted more like mini-adults than small children. Boys in particular might be portrayed as toga-clad, scroll-holding, miniature ideal citizens. Such images represent a prospective view of the career, education and social standing that was denied to the child by premature death. It is also possible to trace a similar theme, derived from Greek literature, of the death of the maiden (Lattimore 1962: 194). Sophocles (Greek playwright of 5th c. BC) has Antigone lament 'I have no bridal song, my marriage is with Acheron' (*Antigone*, 812–13). Similarly in Latin epitaphs and literature the untimely loss of a teenage girl, mature beyond her years, and on the point of marriage, who becomes death's virgin bride, could be a cause of sympathy (**5.14**, **5.26** and **5.27**). Some graves belonging to teenage girls and young women have been excavated, with distinctive grave-goods including amulets and dolls; these childlike items would have been symbolically dedicated to the gods at marriage, an event denied to these girls by premature death (Martin-Kilcher 2000).

5.26 CIL III 2875

Epitaph: 1st or 2nd c. AD. Nedinum (Nadin, Croatia).
  Compare *CIL* V 1710.

> Opinia Neptilia, daughter of Marcus, aged 14 years. A virgin promised in marriage she died with the wedding day approaching. Marcus Opinius Rufus and Gellia Neptilia her parents.

5.27 *Pliny*, Letters 5.16. 1–6

Letter: late 1st or early 2nd c. AD.

Pliny records the death of a friend's daughter, described as not quite 14 years old at the time of her demise. An epitaph discovered in Rome, which is believed to commemorate the same child, records an age of 12 years, 11 months and 7 days (*CIL* VI 16631). In many respects the exact age of the girl did not matter to Pliny as much as the pathos of the picture he was painting (Bodel 1995).

> I write to you in great distress: the youngest daughter of our friend Fundanus is dead. I have never seen such a cheerful and lovable girl, who so deserved a longer life if not an immortal one. She was not yet 14, and yet she was wise beyond her age, combining the dignity of a matron with the sweetness of a girl and the modesty of a virgin. She would hang from her father's neck with great fondness, and greet us, his friends, with affection and modesty. She regarded her nurses, her tutors and her teachers with tenderness and deference for the service given her. She was eager and intelligent in her studies and was moderate and restrained in her play. During her last illness she was patient and, indeed, brave; she obeyed her doctor's orders, spoke cheerful words to her sister and father, and when her bodily strength was exhausted carried on by sheer force of will. This sustained her to her final moments, unbroken by the length of her illness or the fear of death. The memory of her strength makes us miss her and grieve for her all the more. This is a truly sad and untimely end. The timing of the death was more shocking than the death itself. She was already engaged to marry a distinguished young man, the day for the wedding was arranged, and we had all been invited to attend. How joy has been turned to sorrow. I cannot express the grief I felt when I heard Fundanus giving his own orders (for grief is always finding new occasions to pain its sufferers) for the money he had intended for clothing, pearls and jewels to be spent on frankincense, ointment and spices for the funeral.

To mourn for an adult was more acceptable than to mourn for a child. From the philosophical standpoint the adult had more to lose by death and was thus a greater loss to the survivors than the unformed child. The deaths of adults could also be perceived as bitter and untimely, especially if the death was sudden and unexpected. Even the deaths of the elderly could sometimes be characterized in this way. Pliny the Younger justifies his grief for the aged Verginius Rufus because to Pliny it was 'as if he had died before his time' (*Letters* 2.1). In general an untimely death was characteristic of the young while the deaths of those of greater maturity might be more calmly faced and met (**1.15**). To claim great grief for the elderly was to heighten dramatic impact and claim elevated status for the life of the deceased and or their relationship with the bereaved. Authors could reverse the expectation, that more tears would automatically be shed for the young, that parents grieved more for their children than children did for their parents (**5.28**); grief was not simply dictated by age.

5.28 *Statius,* Silvae 5.3, 264–5

Poetry: late 1st c. AD. Lament to the father of Statius.
See also Statius, *Silvae* 3.3, 10–21.

> What lamentation did I make! Forgive me, spirits of the dead. Father
> I may say with truth: you would not have wept more for me!

Nevertheless it was grief for the young, including the grief of parents for their children (of whatever age) that was generally seen as the most poignant and dramatic. Despite the high levels of child mortality, and despite the fact that many parents lost many children, it was still argued that it was not right for a mother or father to bury their offspring. It was perceived to be against the natural order of things for a child to die before its parents (**3.14**). Parents complained in epitaphs, set up to deceased children, that their future security, hopes and happiness had been taken away. Who would now bury them and tend their grave? Grieving for children as a lost support for old age may appear selfish (**5.31**), but for some may have been driven by genuine economic factors.

5.29 CIL X 484

Epitaph: 1st c. AD. Paestum (Italy).
= Lattimore 1962: 189.
The deceased was a man of high standing in the local community, which may have heightened the father's sense of loss.
Compare **5.61** where a mother gives thanks that she did not attend her children's funerals; and contrast **3.14** where a father kills himself in order to predecease his dying son.

> To the spirits of the departed Marcus Vinicius Rufus, son of Marcus, of the Maecia voting tribe, *duovir, quinquennalis,* patron of the colony. The father did for his son what the son ought to have done for his father.

5.30 CIL IX 5407

Epitaph: 1st or 2nd c. AD. Firmum Picenum (Fermo, Italy).
= *CLE* 164; Lattimore 1962: 189.

To the spirits of the departed Spurius Saufeius, son of Spurius, who lived 6 years, 1 month and 5 days. Untimely death made the parent do for the son what the son should have done for his father.

5.31 *Plutarch*, Letter to Apollonius 19

Philosophical consolation: early 2nd c. AD.
  = *Moralia* 111 E-F.

> But do those who mourn for the untimely dead mourn on their own account or on behalf of the departed? If they grieve because they have been deprived of some pleasure, profit or comfort in old age, which they had expected from the dead, then their excuse for grieving is completely selfish. It is clear that they mourn not for the dead, but for their services. But if they mourn on account of the dead, then they should remember that the dead are not suffering and they will rid themselves of grief by following the wise and ancient advice to maximize the good and to minimize and lessen the evil.

Lost love

Love and death are closely aligned in Latin literature; life without love is characterized as little better than death and the loss, or frustration, of love (by death or other means) causes acute grief. Those driven to despair by love might contemplate suicide and choosing to die with your partner could be a romanticized ideal (**1.50–1.52**). Even if you could not die together, to die with your loved one to hand was part of the idealized death scene (**1.55**, **3.11**, **3.13** and **5.32**); what better time and place to die than in the arms of your lover?

5.32 *Tibullus 1.1, 59–68*

Elegiac poetry: late 1st c. BC. Tibullus imagines his own death, taking comfort from the thought of Delia's presence and grief.

> May I look on you when my last hour comes; as I die, may I hold your hand in my failing grasp. Delia, you will weep for me when I'm laid on the funeral couch and you will give me kisses mixed with bitter tears. You will weep: for your heart is not encased in hard iron nor is there flint in your tender breast. From my funeral there will be no young man and no unmarried girl who will return home dry-eyed. Do no violence, Delia, to my spirit; spare your loosened hair and spare your soft cheeks.

Men would not be expected to express their love for a dead partner in such a visible fashion as a woman (see above), although some poets (for example, Propertius) did delight in challenging the boundaries of conventional behaviour. In general, in a literary world populated by male authors it was women who were most often depicted as broken by both love and grief. The defining relationship between life, love and death was epitomized by literary portraits of Dido, the Carthaginian queen, who killed herself after the departure of her lover Aeneas (5.33). Dido was a woman of power and status who was broken by love. Despite the role of the gods in the ill-fated love affair, Dido was viewed as weak; as a woman she could not control her emotions and was overcome to the point of suicidal madness. For Dido, as an abandoned woman, death was the only honourable option.

5.33 Ovid, Heroines 7, 183–96

Poetry: late 1st c. BC or early 1st c. AD. Ovid imagines Dido writing a final letter to Aeneas.
Compare Virgil, *Aeneid* 4, 640–705.

> If you could see now the face of her who writes these words! I write and the Trojan sword is ready in my lap. The tears run down my cheeks and fall on the drawn steel, which will soon be stained with blood rather than tears. In my fated hour your gift is very appropriate. You provide my death at small cost. Nor does my heart now feel for the first time a wound since it already has the wound of cruel love. Anna my sister, my sister Anna, who unfortunately knew my fault, soon you will give my ashes, the final gifts. When I have been consumed upon the pyre, my inscription will not read: Elissa, wife of Sychaeus; let this epitaph be read on the marble of my tomb:
>
> From Aeneas came the cause of her death and the sword; from the hand of Dido herself came the fatal blow.

For women it was acceptable (to some degree) to grieve openly and exhibit signs of loss and mourning. To don widows' weeds and to become a chaste matron, and maintain devotion to a husband's memory could be respected, even if such lasting commitment was rare. The aged widow, for example Cornelia (the mother of the Gracchi) and Livia (wife of Augustus), could be respected for the honour and power conveyed by their husband's memory. Extreme or persistent grief was less often noted, but could have a symbolic or political dimension.

5.34 Tacitus, Annals 16.10

History: early 2nd c. AD. Events of AD 66.

Antistia Pollita is sent by her father, Lucius Antistius Vetus, to plead his case with the emperor Nero. Nero had already ordered the death of Antistia's husband, Rubellius Plautus. Father and daughter were subsequently forced to suicide.

> With him was his daughter, who apart from the imminent danger, was embittered by grief. This had lasted since the day she saw her husband Plautus murdered. She had clasped his bleeding neck and still kept her bloodstained clothes. Widowed, unkempt and inconsolable, she was eating just enough to stay alive. Now at the request of her father she went to Naples and besieged the doors of Nero.

Literature provides us with male perceptions, perspectives and ideals on love, death and grief. By contrast epitaphs could be set up and composed by both men and women. Husbands commemorate wives and wives commemorate husbands. Lattimore notes that 'records of devotion between husband and wife are enormously frequent in Latin inscriptions' (Lattimore 1962: 275). The majority of the epitaphs for wives and husbands are short and use simple and standardized language, such as 'to the best of husbands', 'the sweetest of wives', but as with epitaphs to children we should not dismiss the seemingly formulaic and banal as mere expressionless convention. Most epitaphs say what is expected, but in doing so do not always disguise intense feelings.

5.35 IA 812

Epitaph: 3rd c. AD. Aquileia (Italy).
  See also **6.32**.

> To the spirits of the departed Antonius Castus, who lived 36 years and 5 months. Plotia Callinice made this while living to her sweetest husband with whom she lived for 16 years and 5 months.

But once more, even in epitaphs male expectations of female behaviour were more readily expressed than the converse. Women could be remembered in idealized fashion (**5.36**), as exemplars of traditional morality that served to complement their men folk, or they were made to speak as if from beyond the grave, primarily to comfort their bereaved husbands. In short, the actions and words that men prized were readily celebrated and recorded once women were in the grave. Epitaphs, such as these, with their formal language and idealized behaviour, seem far removed from the poetry of, say, Propertius and Tibullus. There were, no doubt, stereotypes and ideals for wives that ran counter to those for lovers and mistresses.

5.36 CIL VI 11602

Epitaph: 1st or 2nd c. AD. Rome.
= *ILS* 8402.
Compare **3.34**.

> Here lies Amymone, the wife of Marcus, the best and most beautiful. She was good at working wool, pious, modest, frugal, chaste and content to stay at home.

A few epitaphs were more expressive and explored some of the dilemmas and tensions that faced the bereaved. A bereft partner needed to find a balance between remembering the deceased and getting on with life. To stop grieving would be to appear to forget the deceased and to deny their love (**5.37**). Epitaphs sought to express unending devotion by declaring weariness with life and even including wishes to give a life for the life of a loved one; 'I should gladly have exchanged for you whatever time is due to my life' (*CIL* VI 12652; Courtney 1995: n.180). Promises not to remarry, however, were rare (**5.38**).

5.37 CIL VI 15546, 8–12

Epitaph (to Claudia Piste): 1st c. AD. Rome.

> I have lost my wife. Why should I stay longer now? If I had been lucky, my Piste would have been alive. I am gripped by grief, alive when my wife is gone. Nothing is so miserable as to lose your whole life, and yet to go on living.

5.38 CIL VI 35050

Epitaph: 1st or 2nd c. AD. Rome (via Ostiensis).

> To the spirits of the departed Lucius Cornificius Philargyrus who lived 24 years. Articuleia Iris made this for her well-deserving husband. She swears that after his death she will not take another husband. For their freedmen, their freedwomen and their descendants.

Could the ties of love survive the grave? For the romantic at heart, love could convey a sense of immortality and a belief that the bond was so strong that it could not be destroyed by death. There was a paradox; 'the delight of love could be expressed by the feeling of immortality, but equally … by the metaphor of dying' (Griffin 1985: 147). The poet Propertius, who could imagine dying for love (**1.50**), also imagined love conquering death and, all being well, that death would reunite lovers (**5.40**). The ideal that love should transcend death is also expressed in some epitaphs (**5.41** and **5.42**). Poets also toyed with the idea that lovers, those who died in love or who suffered for love, would enjoy a different or special place in the hereafter (**5.43**); that for some, love defined their life and afterlife.

5.39 *Ausonius*, Parentalia 9, 7–14

Poetry: 4th c. AD. A poem in memory of the author's wife.

> As a young man I wept for you, robbed of my hopes in early years, and for 36 years a widower I have mourned for you and mourn for you still. Old age has overtaken me but I cannot stop my pain; for it always hurts and even seems new to me. Time brings comfort to the grief of others, but this wound becomes heavier with length of days. I tear my grey hairs mocked by widowed life and the more I love in loneliness the more I live in sadness.

5.40 *Propertius 1.19, 1–6 and 15–26*

Elegiac poetry: late 1st c. BC.

Compare **6.52** where the dead Cynthia complains that Propertius has all too soon forgotten her.

> I do not fear now the sad shadows, my Cynthia, or care about death fated for the final pyre. This fear is harder to bear than my funeral, that I could go down to the grave unloved by you. Cupid has not clung to my eyelids so lightly that my dust should be empty and love be forgotten.
>
> Nothing will please me more, Cynthia, than your beauty; and (Earth allow this and be just) that although your fated old age keeps you back, the sight of your bones will be dear to my weeping eyes. May you alive feel this while I am dust; then no place of death will be sad to me. But, Cynthia, I have a fear that you may neglect my tomb, and that some cruel passion may draw you away from my ashes, and force you unwilling to dry your falling tears. Constant threats may bend the will even of a loyal girl. So while it can be, let there be joy between lovers. Eternity is not long enough for enduring love.

5.41 *CIL VI 20569*

Epitaph: 1st or 2nd c. AD. Rome (via Labicana). Marble tablet.

Compare Propertius (4.7, 93–4) where the ghost of Cynthia says, 'Other women may possess you now, soon I shall have you to myself. You shall be with me and I shall grind my bones on yours'.

Iulia Methe. Here lie the bones of my dear wife waiting for me to bring mine to them. Tossius promises you often to ask for this: love will survive if only it reaches the shades of the dead.

5.42 CIL VI 24085

Epitaph: 2nd or 3rd c. AD. Rome.

Philemon and Charis, who always loving and living in harmony, could not survive without each other, and in piety their bones rest here together.

5.43 Tibullus 1.3, 57–66

Elegiac poetry: late 1st c. BC. The sick poet writes home to Delia imagining his death.
See also **3.49**.

But me, because I have always been easily held by Love, Venus herself will lead to the Elysian fields. There dancing and singing thrive, and birds fly here and there, singing sweet songs from their slender throats. Untended the field grows cassia and through all the land the kind earth blooms with scented roses. Groups of young men mix in play with gentle girls, and Love continually goes to war. There are all those, to whom Death came because of love; distinguished by wearing myrtle garlands in their hair.

The reality for most widows and widowers, if still young enough, was remarriage, and this was officially encouraged by the Augustan marriage laws. Protestations on the death of a partner that life was no longer worth living may have been genuine at the time, but these would have rarely been permanent feelings. It is striking that literary consolations are rarely addressed to spouses; there are often lists of moral examples of parents and siblings who took grief well, but not husbands and wives. A wife was replaceable unlike a sister, brother, child or parent. Seneca, as noted above, was sceptical for how long even a woman could genuinely weep and grieve (**5.8**). Women could be characterized as fickle in their love and grief. Dido, after all, was a widow devoted to her dead husband Sychaeus until Aeneas came on the scene. The theme of the fickle widow undoubtedly reflected male anxieties about the chastity and faithfulness of wives.

5.44 Petronius, Satyricon 111–12

Satirical novel: 1st c. AD. Some travelling companions are exchanging stories.

There was once a married woman from Ephesus so famous for her virtue that she even drew women from the neighbouring states just to look at her. So when she buried her husband, she was not satisfied with the common custom of following the funeral procession with loose hair and beating her breast in front of the crowd, since she even followed the dead man to his resting place. The corpse was placed in an underground vault, in the Greek fashion, and she watched and wept over it day and night. Neither her parents nor her relations could convince her to stop torturing herself and starving to death … [The woman is eventually seduced by a soldier who is supposed to be guarding the corpse of a criminal. While the soldier is distracted from his duty the family of the criminal remove the corpse for burial. Fearing punishment the soldier convinces the widow to replace the body of the criminal with that of her husband.] … The woman's heart was just as piteous as it was pure: 'Heaven forbid' she said 'that I should look at the same time on the dead bodies of the two men whom I love. I would rather put the dead to use than kill the living'. After saying this she ordered her husband's body to be taken out of the coffin and fixed up on the empty cross.

Cicero and grief

The writings of Cicero provide some fundamental and essential insights into Latin writings on grief and consoling the bereaved. Cicero wrote (and received) consolation letters, a 'consolation' and a philosophical treatise on grief. Cicero was familiar with all the standard themes of consolation, and at times the consolation offered by and to Cicero can seem impersonal and generic; consoling was more about promoting élite male relationships against the backdrop of the uncertain political times than providing real comfort.

5.45 Cicero, Letters to his Friends 5.16.2–3 (187)

Letter (to Titius): 46 BC.
  Cicero does not say who has died; Titius had perhaps lost a son or sons.

There is a very common form of consolation which we should always have on our lips and in our minds. We must remember that we are only men, the law of whose birth tells that our lives will be affected by fortune. We must accept the circumstances to which we are born. We must bear those misfortunes which we cannot in all wisdom avoid. We must remember the events of others, and know that nothing new has happened to us. But more effective, perhaps, than these and other forms of consolation used by the wise men and committed to memory in their writings, ought to be the condition of the state in these unsettled and desperate times. Today, those who have never raised children are blessed, and those who have lost them need to be consoled less than if they had lost them in a good Republic, or indeed in any Republic.

In February 45 BC Cicero's daughter died. The divorced Tullia would have been in her late twenties or early thirties and had not recovered from the birth of her son some weeks before. The child would not long survive her. Cicero was devastated by the death of his daughter; it became a pivotal point in his life, and an experience that would heavily influence his writings and perceptions of grief and death. The consoler became the consoled and in his grief for his daughter, and in how he expressed, suppressed and commemorated this, Cicero charted his own course. Cicero did not parade his grief, but he did absent himself from the city and politics. It was now Cicero's turn to receive letters of consolation filled with uplifting advice, that grief accomplishes nothing and should not be indulged in.

5.46 Lucius Lucceius to Cicero (Cicero, Letters to his Friends 5.14.1–3 (251))

Letter: May 45 BC.

I have often asked after you in the hope of seeing you. I was surprised that you have not been in Rome since you left, and it surprises me now. I do not know what keeps you away. If you enjoy solitude while writing or engaged in one of your usual pursuits, I am glad and make no criticisms of your plan. Nothing is more agreeable, even in calm and prosperous times, let alone these days of mourning; and at this time your mind is weary and needs rest from the heavy weight of business; and it is also an active mind, always creating something to please others and add fame to yourself. If, on the other hand, as before you left, you have abandoned yourself to weeping and sorrow, I am sad for your distress; but, if you will let me speak my mind freely, I will criticize you. For will you, whose intelligence penetrates the most difficult issues, be blind to the obvious? Do you not understand that your behaviour and complaining gain nothing; that you double your suffering when good sense demands that you reduce it?

In his reply to Lucceius, Cicero stressed that his comfort was in books since he could find no comfort in Rome; 'I am mortally weary of times and men, of Forum and Senate House' (Cicero, *Letters to his Friends* 5.15 (252)). Cicero's world was a changing one, both politically and personally; the Republic was failing, Caesar was dictator, his marriage to Terentia was over, his daughter dead and his sorrow and his own justification for it need to be

seen in this broader context. Tullia, her deeds, actions and aspirations, are
rarely mentioned; in fact, after her death Cicero does not mention Tullia
once by name in any of his writings (Erskine 1997: 36). Instead, in these
consolatory exchanges the focus falls on the correspondents. The eminent
Servius Sulpicius Rufus wrote to Cicero (5.47), expressing his condolences,
but also noting his own and Cicero's experiences and setting these up as a
model for imitation (Wilcox 2005: 247–8). In his reply (5.48) Cicero views
his grief as an exceptional one; with his public role diminished he has no
comfort for his grief. For Cicero the death of Tullia symbolized the death of
the Republic.

5.47 Servius Sulpicius Rufus to Cicero (Cicero, Letters to his Friends 4.6 (249))

Letter: March 45 BC.

Servius Sulpicius Rufus was consul in 51 BC. In 46 BC Caesar appointed
him governor of Achaia, from where he wrote to Cicero.

> When I received the news of the death of your daughter Tullia, I was
> indeed duly deeply grieved and distressed, and looked upon it as a
> disaster in which I shared. If I had been at home, I would have been
> at your side, and could have displayed my sorrow to you face to
> face. Yet that kind of consolation can be distressing and painful,
> because the relations and friends who offer it are themselves over-
> come by an equal sorrow. They cannot attempt to console without
> many tears, and seem to need comfort themselves rather than be
> able to offer comfort to others ... [Sulpicius continues to offer
> comfort by placing Tullia's life against the context of the times. The
> loss of a child is an evil, but so is the present political state. Sulpicius
> also notes several Greek cities that had fallen from greatness; people
> like cities are mortal] ... If she had not died now, she would still have
> died in a few years time, for she was mortal. You, too, must remove
> your mind and thoughts from such things, and rather remember
> those things worthy of your life: remember that she lived as long as
> life had anything to give her and that her life outlasted that of the
> Republic; remember that she lived to see you, her father, praetor,
> consul, and augur; and that she married young men of the greatest
> distinction. She had enjoyed nearly all of life's blessings and when
> the Republic fell, she left life. What fault can you find with Fortune
> on that account? Do not forget then that you are Cicero, and a man
> accustomed to instruct and advise others. Do not imitate bad
> doctors, who profess to understand how to heal the diseases of
> others, but are unable to heal themselves. Rather, suggest to yourself
> and place before your own mind the very suggestions which you are
> accustomed to offer others. There is no grief that length of time does

not lessen and soften. It would be better for you, in your wisdom, to anticipate this result than wait for this time to pass. And if there is any consciousness remaining in the world below, such was her love for you and her dutiful affection for all her family, that she certainly does not wish you to act so. Grant this to her, your lost one! Grant it to your friends who mourn with you in your sorrow! Grant it to your country, that if the need arises it may have the use of your services and advice ...

5.48 Cicero, Letters to his Friends 4.7 (250)

Letter (to Servius Sulpicius Rufus): April 45 BC.
  See also Cicero, *Letters to his Friends* 17.1.

Yes, indeed, my dear Servius, I would have wished that you had been with me, as you say, at the time of my sad loss. How much help your presence would have given me, both by consolation and by your sharing, almost equally, in my sorrow, I can judge from the great feeling of relief I experienced after reading your letter. For not only was what you wrote designed to soothe a mourner, but in offering me consolation you demonstrated your own sorrow. Your son Servius, by all the kindnesses he has shown, has made it clear both how much he personally values me, and how pleasing to you he thought such affection would be. His kind gestures have of course often been pleasanter to me, yet never more welcome. For myself, I am not only consoled by your words and (I would almost say) your partnership in my sorrow, but by your character also. For I think it a disgrace that I should not bear my bereavement as you, such a wise man, think it ought to be borne. But at times I am overwhelmed by and scarcely offer any resistance to my grief, because I do not have those consolations which were available to others in similar misfortunes, whose examples I put before my eyes ... [Cicero notes other prominent men who had lost children but found consolation in public life, whereas Cicero in the loss of his public honours had found comfort in Tullia] ... I had a refuge, one bosom where I could find repose, one in whose conversation and sweet ways I could put aside all worries and sorrows. But now, after such a crushing blow as this, the wounds which seemed to have healed have become inflamed. For when I leave my home in sorrow there is no Republic to offer me a refuge and provide consolation by its good fortunes and nor is there, as there once was, a home to receive me when I return saddened by the state of public affairs. Hence I avoid both home and Forum, because home can no longer comfort the sorrow which public affairs cause me, nor public affairs comfort the sorrow which I suffer at home. ...

Cicero's reply to Sulpicius is well considered. In his letters to his good friend Atticus we gain a more vivid sense of Cicero's suffering. In the immediate aftermath of Tullia's death Cicero stayed with Atticus, but from early March 45 BC had left Rome and was corresponding with Atticus regularly. In these letters we see Cicero fighting against his grief, his guilt at both expressing and suppressing his emotions, the comfort he finds in study, the composition of a *consolatio* to himself and his plans to build a memorial shrine (**4.28**). The letters suggest the conflicting relationship between Cicero's public role and his private grief; he is unable to ignore the expectations of others and feels a personal need to justify his approach to mourning. Cicero may be suffering in his grief but he is not overwhelmed by it; he busies himself in practical schemes and literary pursuits, most admittedly centred on grief. At times Cicero speaks of his grief as if it is a sickness or ailment, the cure for which can be found in literary works.

5.49 Cicero to Atticus 12.14.3 (251), 12.20.1 (258), 12.28.2 (267)

Letters: March 45 BC.

It is like you to want me to recover from this grief, but you are my witness that I have not been falling short in my efforts. Nothing has been written by any author on the reduction of grief which I did not read in your house. But my sorrow conquers all consolation. I have even done something which I expect no one has ever done before, I have written a consolation to myself. I shall send you the work as soon as the copyists have finished it. I can assure you that there is no consolation more effective than this. I write all day, not that it brings real benefit, but just for the moment it distracts me, indeed not enough, for grief is powerful, but it helps me to relax; and I try everything to bring my face if not my heart back to composure, if I can. While I do this it sometimes seems that I am doing wrong, at other times that I would be doing wrong if I failed to do it. Solitude helps, but it would be more effective if you were here to share it. That is my only reason for leaving this place, which through these ills has been useful. Yet this is a cause of sorrow, for you will not be able to feel the same towards me. The things that you loved in me are dead.

You encourage me to disguise the intensity of my grief and say that others think I do not do so well. Can I do it more effectively than by spending all my days in literary pursuits? Admittedly I do this not for disguise, but to ease and heal my mind; but even if I myself get little profit from it, at least it cannot be said that I fail to disguise my feelings.

You tell me to return to my old habits. For a long time it was my part to mourn for the Republic and I did so, but less intensely because I had comfort. Now I simply cannot pursue that way of life, and on this matter I do not feel that I must listen to other people's thoughts. My own conscience is more important to me than the comments of everyone else. As to my literary consolation of myself, I am not displeased with what it achieved. I minimized the outward show of sorrow; grief itself I could not reduce, and would not if I could.

Cicero's *consolatio* does not survive, but research for this may have influenced his work on the *Tusculan Disputations*, the third book of which takes grief as its theme. In this work Cicero explored how to put an end to the pain of grief, by considering the beliefs of various philosophical schools of thought (Erskine 1997). Cicero did not focus on his own suffering, but in the conclusion to the *Tusculan Disputations* Cicero highlighted his own varied troubles.

5.50 Cicero, Tusculan Disputations 5.41.121

Philosophical dialogue: 45 BC.

In writing this I cannot easily say how much it will benefit others; but in my own bitter sorrows and the various troubles which have surrounded me no other consolation could have been found.

Philosophical consolation

To console the bereaved was an important responsibility. The person offering consolation and the bereaved person were both expected to behave in certain ways and to say certain things, and the consoler to provide support of both an emotional and practical kind. If one could not be present in person a representative could be used; Cicero mentions the visits of Servius Sulpicius' son and his kind services (5.48). A letter of condolence could also be sent. A handful of original condolence letters, written on papyrus, survives. These date from the Roman period, were composed in Greek and come from Egypt, and thus represent a mixture of cultures and cultural practices. Nevertheless these letters are indicative of the behaviour of people who were not members of the élite, and reflect the support, succour and consolatory thoughts they exchanged. The letters were not penned with subsequent publication in mind and nor were they designed to entertain or to improve the reader, although they may have been composed according to accepted models and criteria.

5.51 SB XIV 11646

Papyrus letter: 1st or 2nd c. AD. Egypt (exact provenance unknown).
= Chapa 1998: n.1.

The papyrus letters often employ standard consolations, such as 'death is common to all' and frequently mention the dispatch of food stuffs. The food may have been intended as a helpful gift for the bereaved or it may have been an offering for the dead. Sarapis was an Egyptian god.

> Isidorus to Taysenouphis, his most treasured friend, many greetings. First of all I hope that you are in good health and I pray for you every day before the lord Sarapis. I was very grieved for your husband, as I was for my brother Germanus. Have courage and take it bravely, for this is common to all. May your children enjoy good health. My mother and brothers greet you. You will receive one hundred walnuts from the carrier of this letter. Write back to me about your health. I greet your children. I pray that you are well.

In contrast to the papyri the other surviving consolation letters are formal, carefully edited for publication and philosophically driven. Offering consolation was part of the services and duties expected in friendship networks and it was occasioned by varied misfortunes, such as political disappointments and exile, as well as bereavement. Consoling was a rhetorical exercise in which the author could display his virtues and standing as much as comfort the recipient (Wilcox 2005). To receive a letter or advice from a prominent man, such as Cicero or Seneca, could give added weight to the standard clichés and themes that the genre often employed. These letters of consolation, or at least the surviving examples, were influenced by or were direct products of philosophical discourse. The philosophically based consolation letter had its own conventions and tended to contain similar elements. These included exhortations not to mourn excessively, examples of people who took their loss well (and sometimes badly), thoughts on the brevity of life, homilies that time lessens grief and ideas that the dead would be spared the problems and disappointments of life. This suggests that a formulaic language of grief existed with stock phrases and expressions that persist to modern times, such as 'time is a great healer'. In many respects letters of consolation were more concerned with how to mourn than healing the real pain of grief.

5.52 *Cicero*, Tusculan Disputations 3.32

Philosophical dialogue: 45 BC. Cicero considers the role of giving consolation and identifies the essential arguments that should be conveyed to the bereaved.

Compare 5.45–5.47.

The first healing step therefore in giving consolation will be to show that either there is no evil or at least very little; the second will be to discuss the common lot of life and any special aspect that needs discussion in the case of the individual mourner; the third is to show that it is very foolish to be uselessly overcome by sorrow when one understands that there can be no advantage.

In his letters of consolation the Younger Seneca did not shy away from what he saw as the primary purpose of the genre, to offer sound philosophical advice. In a letter recorded within a letter, Seneca notes how he was highly critical of a father's grief for his young son (5.16). Mourning has become a vice and Seneca shames rather than comforts the recipient of the letter (Wilson 1997). Seneca acknowledges that grief is a natural human response, and that weeping brings comfort, but nevertheless grief should not be courted or overindulged in. Seneca objects to the theatrical side of emotional display, something that should be ill-suited to the educated élite (see below for opposing views).

5.53 Seneca, Letters 99.16

Philosophical letter: mid 1st c. AD
  Compare Seneca *Letter* 63, 1–2 and Lucian, *On Funerals* (3.20).

> Tears fall, even though we try to hold them back, and by being shed they ease the soul. What then should we do? Let us allow them to fall, but let us not command them to do so; let us weep as emotion affects us, not because imitation demands it. Indeed, let us add nothing to true grief, nor increase it by following the example of others. The display of grief is more demanding than grief itself: few men are sad on their own! They cry louder when they are heard; those who are reserved and silent when alone are excited to new tears when they see others near them! Then they lay violent hands upon themselves, although they might have done this more easily with no one there to stop them; they pray for their own death; and they throw themselves from their couches. But without spectators their grief lessens. In this matter, as in others, we are concerned with conforming to the examples of the many and looking to convention rather than what one should do. We abandon nature and hand ourselves over to the crowd, who are never good advisors in anything, and in this matter, as in all others, are most inconsistent. People see a man who takes his grief bravely: they call him undutiful and hard-hearted; they see a man who collapses and clings to his dead: they call him womanish and weak. Everything therefore should be referred to reason. But nothing is more foolish than to gain a reputation for sadness and to approve tears.

Seneca's words can at times seem severe (**5.16**), but we need to remember that these letters had a philosophical role and in his eyes fitted the needs of the recipient. It is notable that he did not take the same tone with Marcia (**5.5**) as he did with Marullus. Nor did Seneca deny that grief is one element of what makes us human. Seneca acknowledged the human right to mourn, but also that grief passes. Time is a great healer, but it would be more dignified and honourable to give grief up voluntarily than just to allow it to fade away; although, even for Seneca, giving advice could be easier than living up to it.

5.54 Seneca, Letters 63.12 and 14

Philosophical letter: mid 1st c. AD. Written to Lucillius on the death of his friend Flaccus.
Compare Cicero *Tusculan Disputations* 3.30.73.
See also **5.8** and **6.33**.

> You have buried one whom you have loved; look about for someone to love. It is better to replace your friend than to weep. I know what I am about to say is a very common remark, but I shall not omit it simply because it is said by all. A man ends his grief, even if he does not plan it, in the passage of time. But the most shameful remedy for sorrow, in the case of a wise man, is to become weary of sorrowing. I would prefer you to abandon grief than have grief abandon you; and you should stop grieving as soon as possible, because even if you wish to it is impossible to keep it up for long.

> I, the one who writes these words to you, wept immoderately for my dear friend Annaeus Serenus, so that, in spite of my wishes, I must be included among the examples of those who were conquered by grief. But today I condemn myself, and I understand that the cause of my grief was chiefly that I had not believed it possible for him to die before me.

The letter format could be utilized as a guise for philosophical treatises on death, grief and mourning, similar to the *consolatio* that Cicero addressed to himself. Seneca the Younger wrote several *consolationes* and two of these, addressed to Marcia and Polybius respectively, were lengthy works. In these, Seneca included harsh Stoic exhortations about not mourning in excess and drew upon examples of people who coped well with grief to give the bereaved inspiration (**5.5**). However, these works also contained more tender words which acknowledged the genuine pain and loss of the bereaved and consoled them with ideas that their loved ones had lived good lives and were fortunate to have escaped the world.

5.55 Seneca, Consolation to Polybius 18, 7–8

Philosophical consolation: *c.* AD 43.
Compare Seneca, *Consolation to Marcia* 14, 5–6.

> Make yourself often willing to meet the memory of your brother,
> both to speak of him in conversation, and to picture him to yourself
> through constant remembrance. You will be able to achieve this
> only if you make your memories of him more pleasant than tearful;
> for it is natural that the mind will always hide from a subject to
> which it turns with sadness. Think of his modesty, think of his skill
> in life's activities, of his care in performing them, of his constancy to
> promises. Set out all his words and deeds to others and commemo-
> rate them yourself. Think what he was, and what he might have
> hoped to become.

The origins of literary 'consolations' were Greek. Crantor, a philosopher
of the 4th or early 3rd c. BC, had written a work entitled 'On Grief' that was
popular thereafter (Kassel 1958). Unfortunately it does not survive, but it
seems likely that this provided the model for later consolations, with their
stock themes of not mourning in excess and that death is no evil. Plutarch,
writing from the perspective of the Greek world and Platonic philosophy,
followed the conventions of this consolatory genre.

5.56 Plutarch, Consolation to his Wife 3–4

Consolation: late 1st c. AD.
= *Moralia* 608–9. See Pomeroy 1999.
Plutarch advocates setting a good philosophical example at the death of
his daughter (**5.13**), but he also takes comfort from the joy that she had
brought. The child was 2 years old; Plutarch and his wife had already lost
two sons.

> But our daughter was the most delightful thing in the world to
> hold, to watch, to hear; so we must let the thought of her also live
> in our minds and lives, bringing with it joy much more than
> sorrow. If, that is, we can expect benefit in our time of need from
> the advice we have often given to others; we must not be weighed
> down by it, paying for these pleasures with grief many times as
> great. Those who were with you report, with admiration, that you
> did not put on mourning, or allow yourself and your servants to be
> disfigured; nor were there ostentatious or lavish funeral prepara-
> tions; everything was done with decorum and in silence, and in the
> presence of close friends.

Several letters of the Younger Pliny also record the deaths of his friends. These were not addressed to the bereaved so were not consolation letters in the strictest sense. Instead the letters brought the news of the death to other acquaintances of Pliny's and allowed the latter to eulogize the deceased and to record his own feelings of sadness at the loss. In these letters Pliny played the part of the mourner (albeit a somewhat removed one) and he did not lecture himself on how to control his grief; thus the letters appear less philosophically driven than other consolation letters and in places served more as obituary notices. These letters may ostensibly be about grief and loss, but they were also part of how Pliny fashioned his self-image. Indeed, all published letters that took consolation or grief as their theme could form part of the self-definition of, and even competition between, educated men and involve elements of 'rhetorical one-upmanship' (Wilcox 2005: 237). Demonstrating that he had feelings and that he could empathize with the losses of others, while simultaneously demonstrating moderation in grief, and that he knew how to express just the correct amount of emotion, were among the defining features of a Roman gentleman.

5.57 Pliny, Letters 8.23. 7–8

Letter (to Aefulanus Marcellinus): late 1st or early 2nd c. AD. The subject is the death of Junius Avitus, a young senator whom Pliny had supported.
   See also Pliny, *Letters* 1.12, 2.1, 4.21, 5.16 (**5.27**) and 8.5.

> I mourn his youth and the suffering of his family, for he leaves an elderly mother, a wife of only a year, and a daughter just born. So many hopes and joys have been reversed in a single day. He had just been elected aedile, and recently he had become a husband and father: now he has left the office he never held, his mother is childless, his wife a widow, and his daughter is left an orphan, never to know a father. I weep the more because I was away and knew nothing of the illness afflicting him; the news of his sickness and death reached me at same time, before fear could accustom me to this severe sorrow. I am in such anguish as I write that this must be all, for I can think and speak of nothing else just now.

Poetic laments and consolations

The bereaved may have drawn consolation from eulogies and laments to the dead which were in origin associated with the funeral. There were instructions in rhetoric manuals on how to compose a eulogy and praise the deceased (Quintilian 3.7.15). The content of the eulogy would have been defined by the identity of the deceased, their role, age, gender and standing. Subsequently eulogies might be published or their content widely reported. Pliny wrote some sort of eulogy for a friend's son which he intended to publish (*Letters* 3.10; **2.52**); note as well the eulogies to Murdia and Turia published as inscriptions attached to their tombs (**2.26** and **3.34**). Eulogies were formulaic and stylized public statements that were primarily about the life of the deceased, but in the process could also voice the loss and grief of the survivors. Thus the eulogy could have a consolatory element, although this was generally mediated through the formal language of the élite male. Poetic laments or dirges to the dead (*epicedion*) were less constrained in how they gave expression to grief, but like eulogies may have had their origins in the laments and songs performed at the funeral (see **3.20**). Dramatic and often lengthy laments were a characteristic of epic poetry and served to reconcile the participants of the poem, and the reader, to loss. Epic descriptions of public mourning could serve as powerful symbols for communal suffering, defeat, destruction and grief. The epic lament gave voice to the despair, anger and even violence of the bereaved, more than serving to console them; 'revenge is the companion of lament' (Fantham 1999: 228). In the mainly mythical world of Latin epic poetry grief could be raw, and uncontrolled; and it could place private pain in the public domain (Markus 2004: 106).

5.58 *Statius,* Thebaid 3, 114–30

Epic poetry: late 1st c. AD. The subject of the poem is the struggle between the sons of Oedipus for the Theban throne.

For further examples of grief and lament in epic see **3.14**, **3.15** and **3.18**.

> Pale wives and children and sick parents pour from the city into the plain with wilderness everywhere, each rushing to their sorrow in a pitiful contest. Thousands go with them for comfort's sake, some eager to see the deeds of one man and the night's work. The road is loud with laments and the fields echo with the cries of grief. But when they reach the infamous rocks and the cursed wood, it is as if there has been no earlier crying and that no bitter tears have flowed. A pitiful cry rises in a single voice; all are inflamed and maddened by the bloody sight. Grief stands fierce, his bloodied clothes torn and, beating his breast, invites the mothers to mourn. They study the helmets of the cold corpses and point to the bodies they have found, falling down upon strangers and kin. Some press their hair into the blood, some close eyes and wash deep wounds with tears.

Laments, as free-standing poems dedicated to real rather than mythical characters, focused on both the dead and the bereaved, singing the praises of the former to bring comfort to the latter. In some respects these poems represent the middle ground in consolation literature between letters and eulogies on the one hand and epic lament on the other. These poems were less philosophically driven than letters of consolation and less formal than eulogies; they could be emotional and personal, while simultaneously lacking the dramatic excesses of epic. These laments were about grief and its causes and not about moral improvement or a guide to the public face of mourning. Nevertheless, these poems did conform to conventions and expectations of genre. The poems often contained similar elements: an address to the mourners; a commentary on the cruelty of fate; a summary of the career of the deceased or of their virtues; an account of the final moments before death; a description of the funeral; and details of the arrival of the deceased in the next world. The opening lines of one of Statius' dirges capture the context of the poems; they are works written not just to pay tribute to a life lost, but also to commemorate and justify the grief of the bereaved (5.59). Despite the arguments of philosophers such as Seneca there could be pleasure in grief and a therapeutic quality to lament (Markus 2004). The emotion of grief could be savoured, not automatically suppressed and avoided. Grief could be indulged in and even become theatrical (compare 3.20 and 5.53). In poetry Livia is allowed to weep and lament, to put her personal loss before her public image, a seeming lack of self-control that Seneca, in his description of Livia's grief, barely acknowledges (5.5).

5.59 Statius, Silvae 2.1, 1–13

Poetry: late 1st c. AD. Lament to Glaucias, a favourite slave child of Atedius Melior.

For a lament to Melior's parrot see Statius, *Silvae* 4.2.

What consolation can I give you, Melior, for your foster son taken before his time? How can I boldly speak before the pyre, while the ashes are still glowing? Even now the sorrowful wound is exposed, and the great cut lies open to a dangerous path. While I furiously compose my songs and healing words, you prefer to beat your breast and lament loudly; you hate the lyre and turn away with deaf ear. My song is untimely: a defeated lioness or tigress robbed of her cubs would sooner listen to me. Even if the triple chant of the Sicilian maidens [the Sirens] drifted here, or the lyre that is understood by beasts and woodlands, these would not soothe your raging sorrow. Demented grief stands in your heart; at a touch your breast heaves and weeps.

5.60 Pseudo Ovid, Consolation to Livia 113–19

Poetry: mid 1st c. AD? Authorship and exact date are uncertain.

Drusus died in 9 BC, but this poem may have been written much later (see Schoonhover 1992). The consolation contained stock themes such as all men are mortal and also praised the illustrious career and achievements of the

deceased. Simultaneously the poem acknowledged the anguish, disappointments and tears of the bereaved.

> Sometimes Livia makes her tears congeal and harden, holding them
> back, and, braver than her eyes, drives them within: but they still
> burst out, and flood once more her lap and bosom, pouring out
> from heavy and never-failing eyelids. Weeping gains strength from
> the delay; the stream flows fuller, if it has been held back by even a
> brief delay.

A lament sought to bring solace to the bereaved, not to lecture them on
their behaviour. Poetry acknowledged the grief of the bereaved but also
sought to soothe them and to bring consolation, if in a less dogmatic form
than philosophy. It can thus often be difficult to distinguish between poetic
laments and poetic consolations; there is no hard and fast dividing line. So,
for example, the so-called *Consolation to Livia* (**5.60**) and Propertius' elegy
for Cornelia (**5.61**) justify the power of grief and loss, but also provide
comfort and hope. The dead themselves could take on the role of the
consoler, being given a voice from beyond the grave.

5.61 Propertius 4.11, 73–98

Elegiac poetry: late 1st c. BC. A consolation on the death of Cornelia.
   Cornelia, who died in 16 BC, was the wife of Paullus Aemilius Lepidus,
consul in 34 BC and censor in 22 BC. Cornelia was, through her mother, a
half-sister to the emperor Augustus' daughter, Julia. In the poem Cornelia
speaks from beyond the grave, urging her husband to be strong, while taking
pride and consolation from her ancestry, her virtuous life and the children
she bore; this is an idealized view of womanhood and female achievements
written from a male perspective.
   Compare **6.52**. Note as well that Sulpicius imagines what the dead Tullia
might say to Cicero (**5.47**).

> Now I commend our children to you, Paullus, the common pledge of
> our love: this care still stirs, imprinted in my ashes. The father must
> occupy the mother's role: your shoulders must bear all my crowd of
> children. When you kiss their tears away, add their mother's kisses.
> Now the whole household begins to be your burden. And if you
> must weep, do it without their seeing! When they come to you,
> deceive them with tearless eyes as they kiss you. Let those nights be
> enough, Paullus, that you exhaust yourself for me, in the dreams
> where you often believe that you see my face. And when in secret
> you speak to my image, say every word as though to one who could
> reply. But if the couch that faces the doorway should be changed,
> and a careful stepmother occupy my place, my boys, praise and

accept your father's wife: captivated, she will reward your good manners. Don't praise your mother too much: she may be offended by thoughtless speech that compares her with the first wife. Or if your father remembers me, content with my shade, and still prizing my ashes, learn even now to feel how old age advances, and leave no path open for a widower's cares. May the years that were taken from me be added to your years: so my children may delight the old age of Paullus. And it is good that I never dressed in a mother's mourning clothes: all my children came to my funeral.

Poetic laments and consolations captured the emotional paralysis that could affect the bereaved as well as exploring the more well-worn themes of consolation. These were emotive genres, but genres still contained by and responding to poetic conventions. This is well illustrated by the laments composed by Ovid. Ovid employed the form of a lament when writing of the death of his fellow poet Tibullus, but Ovid was also responding to a poem by Tibullus himself, in which Tibullus anticipated his own death away from home (**3.49** and **5.43**; Huskey 2005; Williams 2003). The grief expressed by Ovid may be genuine, but its expression is also part of a dialogue between the poets.

5.62 *Ovid*, Amores 3.9.41–54

Poetry: late 1st c. BC.

Did the flames of the pyre seize your body, poet, and feed upon your breast? Flames that did such an awful wrong would have burned the golden temples of the gods! Venus, who holds high Eryx, turned her face away and some say that she could not hold back her tears. And yet it is better this way than if you had died in Phaecian land [Corfu] and soil had covered your nameless corpse. Here your mother closed your swimming eyes as the spirit left them, and performed the final rites for your ashes. And your sister came, with hair disordered and torn to share your poor mother's grief. And Nemesis and the girl [Delia] you loved before her added their kisses to those of your family. So your pyre was not a lonely one.

Previous to the composition of his lament to Tibullus, Ovid had composed a similar poem on the death of Corinna's parrot. The praise of the parrot, a lover's gift, allowed Ovid to explore his devotion to Corinna, in the playful context of Latin love poetry (James 2006). The poem cleverly adapted the standard elements of the poetic lament: an address to the mourners, an attack on envious fate, a listing of the parrot's virtues, an account of the bird's final moments, thoughts on a bird afterlife and the funeral. Ovid was also responding to an earlier parody of the poetic lament in which Catullus mourned the death of his girlfriend's pet sparrow. These poems remind us that poetry can toy with grief; it may seek to capture emotion more than other more philosophically driven genres, but poetry is still about artistic presentation and thus can be a barrier between the reader and real bereaved Romans.

5.63 Ovid, Amores 2.6 51–62

Poetry: late 1st c. BC.

Compare Catullus 3 and Statius, *Silvae* 2.4. For verse epitaphs to pets see Courtney 1995: n. 200–4.

See also **1.14**.

> There exists, if we may believe it, a place that is the home of pious birds, from which impure birds are kept away. Harmless swans roam there feeding and the long-lived solitary phoenix dwells there as well. Juno's bird [the peacock] spreads out its fantail and the cooing dove gives kisses to its mate. Our parrot is welcome among them in this woodland place, and attracts the feathered faithful to hear his words. His bones are covered by a mound, just big enough to cover his body, on which a small stone bears these words: 'This very monument shows that my mistress loved me well. I was skilled in speech beyond a common bird'.

6

THE AFTERLIFE

Introduction

What did the inhabitants of the Roman world believe happened after death? There is no simple or short answer to this question. Roman beliefs were varied and ranged from the idea that death was a complete end, to a well-developed geography for a separate world of the dead. We can gain a taste here for some of these views, but it remains difficult to assess how many people believed in what, exactly how these beliefs developed and changed across time, and the extent to which they varied by geographic region.

For the afterlife, perhaps more so than in any other aspect of Roman death, we face the challenge of bridging the gap between élite discussions and the real thoughts of the mass of the population. The great philosophical writers debated whether the human soul survived death and, if so, what happened to it. These intellectual discussions reveal little about what most people actually did or did not believe. Epitaphs provide a more diverse spectrum of people's expressed views, opinions and hopes, but these can be stylized and constrained by convention. What does become clear, however, is that there was no consensus in either genre; there was not one view about what happened after death that was either accepted or challenged. Death remained the great unknown and in general pagan religion, unlike Christianity, offered no definite answers and made no promises. Nevertheless, the living still had intense feelings for and about the dead, and the dead did live on in the minds of those who survived them. This meant that even sceptics could retain a vague hope for some sort of continuity for the dead, and even for a future reunion with them.

The most comprehensive survey of Roman views on and attitudes towards life after death remains Cumont's book first published in 1922. The lack of a more recent synthesis reflects the broad nature of the topic. Scholars have tended to explore certain aspects of Roman views on life after death, such as philosophical discourses (Warren 2004), religious attitudes (Knight 1970; Davies 1999; Bremmer 2002), representations of the underworld (Bernstein 1993), ghosts (Felton 1999; Ogden 2002) and necromancy (Ogden 2001). Ghost stories can be as informative and suggestive as descriptions of Hades, since belief easily faded into superstition and in the Roman era there was no hard line between the two. The range of opinions about the afterlife, the soul, spirits, gods and ghosts was part of the reality of dealing with death in the Roman world. Everyone did not believe the same things and some people may have given little thought to what they did believe. Nevertheless, a relationship existed between the living and the dead which placed a burden of responsibility with the living. The dead needed to be treated with respect and buried properly; the dead needed to rest secure; and ideally, the dead needed to be honoured and remembered. The living gave thanks for the dead who had preceded them, even if they were not sure where, if anywhere, they had gone.

The soul

Cicero, when discussing whether death is an evil and the dead wretched, considered different views on the nature of the soul (*animus*; *anima*) and its continuity after death (**6.1**). It is clear that among philosophers at least there were diverging definitions of the soul and contrasting opinions about its fate.

6.1 *Cicero,* Tusculan Disputations *1.9.18*

Philosophical dialogue: 45 BC.

> We must first then consider what death, which seems to be a subject well-known to all, is in itself. Some think death to be the separation of the soul from the body; some believe there is no separation, but that soul and body die together and the soul is annihilated with the body. Of those that think that the soul is separated, some believe that it is at once dispersed, others that it survives a long time, others that it survives for ever. Further, as to what the soul is in itself, or where it is in us, or where it came from, there is much disagreement.

Cicero continued by summarizing different definitions of the soul. Some thinkers believed that the soul was located in the heart, some in the brain, while others identified the soul with breath; the Stoics held the soul to be fire, while other individual thinkers equated the soul with musical harmony, numbers and movement (Cicero, *Tusculan Disputations* 1.10). Whatever its nature, the central issue was what happened to the soul at death. Was the soul immortal? The great Greek philosopher Socrates had provided the basis for much subsequent philosophical thought: 'Death is one of two things. Either the dead man no longer exists and has no sensation at all; or other-wise, as men say, it is a change and migration of the soul from here to some-where else' (Plato, *Apology* 40c). Different philosophical schools provided different ideas and perspectives on this issue (for an overview see Corrigan 1986; Poortman 1994; Warren 2004): followers of Epicurus and Aristotle

212

believed that death was annihilation (**6.2**); followers of Plato that the soul was immortal (**6.3**); Orphic-Pythagoreans in a sort of cyclical reincarnation; and the Stoics that souls might be liberated but had little subsequent independent being (**6.5** and **6.6**).

6.2 *Lucretius*, On Nature 3, 323–8

Philosophical (Epicurean) poetry: 1st c. BC.

> So the soul is held together by all of the body, and is itself the guardian of the body and the source of its safety; for soul and body cling together with common roots, and it is apparent that they cannot be torn apart without being destroyed.

6.3 *Plutarch*, Letter to Apollonius 36

Philosophical consolation: early 2nd c AD.
= *Moralia* 121D.
Plutarch is quoting Plato and Socrates, and prior to this comment has been describing the just judgement of souls in the underworld.

> It seems to me that death is no more than the severing of two things, soul and body, from each other.

6.4 CIL *III 3247*

Epitaph: 2nd c. AD. Colonia Flavia Sirmium (Sremska Mitrovica, Serbia).
= *CLE* 1207.
For the theme of separation of body and soul in epitaphs see Lattimore 1962: 29–43.

> To the spirits of the departed. The ground holds the body, the stone the name and the air the soul. For the slave Quintus Ammerus.

6.5 *Epictetus*, Fragment 26

Philosophy (Stoic): late 1st or early 2nd c. AD.
See also **6.30**.

> You are a small soul, carrying around a corpse.

6.6 *Marcus Aurelius*, Meditations 4.21

Philosophy (Stoic): 2nd c. AD.

If souls continue to exist, how has the air found room for them all since the beginning of time? Also how does the earth find room for all the buried bodies from across the ages? The earth, after a short period, through change and decay of these bodies makes space for other dead bodies. Similarly, souls removed into the air exist for a while before being changed and diffused, and are then transferred into fire and taken back into the creative intelligence of the universe, and in this way room is made to receive new souls.

The nature, location and length of the soul's new life were often ill-defined by those who believed in its liberation at death. In many ways the fate of the soul was a secondary issue; what mattered was how belief in the soul and its survival (or not) impacted upon how people lived their lives. Some great thinkers can appear to hedge their bets as to whether and in what form the soul survived. However, this acknowledgement of uncertainty could be coupled with the ethical certainty that death in itself was not a bad thing and should not be feared (**2.16–2.18**). Death could provide an end to suffering, and even if this meant that the soul did not survive, no existence was better than a miserable existence.

6.7 *Cicero,* Tusculan Disputations *1.11.25*

Philosophical dialogue: 45 BC.
    For Cicero on souls in heaven see **6.17**.

> Therefore in what way or for what reason do you say that you consider death an evil, when it will either make us happy if our souls survive, or free us from misery if we are without sensation?

6.8 *Seneca,* Letters *91.21*

Philosophical letter: mid 1st c. AD.

> Death also has a bad smell. But none of the people that condemn it has put it to the test. Meanwhile it is madness to condemn that of which you are ignorant. However, you do know this one thing, that death is beneficial to many, that it frees many from torture, want, sickness, suffering and weariness.

Those who were more categorical that death was an absolute end could argue that if the soul does not survive then 'death is nothing to us' (Lucretius, *On Nature* 3, 830; see also **3.37**). Man is mortal and once life is taken away he is nothing and can endure no pain or misery; beyond death there is nothing, neither happiness nor unhappiness.

6.9 Sallust, Conspiracy of Catiline 51.20

History: mid 1st c. BC. Events of 63 BC, Julius Caesar speaks against the execution of the conspirators.

> To men in grief and distress death comes as a release from suffering, and is not a punishment; death puts an end to all human worries, and beyond it there is no place for either sorrow or joy.

Heaven or hell?

It was the issue of the soul's survival that informed discussions about the afterlife and the form that this afterlife might take. Philosophers were often more concerned with ethical issues centred on the soul than with picturing the soul in its disembodied state. For others, imagining what might happen to the soul, and all the uncertainties that this embraced, was a fundamental aspect of facing death. If the soul did exist and if the soul did survive, what happened to it?

6.10 Scriptores Historiae Augustae, Hadrian 25.9

Biography: 4th c. AD. Events of AD 138.

The emperor Hadrian allegedly composed this poem on his deathbed. It suggests a playful attitude to the soul and its survival, tinged with a note of pessimism.

Note also that Hadrian is believed to have created his own 'Underworld' at his villa in Tivoli, in a series of dark grottoes and underground corridors; Macdonald and Pinto 1995: 131–8.

For Hadrian on death see also **6.22**.

> Little spirit, dear wanderer, guest and companion of the body, to what pale, stern and bare places have you now flown? You will not, as you were used to, joke and play.

The traditional view was that the souls of the dead went to Hades, an underworld kingdom; a vision of life after death that was itself heavily influenced by the Greek world. Constructing a coherent view of what the 'Roman' underworld was supposed to be like is complicated. There were, for example, different opinions as to whether the underworld was a place of joy or punishment (see below). In addition, some of the best descriptions of the underworld originate either from authors who were clearly sceptical about and dismissive of conventional views, or from descriptions representing artistic inventions – what Cicero describes as 'the monstrosities of poets and painters' (Cicero, *Tusculan Disputations* 1.6.11). As a starting point we can consider the poet Ovid's view of the afterlife, which was basically a continuation of earthly life, with the dead still pursuing their worldly employment (**6.11**). Such a view offered no escape or rest for those who had toiled in life, although justice was served on the wicked.

6.11 Ovid, Metamorphoses 4.430–46

Poetry: late 1st c. BC or early 1st c. AD. The goddess Juno visits the underworld.

Dis is Pluto, king of the underworld.

> There is a path that slopes downhill, gloomy with deathly yew. It leads to the underworld, through mute and silent regions. There the sluggish Styx breathes forth vapours, and by that way the shades of the newly dead descend, the ghosts of people laid to rest in their tombs with full rites. The wide and desolate place is cold and gloomy. The recently arrived ghosts do not know where the road is which leads to the Stygian city, nor where to find the cruel palace of black Dis. His populous city has a thousand entrances, and open gates on every side. Just as the sea absorbs rivers from all over the earth, so that place accepts all souls: it is never too small, however great the numbers, and does not notice the arriving crowds. Lifeless shadows without flesh or bones wander about, some jostling in the Forum, some round the palace of the underworld's ruler, while others pursue the trades, imitating their old lives. Others are punished according to their crimes.

Ovid plays with the familiar, whereas most descriptions of the underworld created an environment that was fundamentally different to the world above. Common elements such as topographical details (for example, Acheron and Styx) and characters (for example, Charon) characterize many descriptions, but it remains difficult to standardize the features or create, as it were, some sort of map of the underworld. Lucian, albeit in jest of the believers and in a Greek context, provides a useful summary of what he claims were the widespread beliefs about Hades.

6.12 Lucian, On Funerals 2–9

Satirical essay: 2nd c. AD.

Homer and Hesiod were the fathers of Greek literature and admired across the generations, but whether people took the myths literally, as Lucian implies, is another matter. The three-headed dog was known as Cerberus. Alcestis, Protesilaus, Theseus and Odysseus were all Greek mythological characters who were supposed to have visited the underworld; compare the visit of Aeneas in Virgil, *Aeneid* 6. Ixion, a legendary king of Thessaly, attempted to rape Hera and in Hades was crucified on a burning wheel that was to spin for all eternity. Sisyphus was the legendary king of Corinth who tried to cheat death and was punished in Hades by having to roll a large boulder up a hill, to have it continually roll back again. Tantalus, a legendary king of Sipylus, abused the privilege of dining with the gods and was punished eternally by water and fruit that disappeared when they were almost within his grasp.

The general crowd, whom philosophers call the laity, taking on trust, almost as law, the fiction of Homer and Hesiod and the other myth-making poets, believe that there is a hole deep under the earth called Hades, which is spacious, murky and sunless; but somehow mysteriously lit up so all its details can be seen! The king there is a brother of Zeus, called Pluto, whose name, so I was told by an expert in such matters, is an allusion to his wealth of corpses. As to the nature of his government and his subjects, this Pluto has authority over all the dead, whom he keeps under control, securely chained. The shades are not allowed to return to Earth; in all time there have been only a few exceptions and these for very important reasons. Pluto's kingdom is surrounded by great rivers, the names of which even inspire fear: Cocytus ['Wailing'] and Pyriphlegethon ['Burning Fire'] and the like. But the most formidable feature is Lake Acheron which first confronts and receives the newcomer; it cannot be crossed without the ferryman; for it is too deep to wade across and too wide to swim; indeed, even dead birds cannot fly across it. At the beginning of the descent is a gate made of adamant where the king's nephew, Aeacus, stands guard with a three-headed dog at his side. This long-toothed beast is friendly enough to those who come in but barks and shows his teeth to those who try to run away. On the other side of the lake is a meadow overgrown with asphodel and a spring that makes war on memory which is called Lethe ['Oblivion']. All this was known by the ancients from those who had visited; Alcestis and Protesilaus of Thessaly, Theseus, son of Aegeus and Homer's Odysseus. These witnesses, trustworthy I'm sure, presumably did not drink from the spring or else they would not have remembered it all! According to them supreme power is entirely in the hands of Pluto and Persephone who are, however, aided in the administration by a great crowd of assistants: such as the Furies, the Tormentors, the Terrors and also Hermes, although he is not always with them. Judicial powers are held by two satraps or judges, Minos and Rhadamanthus of Crete, who are sons of Zeus. All good and just men, who have lived virtuously, are gathered and sent by these judges as colonies to the Elysian Fields to lead the perfect life. By contrast any evil-doers are handed over to the Furies who take them to the place of the Wicked, where they are punished in proportion to their wrong-doings. What a variety of torments they may endure! There are racks, fires and gnawing vultures. Here Ixion is turned on a wheel and Sisyphus rolls his stone; not forgetting Tantalus who stands on the edge of the lake, with a dry throat, as if the wretch will die from thirst. But those who have followed the neutral path in life, and there are many of them, wander about the meadow without their bodies, shapeless phantoms, that vanish like smoke at a touch. These get their nourishment, naturally, from the libations and offerings left by us at their tombs; so a shade who has no surviving friends or relations on earth has a hungry time of it in the lower world.

In traditional descriptions of the underworld the dead continued to have emotions and were still susceptible to pleasure and pain. The souls of the dead enjoyed or suffered according to the life they had led. For the wicked the underworld was often perceived as a place of punishment. The famous ill-doers and their excruciating or frustrating punishments were well known (see **6.12**), but it was less clear what happened to ordinary sinners. Virgil, in Aeneas' visit to the underworld, suggested that the dead were divided by how they had lived and died. For the isolation of suicides see **1.41**. Virgil also described a separate terrifying area set aside for sinners where the blood-stained Tisiphone stood guard. Here were to be found the characters of Greek myth who were condemned to enduring eternal torments, such as Tityos, the son of Earth who, as a punishment for assaulting Leto, the mother of Apollo, had become a constant feast for vultures (*Aeneid* 6, 595–600). Virgil does suggest that there were others too in this region of the underworld, less infamous, but still suffering.

6.13 Virgil, Aeneid 6, 608–17

Epic poetry: late 1st c. BC.

> Imprisoned here and awaiting punishment are those who in life hated their own brothers, hit their fathers, cheated their dependants and found wealth and kept it close without sharing it with their family. These latter are the most numerous of all. Also those killed for adultery, men who took up arms against their own people and those who abused their master's trust. Do not ask to know what their punishments are, what form of torment and what misfortune awaits each of them. Some have to roll huge rocks and some spin spread-eagled on the spokes of wheels.

This theme of punishment in death for the sins of life was a common one, with the punishments often being designed to fit the crime or the extent of the ill-doing. Plutarch, in discussing divine vengeance, does not paint the traditional view of Hades (see below for alternative beliefs), but the typical features of judgement and suffering are paramount. Plutarch suggests that there were harsher punishments for those who on earth had pretended to be good and that when someone's wickedness had brought suffering for his descendants, the souls of these descendants berated him.

6.14 Plutarch, Divine Vengeance 30

Dialogue on punishments after death: early 2nd c. AD.
= *Moralia* 566F.

Plutarch tells the story of Aridaeus from Soli who, after a near death experience and a vision of the afterlife, became a reformed character. Aridaeus claimed that his soul had gone up among the stars where he saw other souls moving about aimlessly and crying in terror. Other higher souls were joyful and among these Aridaeus recognized a kinsman, who renamed him Thespesius and then served as his guide. Here souls are punished between lives.

> They now turned to look at those who were suffering punishment. At first these presented only an unpleasant and piteous sight; but then Thespesius kept meeting friends, relatives, and comrades who were being punished, something he would never have expected; and these lamented to him and cried out as they endured awful torments and humiliating and painful penalties. Finally Thespesius caught sight of his own father emerging from a pit, covered with burns and scars, stretching out his arms to him and not allowed by those in charge of the punishments to keep silent. He was forced to confess his terrible wickedness to certain guests whom he had poisoned for their gold. This crime had not been detected in the lower world, but here it had been brought to light, and having suffered part of his punishment he was now being taken away to suffer more.

The underworld, and other variations on the afterlife, was not all hell and damnation. Rewards were also believed to come the way of the deserving. The Elysian Fields were the happy part of the underworld (see **6.12**), although the term is also used to refer more generally to a place for the blessed without specific reference to the underworld. Elysium was first mentioned by Homer as a home for those blessed by connections with the gods (*Odyssey* 4, 561–9). In Virgil's epic, Elysium had a moral dimension; it was here that morally pure souls were to be found (Molyviati-Toptsis 1994: 37). Virgil suggested that the 'home of the blest' was a special place, but not beyond the reach of some ordinary souls (**6.15**). The bereaved may have taken comfort from the thought that a type of 'heaven' was within the grasp of ordinary men and women, and that good and moral behaviour would ultimately be rewarded. The potential wonders of the Isles of the Blest were, however, also ripe for parody (**6.16**).

6.15 Virgil, Aeneid 6.638–692

Epic poetry: late 1st c. BC.

They entered the land of joy, the lovely green glades of the fortunate and the home of the blest. Here an open sky provides the plains with bright light and this place has its own sun and stars ... [Here spirits exercise and sing; and here are found the legendary heroes] ... Here were armies of men who had suffered wounds while fighting for their country, priests who had led pure lives, and true poets whose words were worthy of Apollo; then those who had improved human life by the skills they had discovered and those who are remembered for their goodness to men.

6.16 Lucian, True Story 2.14–15

Satirical essay: 2nd c. AD.

Lucian turns the 'Isles of the Blest' into a fantasy land where the inhabitants wore clothes spun from spider webs, bathed in hot dew and no one grew old.

The place for banqueting is outside the city in the Elysian Fields, a very beautiful meadow surrounded by thick-growing trees of every kind, which shade the guests. The couches that the guests lie on are made of flowers, and they are waited on and served by the winds. Except that no one needs to fill their wine cups, for all around are great trees of the clearest glass, whose fruit is cups of all shapes and sizes. When anyone arrives he picks one or two of the cups and puts them at his place, where they at once fill with wine ready to drink. Instead of garlands, the nightingales and other song birds pick flowers with their beaks from the fields around, and flying over drop them like snow, while singing all the time. Perfume is not forgotten; thick clouds draw up scent from the springs and river, and hanging over the tables are gently squeezed by the winds until they spray it down as delicate dew. During the meal there is poetry and song ... [all the famous poets, Homer included, are present] ... When they stop singing a second chorus appears of swans, swallows and nightingales, and as they sing the whole wood provides the accompaniment, with the winds conducting. But the most important thing that the guests have for ensuring a good time are two springs close to the table, one called the Fountain of Laughter, the other the Fountain of Enjoyment. They all drink from each of these when the party begins, and afterwards enjoy themselves, laughing all the time.

Lucian may be playing with people's hopes and beliefs and the literary creations of other authors, but not all who believed in 'heaven' may have equated it to a fantasy land of feasting and pleasure. Heaven could be defined as a place where the souls of the righteous and illustrious passed at death, a celestial space far removed from the tradition of Hades. This 'heaven' may be vaguely conceived, but the sense of immortality and unending glory could be a source of inspiration to the great and the patriotic.

6.17 Cicero, On the Republic (Scipio's Dream) 6.13

Political and philosophical dialogue: 51 BC.
Cicero, in discussing the qualities of a statesman, has Scipio Aemilianus (185–29 BC) narrate how, when on campaign in Africa, he had a dream vision of his adoptive grandfather, Scipio Africanus (236–183 BC). This vision of dead members of his family and also the heavens inspired him to greatness.
Compare Cicero, *Tusculan Disputations* 1.12.27 and Tacitus, *Agricola* 46.1.

> Be certain of this so that you will be even more eager to defend the Republic: all those who have saved, helped or extended their country have a special place fixed for them in the heavens, where they will enjoy a life of eternal happiness.

Visions of the hereafter tended to polarize earthly behaviour and its afterlife consequences. Pain and pleasure, vice and virtue, lent themselves well to literary flights of fancy. For the mass of ordinary souls who had followed 'the middle way', as Lucian (**6.12**) and Ovid (**6.11**) imply, Hades was neither full of punishment or pleasures; the fate of these souls had little literary or philosophical appeal. The extent to which people subscribed to the ideal that how one lived in life affected how one 'lived' after death is hard to evaluate. Some epitaphs do suggest belief in afterlife justice and even imbue the dead with a sense of physical well being.

6.18 CIL VI 2489

Epitaph: AD 29. Rome (Porta Collina).
= *CLE* 991.
Rubellius and Fufius Geminus were consuls in AD 29.

> To the spirits of the departed Quintus Caetronius Passer, son of Quintus, of the Publian voting tribe, a soldier of the Third Praetorian Cohort, for 18 years. He was discharged under the two Gemini. He made this for himself and Masuria Marcella, daughter of Marcus. I always lived well, as I wished, poor but honest. I cheated

no one, which is a pleasure to my bones. In front 11 feet, into the field 3 feet.

Indeed the continuing physical nature of the dead, at least in the imaginations of the living, could lead to inconsistencies in both belief and literary creations. The shades which inhabited the underworld were usually viewed as recognizable in form, but were without flesh and blood, and so Virgil's Aeneas unsuccessfully tries to embrace the ghostly figure of his father Anchises (**6.19**). There was an anomaly that the shades of the dead were insubstantial and yet some at least were supposed to suffer physical pain and pleasure (**6.20** and **6.21**).

6.19 Virgil, Aeneid 6, 698–702

Epic poetry: late 1st c. BC.

'Let me take your right hand, father. Give it to me and do not avoid my embrace.' As he said these words his cheeks were wet with tears. Three times he tried to put his arms around his father's neck. Three times the phantom slipped through his hands, insubstantial as the wind, as light as a passing dream.

6.20 Lucretius, On Nature 3, 624–33

Philosophical (Epicurean) poetry: 1st c. BC.

Besides, if the soul is immortal and is able to feel when it is separated from the body, we must then assume, I think, that it is endowed with the five senses; how else can we imagine the souls of the dead wandering about Acheron? So the artists and the earlier generations of poets have pictured the souls endowed with senses. But, when it is apart from the body, the soul cannot have eyes or nose or even hands, let alone tongue or ears. Souls by themselves can have neither sensation nor existence.

6.21 Cicero, Tusculan Disputations 1.16.37

Philosophical dialogue: 45 BC.

And such was the extent of the error, now it seems to me dispelled, that although people knew that the bodies of the dead were cremated, they still imagined that events took place in the underworld which cannot take place and are not intelligible without bodies; for they were unable to understand the idea of souls living by themselves and tried to find for them some sort of appearance and shape.

Alternative beliefs

For those who dismissed Hades but still believed in the continuity of the soul, other philosophical and religious ideas could bridge the gap. These beliefs were not always well developed or extensively discussed in literature, and indeed many of these beliefs, perhaps with the exception of the Mystery Cults, may have been underpinned by hope rather than doctrine. Suggestions included the idea that the souls of the dead went to be near the moon or sun (**6.14**), or that a soul could become a star. A comet seen soon after Caesar's death was thought to be his soul (Suetonius, *Caesar* 87; compare Plutarch, *Caesar* 69). The Emperor Hadrian thought that the soul of his lover Antinous was a new star.

6.22 Cassius Dio 69.11.4

History: late 2nd or early 3rd c. AD. Events of AD 130.

Antinous drowned in the Nile while accompanying Hadrian on a tour of the provinces.

> He honoured Antinous, either because of his love for him or because the young man had died voluntarily, believing that a life must be given freely for Hadrian to accomplish his ambitions. Hadrian built a city on the spot where Antinous had suffered his fate and named it after him; and he also set up statues, or more accurately sacred images, of him, practically all over the world. Finally, Hadrian announced that he had seen a star which he believed to be that of Antinous, and willingly listened to the false tales, created by his followers, that the star had come from the spirit of Antinous and had now appeared for the first time. On account of this, Hadrian became the object of some ridicule, especially since at the death of his sister Paulina he had not immediately paid her any honour.

The so-called Mystery Cults seem to have promoted an ultimate union with the divine. The Syrian cults and Mithraism taught that the soul rose to the sky, 'there to enjoy divine bliss in the midst of the stars in the eternal light' (Cumont 1922: 37). However, direct evidence for what adherents of these cults believed and expected is extremely limited (MacMullen 1981: 55). In Apuleius' *Metamorphoses* the hero becomes an initiate in the cult of Isis, but makes it clear that it would be sacrilege to speak of what was revealed to him; he does, however, indicate that he was brought to 'the boundary of death' and met the gods 'face to face' (*Metamorphoses* 11.23). Some individuals cultivated connections with the divine; the emperors could be viewed as present gods, saviours, or incarnations of gods such as Zeus or Apollo. The first emperor Augustus associated himself heavily with the god Apollo and encouraged at least some of his subjects to worship his spirit or *genius*. At death the soul of an emperor was supposed to be borne away by an eagle released from the pyre (see Chapter 3) or was thought to rise heavenwards in the sun's chariot. Apotheosis could also be extended to members of the Imperial family (**5.17**). The emperors were aligned with the powers that controlled the universe and particularly with the Sun god. The divine aura made the emperors immortal, while alive the allusion was that they could create heaven on earth.

6.23 Martial, Epigrams 9.1, 8–10

Poetry: late 1st c. AD.
  Vespasian, Titus and Domitian were the Flavian emperors.

> The exalted glory of the Flavian race will endure together with sun and stars, and with the light of Rome. Whatever an unconquered hand has founded belongs to heaven.

There was undoubtedly much of the political rather than the spiritual in the divine imagery of Rome's rulers, but it may have had some influence upon popular beliefs about the nature of life after death. Portraiture could show the deceased in the guise of a god (Wrede 1981) and sculpted reliefs on sarcophagi could suggest parallels between the life and the afterlife of humans and the divine. Detailed scenes depicting the myths of Adonis and Endymion, for example, could hint at a hoped-for immortality, or in the case of Endymion eternal rest or sleep (Koortbojian 1996). Such mythological allegories and the apotheosis of the emperor underline the fluidity in Roman beliefs about the nature of death and the god–human relationship (Tertullian, *On nations* 1.10.26–9). Another possibility was reincarnation (or metempsychosis), which could be viewed as a reward or punishment. This was of interest to philosophers, especially the Orphic-Pythagorean idea that souls could be reincarnated until they became pure (**6.24**). It is hard to judge how seriously others in non-philosophical circles took it, but the prospect of reincarnation did create some striking literary images (**6.25**).

6.24 Seneca the Younger, Letters 108.21

Philosophical letter: mid 1st c. AD.
  Seneca quotes the words of one of his teachers (a follower of Pythagoras), which inspired him to become a vegetarian for fear of inadvertently eating the flesh of another. Seneca maintained his special diet for a year before bending to pressure from his father to abandon this particular philosophical affectation.
  Compare Ovid, *Metamorphoses* 15, 75–160.

Therefore while holding your own view, keep the whole issue fresh in your mind. For if these ideas are true, it is a sign of purity to abstain from eating the flesh of animals; and even if they are not, it will still be an economy. What harm will believing do to you? All I am depriving you of is the food of lions and vultures.

6.25 Virgil, Aeneid 6, 743–51

Epic poetry: late 1st c. BC.

Book 6 tells of the visit of Aeneas to the underworld. Virgil uses the idea of reincarnation as a literary device to allow Anchises to foretell the future by recounting the future lives of some of the souls of the underworld.

Compare Plutarch, *Divine Vengeance* 32.

Each of us finds his own fate in the afterlife. From here some are sent to wander over the broad plains of Elysium and to enjoy these fields of happiness until the circle of time is completed, and the long days have removed ingrained corruption, and nothing is left but pure ethereal sense and the spirits' essential fire. All these souls whom you see, when they have completed a thousand year cycle, are sent for by God to come in great crowds to the river Lethe, so that with their memory washed away, they may go back to the earth, and become willing to return to bodies.

Reincarnation does not feature in epitaphs, but some people may have derived comfort from the cycle of nature, that their remains would nourish the earth, or failing this that death did reunite loved ones, if only as bones, ashes and earth.

6.26 CIL XII 4015

Epitaph (in Latin and Greek): 2nd c. AD. Nemausus (Nîmes, France). A funerary altar; the epitaph is surrounded by an ornate floral border.
= *EG* 548. For funerary gardens see **4.33–4.35**.

To the spirits of the departed Caius Vibius Licinius, aged 16 years and 6 months. Caius Vibius Agathopus and Licinia Nomas made this for their devoted son ... May all about you, Vibius, become violets, marjoram, and water-narcissus, and roses.

6.27 CIL XII 5193

Epitaph: 1st or 2nd c. AD. Narbo (Narbonne, France). A funerary altar, with portraits of husband and wife.

Valerius Philolocus, freedman of Lucius, to Quieta Silvana his wife.
I wait for my husband.

Belief and disbelief

It is very difficult to judge how many people believed in Hades, Elysium, or in rewards and punishments after death. Some writers imply that they are describing what everyone thinks (**6.12**), but we may doubt the veracity of such claims. Epitaphs do provide some insights into the views of 'ordinary people', but even these rarely provide any direct indication of beliefs. Thousands of epitaphs begin with the invocation *Dis Manibus* which roughly translated means 'to the spirits (or shades) of the departed'. The expression became so common that it was frequently abbreviated to the letters DM, suggesting that the term came to be employed through convention rather than deep-seated belief. The same may also be true of more direct or detailed references to life after death found in some epitaphs. It can be difficult to judge the tone and circumstances in which individual epitaphs were written; should we take literally common phrases such as 'you live in eternity' (*CLE* 2270, 1) or 'may the gods preserve you' (*CIL* III 10501)? Did people believe what they wrote (or commissioned) or were they conforming to traditional expectations and clichéd imagery?

The circumstances of an individual's life may have affected their belief (or the extent of belief) in the afterlife; regional origins, wealth, education, social status and so forth would have influenced their views. Chronology may also have played a role. Cumont argued that the belief in an afterlife became increasingly common in the 2nd c. AD, 'as present life came to seem a burden harder and harder to bear' (1922: 39). Such an assertion is difficult to quantify with any accuracy, but the growth in mystery cults may support an increased search for spirituality. After the mid 1st c. BC (if not before) many of the intellectual élite already held that the traditional view of the underworld was at best flawed; even if the soul continued to exist it did not go down to Hades.

6.28 *Cicero,* Tusculan Disputations *1.5.10*

Philosophical dialogue: 45 BC.

Cicero mocks the fact that the 'Roman' underworld was a Greek invention by mentioning the famous Athenian orator Demosthenes (384–22 BC). For Cerberus, Cocytus, Acheron, Tantalus, Sisyphus, Minos and Rhadamanthus see **6.12**.

For Cicero on 'heaven' see **6.21**; and see also Cicero, *For Cluentius* 171 and *Catiline* 3.8. Contrast these with Cicero, *Philippics* 14.12.32, where for impact Antony's soldiers are condemned to underworld punishments.

MARCUS: Tell me, you are not frightened, are you, by the stories of three-headed Cerberus in the lower world, the roar of Cocytus, the passage of Acheron, and 'the water touching Tantalus, exhausted with thirst'? Again, are you frightened at the tale that Sisyphus 'who sweats with the toil of rolling the stone that never moves'? Or perhaps you are scared of the merciless judges Minos and Rhadamanthus? At whose bar Lucius Crassus will not defend you, nor Marcus Antonius, nor, since the case will be before Greek judges, will you be able to employ Demosthenes: you will have to plead your cause in person before a huge audience. Maybe you shrink from these prospects and therefore consider death an eternal evil.
ATTICUS: Do you think I am crazy enough to believe such tales?

6.29 Seneca, Consolation to Marcia 19.4–5

Philosophical consolation: AD 39/40.

Know that there are no ills to be suffered after death, that the reports that make the underworld terrible to us are only tales, that no darkness awaits the dead, no prison, no blazing streams of fire, no river of oblivion, that no judgement seats are there, nor culprits, nor in that lax freedom are there any tyrants. All these things are the fancies of the poets, who have worried us with false terrors. Death is a release from all our suffering, a boundary beyond which our ills cannot cross; it restores us to that peaceful condition in which we were before birth.

6.30 Epictetus, Discourses 3.13.14–15

Philosophy (Stoic): early 2nd c. AD.
For Acheron, Cocytus and Pyriphlegethon see **6.12**.
Compare also Epictetus, *Discourses* 4.7.15–16.

You do not go back to something you must fear, but back to that from which you came, to what is friendly and familiar to you, to the physical elements. What there was of fire in you shall return to fire, what there was of earth to earth, what there was of air to air, what there was of water to water. There is no Hades, Acheron, Cocytus or Pyriphlegethon.

6.31 Juvenal, Satire 2, 149–52

Satirical poetry: early 2nd c. AD.

These days not even children, except those small enough to get a free bath, believe in such things as spirits, or underground kingdoms and rivers, or the waters of Styx black with frogs, or thousands of dead men crossing in a single boat.

Whether 'ordinary people' shared the élite view is difficult to evaluate. As noted above some epitaphs can seem to endorse the traditional views of Hades and the continuity of the soul. However, the vast majority of the epitaphs provide no clues as to the beliefs of those who commissioned them and were commemorated by them. Beyond the use of the opening formula 'DM' epitaphs in general did not contain a spiritual dimension. It is possible that mourners expressed their beliefs more openly through graveside rituals rather than through lapidary texts (see below). Tombstones and tombs, as explored in Chapter 2, were more about remembering the dead in the context of their life on earth rather than any future life in the hereafter. Indeed, the idea of being remembered by the living may have been perceived as a compensation for the lack of an afterlife. The body and soul might perish, there might be no Hades or Elysium, but you could be remembered forever through an inscription or tomb or foundation or through a good reputation. A few epitaphs do dismiss the underworld and all its traditional trappings categorically, but in doing so suggest that perhaps others did believe in it.

6.32 CIL I 6298

Epitaph: 2nd c. AD. Rome. Latin epitaph, with a poem in Greek.
  = EG 646; Lattimore 1962: 75.

To the spirits of the departed, Cerellia Fortunata, a very dear wife, with whom I lived 11 years without quarrel. Marcus Antonius Encolpus made this for himself and Antonius Athenaeus, his very dear freed slave, and for his freedmen and freedwomen and their descendants, except Marcus Antonius Athenionus.

Traveller, do not pass by my epitaph, but stop and listen, and then, when you have learned the truth, carry on. There is no boat in Hades, no ferryman Charon, no Aeacus holder of the keys, nor any dog called Cerberus. All of us who have died and gone below are bones and ashes: there is nothing else. What I have told you is true. Now leave, traveller, so that you will not think that, although dead, I talk too much.

Many may have been sceptical about the underworld and even the continuity of the soul, but perhaps retained an open mind, or at least a vague hope, that there might be something after death. Seneca the Younger, as many others, was dismissive of the traditional horrors of the underworld, but acknowledged that to deny its existence raised other questions and fears, 'For the fear of going to the underworld is equalled by the fear of going nowhere' (Seneca, *Letters* 82.16). Seneca did believe in the immortality of the soul (*Letters* 65, 57, 92), but also equated death to the state of non-existence before birth, 'whatever condition existed before our birth is death' (*Letters* 54.5). Yet even Seneca seems to imply a hope for some sort of continuity (although note the 'if only') when concluding a letter about the recent death of a friend. These ifs and buts also find parallels in epitaphs.

6.33 Seneca, Letters 63.16

Philosophical letter: mid 1st c. AD.
See also **5.8** and **5.54**.

> Let us therefore reflect, my dear Lucilius, that we shall soon come to the place which this friend, for whom we sorrow, has reached. And perhaps, if only the story told by wise men is true and there is a place to welcome us, then he whom we suppose we have lost has only been sent on ahead.

6.34 CIL VIII 27279

Epitaph: 2nd or 3rd c. AD. Thugga (Dougga, Tunisia).
= *CLE* 2146.

> To the spirits of the departed. If the soul [*animus*] lives without the body, our father lives, but without us.

6.35 CIL VIII 11594

Epitaph: 2nd or 3rd c. AD. Ammaedara (Haidra, Tunisia).
= *CLE* 1328.

> To the spirits of the departed Caius Iulius Felix who lived 82 years and 7 months ... you ought to have lived to be 100 years, if it was allowed. If there are spirits [*manes*] may the earth lie light upon you.

There were some who refused to believe or hope or even keep an open mind. For an Epicurean such as Lucretius, comfort and courage could be taken from the continuity of the atoms of the Universe (**6.36**), while others were clear that belief in the survival of the soul and an afterlife were just part of human vanity, an aspect of man's arrogant sense of self-importance and worth (**6.37**). A few epitaphs also echo the belief that death was an absolute end, and life little more than a short period between two nonentities (**6.38–6.40**).

229

6.36 *Lucretius*, On Nature 2, 573–80

Philosophical (Epicurean) poetry: 1st c. BC.
For Lucretius' bleak view on the survival of the soul see **6.2**.

> Thus this long and equal struggle of the elements, a war that began in the distant past, goes on and on. Now here, now there, the forces that give life are victorious and simultaneously are defeated. The first cries of babies when they see the light are mixed with the funeral; every night that follows day and every sunrise that follows dark has heard the feeble crying of infants', blended with the lamentations that follow death and its black rites.

6.37 *Pliny the Elder*, Natural History 7.55.188–9

Natural history: 1st c. AD.

> All men are in the same condition from their final day as they were before their first day. Neither body nor mind has any sensation after death, any more than it did before birth. It is vanity that extends itself into the future and creates for itself a life lasting beyond death, sometimes giving the soul immortality, sometimes transfiguration, sometimes giving senses to those below, and worshipping ghosts and making a god of one who has already ceased to be even a man. It is as if man's method of breathing were different from that of other animals and no one predicts a similar immortality for other animals that live as long. But in itself what is the substance of the soul? What is its material? Where is its thought? How does it see, hear and touch? What use does it get from these senses, or what good can it have without them? Next, where is the home and how great is the crowd of all the souls and shades of the ages? These are childish delusions and the inventions of mortality greedy for unceasing life.

6.38 CIL *XIII 530*

Epitaph: 2nd c. AD. Lactora (Lectoure, France). A funerary altar.
Note that despite the expressed sentiment this epitaph and **6.39** still begin with the letters DM!
See also *CIL* V 1813, 2893.

> To the spirits of the departed. I was not, I was, I am not, I don't care. Donnia Italia aged 20, rests here. Caius Munatius and Donnia Calliste for a devoted freed slave.

6.39 CIL VIII 3463

Epitaph: 2nd c. AD. Lambaesis (Tazoult, Algeria).

To the spirits of the departed, Aurelia Vercella, a very sweet wife
who lived more or less 17 years. I was not, I was, I am not, I don't
mind. Anthemus her husband made this.

6.40 CIL VI 26003

Epitaph: 1st or 2nd c. AD. Rome.
= CLE 1495.

Lucius Scaterius Celer. We are and we were nothing. See, reader,
how quickly we return from nothing to nothing. Lucius Scaterius
Amethystus made this according to the will.

Ceremonies for the dead

Whatever the level of belief or disbelief entertained by the individual, the
dead were not forgotten. The domestic shrine (lararium) of the household
gods (lares) could act as a focal point for the family to honour their ancestors, as could the masks (imagines) of former family members which were
displayed in élite households and at funerals (see Chapter 3). Such shrines
and masks promoted the shared past of the family and the connections
between the dead and the living. The living could also visit the tombs of the
dead and participate in certain annual rituals. Some of those who performed
these rituals may have firmly believed that their loved ones felt their presence, but others may have performed the rituals more from habit than belief,
or from a sense of duty to remember the deceased, even if body and soul were
both long gone. For the modern observer it is difficult to establish whether
the actions of individuals were motivated by belief, superstition, duty, tradition or the desire to honour and respect the dead, or indeed a mixture of
these motives.

6.41 Catullus 101

Poetry: 1st c. BC.
The epigram suggests the importance of ritual communication between
the living and the dead performed from affection and tradition rather than
belief. The poem plays with epigraphic conventions, especially in the final
words 'ave atque vale', found in many epitaphs; the poem becomes a monument to Catullus' dead brother; see Feldherr 2000.

Elsewhere Catullus is more categorical about the finality of death; 'suns can set and rise again, but for us, when our short light has set, there remains the sleep of one everlasting night' (5, 4–6).

> Carried through many lands and many seas, I come, brother, to these sad rites, to give to you the final gift of death and to speak in vain to your silent ashes. Fortune has taken you away from me. My brother, you are cruelly torn away! Now, however, take these offerings, which by ancestral custom are handed down; they are a sad gift for these rites. Accept them, wet with many tears of a brother, and forever, brother, hail and farewell.

6.42 Ausonius, Epitaphs 31

Poetry: 4th c. AD. An epitaph to a 'happy man',

Note, in composing this series of poems Ausonius is evoking the past; in his day most bodies would have been inhumed rather than cremated.

> Sprinkle my ashes with good wine and perfumed oil. Stranger, bring balsam too and red roses. Perpetual spring pervades my tearless urn. I have changed my state, not died. The joys of my old life have not gone, whether you think I remember everything or nothing.

Cicero emphasized the veneration with which graves should be treated and suggested that this was because the ancestors believed that 'the dead should be included among the gods' (Cicero, de Legibus 2.22.55). Whether this was widely believed or not, it is clear that the dead were the focus for respect and religious solemnity. Regular festivals and events suggest the public regulation of communication between the living and the dead and the perceived importance of showing piety to the ancestors. In the centre of the city of Rome was some sort of chamber or pit, the mundus, with a key stone known as the lapis Manalis. The tradition was that the latter was raised three times a year so that the dead could briefly access the world of the living. Other Roman towns may also have had a mundus, although it remains difficult to evaluate whether the tradition of opening the mundus was widely observed and if people believed that, at these regulated times, the souls of the dead could rise through 'these mouths of hell' (Cumont 1922: 71). In the early tradition the mundus was also associated with fertility and the harvest, suggesting connections between the earth, the dead and rebirth, especially at the foundation of a city (Ovid, Fasti 4.820–4; Plutarch, Romulus 11).

6.43 Festus 156 (Paulus 148)

On words: late 2nd c. AD.

> The *mundus* is thought to have been opened three times a year on
> the 24th of August, the 5th of October and the 8th of November.
> For the lower region, consecrated to the spirits of the dead, was
> closed all the time except on these days. Then the religious judged
> that the spirits hidden and concealed with the gods could be exposed
> and brought out into the light, and at these times no state business
> was to be carried out. There was to be no fighting with an enemy, no
> legal work, no assemblies; nothing whatsoever, unless of the utmost
> necessity, was to be done.

The annual official commemoration of the dead was the *Parentalia,* held
between the 13th and 21st of February. The observance of the *Parentalia* is
mentioned in literature and epitaphs (**2.43**), suggesting that it remained an
important time to remember and honour the dead well into the imperial
period. It was in theory an inauspicious time, since the spirits of the dead
could be feared; but above all the festival underlined the important connections between the living and the dead and the continuity of the family.

6.44 Ovid, Fasti 2, 533–70

Poetry: early 1st c. AD.

Hymen was a god of marriage. A bride wore her hair in six braids, the
partings for which were made with a spear. After the marriage ceremony
husband and wife processed to their new home by torchlight.

> Honour is paid to the tombs. Placate the souls of your fathers and
> bring small gifts to the extinguished pyres. The spirits [*manes*] ask
> for little: they value piety more than an expensive gift; the Styx
> below does not have greedy gods. A tile wreathed with votive
> garlands, a handful of corn, a few grains of salt, bread soaked in
> wine, and some loose violets, are offerings enough. Put these on a
> potsherd and leave them in the middle of the road. I do not forbid
> larger offerings, but these will suffice to appease the shades; and add
> prayers and suitable words at the hearth. This custom was intro-
> duced into the land, righteous Latinus, by Aeneas, the author of
> piety. He brought solemn offerings to his father's spirit [*genius*] and
> from him the people learned the pious rites. Once, while fighting
> long wars with arms, the people neglected the *Parentalia*. It did not
> go unpunished. For it is said that for this lack of piety, Rome grew
> hot from the funeral pyres outside the city. They say, although I can
> hardly believe it, that the ancestors came out from the tombs and

lamented in the silent night, and that hideous ghosts howled through the city streets and the wide fields, a shadowy crowd. After that, the honours which had been omitted were again paid to the tombs, and a limit was set to prodigies and funerals. But while these rites are being performed women should remain widows and the marriage torch wait for pure days. Do not let girls, who seem ready for marriage in their mother's eyes, have the spear comb their virgin hair. Hymen hide your torches and take them away from these solemn fires. For other torches are lighting up the sad graves. Screen the gods as well by closing the temple doors. Do not let incense burn on altars or fire upon the hearth. At this time the slender souls and buried dead wander about, and the ghost feeds upon the offered food. However, this only lasts until there remain as many days in the month as there are feet in my verses [i.e. eleven]. That day is called the *Feralia*, because the people carry gifts to the dead; it is the final day for appeasing the spirits.

The *Lemuria*, held on 9th, 11th and 13th of May, was when ghosts (*lemures*) were thought to wander around the house. The associated rites were private and domestic in character and happened at night.

6.45 Ovid, Fasti 5, 429–44

Poetry: early 1st c. AD.

The souls of the dead were thought to be contained in beans (Pliny, *Natural History* 18.118). In this ritual perhaps the beans were viewed as substitutes for the living who might otherwise be harmed by the ghosts. Temesa in southern Italy was famous for its copper mines.

At midnight, when there is a deep silence, and dogs and all birds are quiet, the man, who keeps the old rites in mind and fears the gods, gets up (having nothing to hold his feet) and makes a sign with his thumb in the middle of his closed fingers, in case in the silence a slender shade should meet him. When he has washed his hands clean in spring water, he turns and is given black beans which he throws away with his face averted. While he throws the beans he says 'I send these and with them I redeem myself and my family'. He says this nine times without looking back. The shade is thought to collect the beans and follow behind unseen. He then touches water and clashes Temesan bronze, asking the shade to leave his house. When he has said nine times 'Ghosts of my fathers, leave', he looks back and believes that he has performed the sacred rites appropriately.

Other occasions to honour the dead and visit the tomb included significant familial dates such as the birthday of the deceased or the anniversary of the death (see, **2.34, 2.37, 2.41, 2.43** and **4.35**). The *Rosalia* (feast of the roses) held in May and June was also a time to scatter roses at the tomb and wreathe statues and images of the dead. All these occasions and festivals indicate that traditionally a dialogue or relationship was expected between the living and the dead, and such traditions could persist even if the underlying beliefs were questioned. The remains of Roman cemeteries indicate an expected interaction between the living and the dead (see Chapter 4). Tomb design, structure and décor suggest that ideally the living would visit the dead and bring offerings of wine, food and flowers. Tombs were furnished with cooking and dining areas while libation pipes 'fed' remains (**Figure 19**) and images of flowers, painted and sculpted, evoked floral tributes (Jashemski 1979: 151). The dead could be imagined as having a good time, or at least as benefiting from the actions of the living.

6.46 CIL XIII 8283 and Figure 20: Tombstone of Marcus Valerius Celerinus

Tombstone: 1st c. AD. Colonia Agrippinensis (Cologne, Germany).
    = Galsterer and Galsterer 1975: n. 219.
    The stele is decorated with a so-called 'totenmahl' relief. This depicts the commemorated man reclining on a couch as if at a banquet. A three-legged table is in front of the couch and this supports food and vessels. To

Figure 20
The tombstone of
Marcus Valerius
Celerinus, Cologne.

the right of this is a large jug. At the foot of the couch a female figure (the wife of the commemorated man) sits in a high-backed chair. A shallow basket holding fruit rests in her lap and a further tall basket is to the side of the chair. At the head of the couch stands a small figure; the diminutive stature used to depict this figure may suggest a slave waiting on his master and mistress. It remains uncertain if 'totenmahl' reliefs such as this were intended to represent the dead enjoying a meal in this or the next life, but they are suggestive of the interaction between the living and the dead, and the idealized role that the dead might play in the rituals and offerings made at the grave. The design may also be aspirational, celebrating the real or desired wealth and status of those commemorated. See Carroll 2005; Dunbabin 2003: 103–40; Noelke 1998.

> Marcus Valerius Celerinus of the Papirian voting tribe, from Astigi [Écija, Spain], citizen of Colonia Agrippinensis [Cologne], a veteran of *legio X Gemina Pia Fidelis*. He made this while living for himself and for his wife, Marcia Procula.

For many people, making offerings to the dead may have been tied more to status display and memory promotion than to a real belief in 'feeding' the souls of the dead (see Chapter 2), the offerings fulfilling a symbolic role. After all, how could the dead partake of them? Once more the sceptics could find entertainment value in poking fun at what could be portrayed as pointless behaviour that revealed inconsistent beliefs about what happened to the dead.

6.47 Lucian, Charon 22

Satirical dialogue: 2nd c. AD. An imagined exchange between Charon (the underworld ferryman) and Hermes, set in the 6th c. BC.

> They eat and drink, when their skulls are nothing but dry bone? But I'm wasting my time telling you that since you bring them down below every day: you know whether they can come back up again once they've gone underground! I should be in a fine mess, Hermes, and should have lots of extra work if we not only had to bring them down but to bring them back up again for a drink. What foolish idiots! They do not know how great a gulf divides the world of the dead from the world of the living.

Ghost stories

The cemetery could be perceived as an eerie place. As noted in Chapter 4, the cemetery was often an active, if marginal area. The dead, and those of the living who frequented the zone at unsociable hours, could be viewed with suspicion and superstition. Tombs were the haunts of unsavoury characters such as tramps, thieves, prostitutes and witches (**4.57**, **4.58** and **6.60**), but were also characterized by the ghostly presence of the dead. Epitaphs and tombs sought the attention of the living, but the living may have been wary of them. To read an epitaph, to say the dead person's name, perpetuated memory, but for some the same reading might also evoke the spirit of the dead, and spirits could be malevolent (Davis 1958). The dead could be imagined as 'living' a shadowy existence in or near the tomb or grave, and this is supported by the rituals which occurred there (see above). The tomb could also be viewed as a house for the dead, where they received food and drink and some of the comforts of home; 'this is an eternal home, here I am, here I will always be' (*CIL* IX 4796). Epitaphs could contain the formula STTL (*sit tibi terra levis*), 'may the earth lie lightly upon you', suggesting that the dead retained sensations and were resting at their tomb (note this sentiment is echoed by the poet Martial, see **5.19**). In short, for those who believed in the afterlife, whether in Hades or something else, the soul might be perceived as lingering at the tomb or the deceased might even be believed to be 'sleeping' there.

6.48 CIL XII 5102

Epitaph: 1st c. AD. Narbo (Narbonne, France).
  Compare with **2.13–2.15**.

> Lucius Runnius Pollio, son of Cnaeus, of the Papinian voting tribe. I continue drinking in this tomb, more eagerly because I will sleep and remain here for ever.

6.49 CIL VIII 212, 38–42 and 55–61

Epitaph: mid 2nd c. AD. Cillium (Kasserine, Tunisia).
  = Lassère et al 1993; Davies 1999: 221–4.
  The long epitaph, in the form of a poem, was inscribed on a large tower tomb. It was set up by Titus Flavius Secundus to his father. Tomb and epitaph celebrate the success of the family and suggest various cultural fusions (Hitchner 1995). The epitaph reveals some uncertainties about life after death, but promotes the immortality of the deceased through the tomb (see Chapter 2).

> I do not doubt that in the silent darkness of Acheron, if feeling remains after death, your father must often feel joy, Secundus, and look down on the crowd of the other shades, for he knows that here his tomb continues to exist, perpetually new in all its grandeur.
>   Now is the time to hold that your father is immortal, that he has abandoned the underworld and fled its sinister palace, since he prefers, for all time, to follow the fate of this monument and live,

thanks to these names written here eternally, to inhabit these familiar woods, to contemplate from here with tenderness the hills of his fatherland and remain, as it were, the master of the household that he passed on to his children.

Some may have believed that the dead were present at the grave, while for others terms such as 'the eternal home' and 'sleep' were euphemisms for the all-encompassing finality of death and the tomb. Whether 'sleeping' at the grave or not, the dead were separated from the living by a series of traditional rituals and ceremonies that set up boundaries between the living and the dead and sought to regulate contact between them. The idea that the dead might seek to cross these boundaries was a source of popular stories and literary inspiration. Ghost stories were frequently told and were part of Roman folklore and tradition. In literature ghosts made for dramatic content; they were vehicles of high drama on the stage, provided stories within stories in novels and dialogues, and were emblematic of a troubled mind or guilty conscience in genres such as biography and history. Even those who were seriously minded could give credence to the stories; the Younger Pliny, for example, stated that on balance he did believe in spirits (*Letters* 7.27). Others were more sceptical and thus Plutarch (**6.55**), through Cassius, puts forward the voice of reason, while some mocked the superstitions of others (**6.51**), but as with so much about the afterlife, many people may have been prepared to keep an open mind. The literary ghost stories may not reveal how many people believed in them, but they do suggest that ghosts were a talking point, and that in literature a good ghost story played on people's superstitions to create tension and entertainment.

It is notable that most ghost stories were not set in or near tombs or cemeteries. Ghosts were believed mainly to seek out the living in the spaces of the living, invading their homes and sleep. It was among the living that ghosts could seek revenge or issue dire warnings with maximum impact. Besides, it was often people who had not received a proper tomb and burial who did the haunting (Felton 1999: 8–12). A common theme was ghosts appearing to the living to tell of who had killed them and where their body was to be found.

6.50 Cicero, On Divination 1.27.56–7

Dialogue on religious philosophy: mid 1st c. BC. Here Cicero's brother Quintus tells two stories about dream apparitions.
Compare Apuleius, *Metamorphoses* 9.30–1.

Simonides once saw a dead body of an unknown man lying exposed and buried it. Later, when he was considering going on board a ship, he was disturbed by a vision of the person he had buried, and warned not to do so, because if he did he would die in a shipwreck. Therefore Simonides turned back and all the others were lost.

The second dream is very well known. Two friends from Arcadia who were travelling together came to Megara. One traveller put up at an inn, and the second went to the home of a friend. After they had eaten supper they went to bed. In the middle of the night the second traveller dreamed that his companion was begging him to come to his aid, since the innkeeper was planning to murder him. At first, very frightened by the dream, he woke and got up. But then, having regained his composure, decided that there was nothing to worry about and went back to sleep. While he slept the same person appeared to him again and begged him not to leave his death unavenged, since he had not rescued him while still alive. He told him that having killed him, the innkeeper had thrown the body into a cart and covered it with dung. He asked him to be at the city gate in the morning before the cart left town. Disturbed by the second dream he met the cart driver at the gate in the morning, and asked him what he had in the cart. The driver fled in terror. The crime was reported to the authorities and the innkeeper punished.

Other ghosts complained that funerary rituals had not been performed properly or that the commemorative rites were being neglected. Such neglect of the rituals could prevent the entry of the soul of the deceased to the afterlife.

6.51 *Lucian,* The Lover of Lies 27

Satirical dialogue: 2nd c. AD. The subject is why men tell lies and make up outrageous stories. Among such storytellers are a group of philosophers who believe in the supernatural and recount their experiences. Lucian is satirizing irrational beliefs.

'Everyone knows how I loved my dear wife, the mother of these children. I showed my devotion in everything I did for her, not only when she was alive, but also after death; for I ordered all her jewellery together with the clothes she had liked when she was alive to be burnt upon the pyre. On the seventh day after she died, I was lying here on this very couch consoling myself by quietly reading Plato's book on the nature of the soul, when Demainete herself came in and sat down nearby, where Eucratides is sitting now', he said, pointing at the younger of his sons. The boy immediately shuddered childishly, having already turned pale during the story. Eucrates continued, 'I embraced her, and weeping, wailed aloud. But she told me to stop crying, and complained that, although I had freely given everything else to her, I had neglected to burn one of her gilt sandals. It had fallen under a wooden chest, and because of this we had been unable to find it, and had burned only the one.

We were still talking when a hateful little Maltese dog that was lying under the couch started barking and she vanished. But the sandal was found under the chest, and later burned.'

6.52 Propertius, 4.7, 1–34

Elegiac poetry: late 1st c. BC. The recently deceased Cynthia returns to Propertius in a dream to complain about her funeral; she goes on to demand good treatment for her slaves, better care of her tomb and a suitable epitaph.

Compare Propertius 4.11,1 where the spirit of Cornelia knows that her husband weeps at her tomb. See also Virgil, *Culex* 210–384.

> Shades do exist: death is not the end of all, and a pale ghost escapes the extinguished pyre. For I dreamt that Cynthia was leaning over my bed, she who had lately been buried near the busy road, as fresh from love's burial I slept a broken sleep and mourned that the kingdom of my bed was empty and cold. Her hair, her eyes were the same as when she was carried to the grave: her dress was charred at the side, and fire had eaten at the familiar beryl [ring] on her finger, and the water of Lethe had withered her lips. Voice and spirit still lived but her fragile fingers cracked with a snap of her thumb. 'Treacherous one, from whom no woman can expect better, can sleep have power over you so soon? ... [Cynthia complains that their night-time escapades have all too quickly been forgotten, that no one performed the *conclamatio* at her deathbed and that Propertius did not attend her final rites.] ... Why, ungrateful man, did you not call the winds to fan my pyre? Why was my funeral pyre not scented with spice? Was it then too much of a burden to cast hyacinths, an inexpensive gift, upon me, and to appease my ashes with wine from a shattered jar?'

Some ghosts were more benign in intent, wishing to warn the living about impending danger. Ghosts could also repay favours and act out of love or filial devotion. Note, for example, the ghost that appeared to Simonides to tell of the impending shipwreck (6.50). These benign ghosts generally appeared as they did in life, and did not have a frightening appearance or demeanour (see for example, Quintilian, *Declamation* 10.5). The most ominous, and the most likely to walk, were the ghosts of those who had suffered a violent or premature death. The cause of their death could bode ill for the nature of their afterlife. The victims of violence might haunt the perpetrator of the crime, striking fear or doubt into the hearts of the living (6.54). In literature these hauntings were emblematic of a troubled conscience (6.54, 6.55, 6.62 and 6.63). Some of these ghosts explicitly sought revenge upon the living or continued some of the unpleasant traits of the person they had been (**6.53**). Even in death the malevolence of certain characters could be imagined or even believed to have continued.

6.53 Suetonius, Gaius 59

Biography: early 2nd c. AD. Gaius (Caligula) was assassinated in AD 41. For Gaius see also **2.63**.

> The body of Gaius was moved secretly to the Lamian Gardens, half-cremated on a hastily built pyre, and then buried beneath a light covering of earth. Later, when his sisters returned from exile, they dug up the body, cremated and entombed it. Before this all the city knew that the caretakers of the Gardens were disturbed by ghosts, and that in the house where he had been killed a horrible apparition was seen every night until the house was destroyed by fire.

6.54 Suetonius, Otho 7.2

Biography: 2nd c. AD. Otho was tormented by the ghost of his predecessor Galba.
For the deaths of Galba and Otho see **1.53**, **4.51** and **1.58**.

> It is said that Otho had a fearful dream that night; he cried out loudly and was found by those who ran to help him lying on the ground beside his bed. After this he did everything he could to placate the ghost of Galba whom he dreamed would cause him to fall; but next day, while he was taking the auspices, a great storm arose knocking him over.

6.55 Plutarch, Brutus 36–7

Biography: early 2nd c. AD. Brutus sees a frightening apparition before Philippi (42 BC), which is suggestive of a troubled mind that the Epicurean Cassius seeks to soothe with logical explanations.
See also Plutarch, *Caesar* 69. Compare Lucan, *Civil War* 3.28, where Julia's ghost appears to Pompey warning him of and blaming him for the impending disaster at Pharsalus.
For the death of Brutus see **1.54**.

> In the middle of his thoughts and meditations, he [Brutus] thought he heard someone enter the tent. He looked towards the entrance and saw a strange and horrible apparition, a monstrous and terrifying figure standing silently by his side. Plucking up the courage to question it, he asked, 'What man or god are you, and what do you want with me?' The phantom answered 'I am your evil spirit,

Brutus: you shall see me at Philippi.' Brutus remained calm and replied, 'I shall see you then.' When the figure had vanished, Brutus summoned his servants, but they assured him that they had heard no voice and seen nothing. Brutus stayed awake for the rest of the night, but as soon as it was light he found Cassius and described what he had seen. Cassius, who was a follower of the doctrines of Epicurus, and who used to take issue with Brutus on such subjects, said to him, 'Our opinion, Brutus, is that by no means everything we see or experience is real. The perceptions that come to us through the senses are deceptive and changeable, besides which our intelligence is quick to transform the experience itself, which may have no real existence, into a whole variety of forms ... [the imagination and dreams can overstimulate and trick the mind] ... In your own case your body has suffered the strain of many hardships, and this condition both excites and distorts the intelligence. As for spirits, I do not believe that they exist, and even if they do, they cannot take on the appearance and speech of people, or exert any influential power over us.'

Raising and laying ghosts

The fears and superstitions surrounding ghosts and spirits are suggested by stories about how to get rid of them. Malevolent spirits of the dead could possess people who could only be cured with the help of a suitable exorcist (6.56), or a scene of violent death might become occupied by a threatening presence that only a brave, wise or superstitious person could remove. Haunted houses, in particular, could provide a locus for the unwelcome presence of the dead and their interactions with the living. Ghosts could frighten people away from houses until the wrong done to the dead, usually non-burial, was put right and equanimity restored (6.57 and 6.58). One modern commentator has argued that haunted houses may have been an economic reality, if an unusual one (Felton 1999: 45). People had a moral, but not a legal, duty to disclose information when selling or renting property. Such tales about haunted houses and possessed individuals were often intended primarily to be entertaining, but simultaneously they do suggest a level of belief in spirits, ghosts and miracle workers.

6.56 *Philostratus,* Apollonius 3.38

Biography: early 3rd c. AD.

Apollonius of Tyana, who lived during the 1st c. AD, was a neo-Pythagorean famous for his beliefs in reincarnation, his healing of the sick, and the performance of miracles. This incident allegedly took place during a visit to India; a mother has approached Apollonius claiming that her son is possessed.

Apollonius eventually sends a threatening and ominous letter to scare away the demon.

See also Philostratus, *Apollonius* 3.38–9 and 4.25.

> The spirit told me that he was the ghost of a man who had long ago fallen in battle. At death he had been passionately attached to his wife, who only three days after his death had insulted their marriage by marrying another man. As a consequence of this he had come to hate the love of women and had transferred himself wholly into this boy. He promised he would endow the boy with many blessings provided I did not denounce him. I was influenced by these promises, but he has stalled me for such a long time now to the point that he has control of my house when he has no honest or good intentions.

6.57 *Plautus*, The Haunted House 496–505

Comic play: late 3rd or early 2nd c. BC.

The slave, Tranio, has claimed that a previous house-owner had murdered a guest and buried him on the site and that this dead man had appeared to Philolaches (his master's son) in his sleep. Tranio uses this story to keep his master out of the house.

> And this is what the dead man said to your son in his sleep: 'I am Diapontius, a stranger from over the seas. I live here since this is my appointed home. For Hades will not allow me to cross Acheron, since I was killed before my time. I trusted and was deceived. My host murdered me in this house, and buried me, without rite or ceremony, secretly, in this very house. He did it for my gold. You must leave, for this house is defiled and cursed.' That is what the ghost said and as for the strange things that have been going on it would take more than a year to describe them all.

6.58 *Pliny,* Letter 7.27. 5–11

Letter: early 2nd c. AD.

Compare Lucian, *Lover of Lies* 30–1. See also Pliny, *Letters* 3.5 and 5.5.

> In Athens there was once a remarkable house; it was large and spacious, but had a reputation for being dangerous. In the dead of night its occupants would hear the clanking of chains, some way off to start with but then getting closer. Then the ghost of an old man would appear, emaciated and dirty, with long hair and a beard. At his hands and feet were shackles, the source of all the noise. The occupants would stay awake and some became ill due to

lack of sleep and even died. Fear did not leave them during the day when the apparition had gone, because they still remembered what they had seen. Eventually the house was empty; deserted, it was abandoned to the ghost. It was advertised for sale or let in the hope that someone ignorant of its reputation would take it. One day Athenodorus, the philosopher, came to Athens and saw the notice. He was suspicious of the asking price and soon found out the whole story, but still decided to go ahead and rent the house ... [Athenodorus sees the ghost and follows it the courtyard of the house where it disappears] ... The next day, Athenodorus called the magistrate and suggested that the place where the ghost had vanished should be dug up. There they found chains twisted around bare bones, the soil having rotted away the body. The bones were collected and given a proper burial and the ghost, having been laid to rest, was never heard from again.

The dead and their spirits were not always perceived as a menace since they could potentially be beneficial. Some believed that the dead were imbued with special powers that could be harnessed by the living. The fact that this was more than just literary fancy is confirmed by the recovery of spells and curse-tablets (*defixiones*) which could make requests for assistance to the dead. The burials of those who died premature or violent deaths, whose souls were thought to be discontented and trapped between the world of the living and the dead, may have been particularly targeted as a means for conveying messages to the gods of the underworld (Gager 1992: 18–20). Love was often the subject; for example, a spell found in a Romano-Egyptian cemetery, which had been placed in a vase with a female figure pierced with needles, invoked numerous gods and the spirit of a dead man to win the writer the exclusive love of a girl; 'drag her by the hair, the guts until she does not reject me' (Gager 1992: n.28). The dead and the gods could also be asked for help in matters of gambling, the recovery of property and revenge.

6.59 Gager 1992: n.101

Curse: 1st or 2nd c. AD. Veldidena (Wilten, Austria). A lead curse tablet found in a graveyard.
 = Versnel 1991: 83.
 The god Mercury was associated with theft. Moltinus was a Celtic deity. Cacus was a fire god of the Palatine in Rome, known for stealing cattle from Hercules. Here the stolen property is dedicated to the gods so that the loss also becomes theirs.

Secundina commands Mercury and Moltinus, that whoever stole two necklaces worth fourteen denarii, that deceitful Cacus take him away and his fortune, just as hers were taken, the very things which she hands over to you so that you will track them down. She hands them over to you so that you will find him and separate him from his fortune, from his family and from those dearest to him. She commands you on this; you must bring him to justice.

A step further in these ideas was the raising of the dead, most frequently to predict the future, since the ghosts or spirits of the dead were perceived as wise, all-knowing and unable to tell lies. Exploiting the dead in this way was a literary theme that allowed the exploration of the darker side of ancient society. This world of witchcraft and wizardry created some of the most graphic images in Latin literature; to raise up the dead, to hear them speak and walk again was the stuff of high drama.

6.60 Horace, Satires 1.8, 17–29

Satirical poetry: late 1st c. BC. A wooden image of Priapus located on the Esquiline describes what he has seen in the old cemetery. See also 4.8.

Compare Tibullus 1.2, 41–5 and 1.5, 51–2; Seneca, *Oedipus* 530–626; Philostratus, *Apollonius* 4.11.16.

For myself, it is not so much the thieves and animals who infest the place that worry and annoy me, but the witches who with spells and potions plague human souls; these I cannot stop in any way from gathering bones and harmful herbs, as soon as the wandering moon has shown its lovely face. I myself saw Canidia with her black gown tucked up, walking barefoot and with dishevelled hair, yelling together with the elder Sagana. Paleness had made them both horrible to behold. They began to claw up the earth with their nails, and to tear a black lamb to pieces with their teeth. The blood was poured into a ditch, from where they might summon up the shades of the dead that were to answer their questions.

6.61 Lucan, Pharsalia 6, 667–717

Epic poetry: mid 1st c. AD. After the battle of Pharsalus (48 BC) Sextus Pompey asks the witch Erictho to foretell the future by reanimating a corpse.

Compare Heliodorus, *Aethiopica* 6.12–15.

Then she began by piercing the chest of the corpse with its fresh wounds, which she filled with hot blood. She washed the innards clean of clotted gore and poured in generously the poison supplied by the moon. With this was mixed all those things made inauspiciously by Nature ... [Erictho uses strange poisons and potions and makes animal noises] ... She continued by saying plainly a Thessalian spell in a voice that went down to Tartarus: 'I call upon the Furies, the horror of Hell, the punishments of the guilty, and Chaos, eager to unite numerous worlds in ruin; I cry to the Ruler of the World below, who endures eternal pain because gods are so slow to die; to Styx and Elysium where no Thessalian witch may enter ... [Erictho invokes other deities] ... If these lips of mine that call you have been tainted enough with horror and pollution; if I have always eaten human flesh before chanting these spells; if I have cut open human breasts still full of divine life and washed them out with warm brains; if any baby could have lived, once his head and inner organs were laid on your dishes; then grant me my prayer! I am not asking for a shade lurking in the depths of Tartarus, a shade that has become long-accustomed to darkness, but for one that has just left the light and was on his way down; he still lingers at the entrance of the chasm that leads to gloomy Orcus, and, even though he obeys my spells, he will go only once to join the shades. Let a shade who was just recently one of Pompey's soldiers tell Pompey's son the whole future.

These may be striking and entertaining literary images, but attempts at raising the spirits of the dead were not unheard of, even if largely recounted for rhetorical impact. Such black magic was used to characterize some of the more suspect figures of Roman history and to suggest associations between them and oriental, foreign and strange practices. Bad emperors in particular could be depicted as dabbling with the black arts; as Ogden has noted it was part of how emperors were portrayed as 'distracted, desperate and excessive' (2001: 149). To try to transcend the natural and spiritual boundaries between the living and the dead was the act of the wicked and the tyrannical. That necromancy, or at least other suspect magical activities, may have been practised in the cemetery is suggested by anti-magic laws (*Theodosian Code* 9.16.7). The practitioners may have also been liable for breaking laws against tomb violation. However, such legislation may reflect the concerns of the emperors who were afraid that people might use the dead to divine the time of their death and who would succeed them, thereby undermining their position and the stability of the state.

6.62 *Suetonius*, Nero 34.4

Biography: early 2nd c. AD. Events of *c.* AD 59. Nero had murdered his mother Agrippina.

See also Tacitus, *Annals* 14.9–10 and Pliny *Natural History* 30.14–18. Compare emperor Otho's attempts to placate the ghost of Galba, **6.54**. See also Cicero, *On Vatinius* 6.14; Cicero, *Tusculan Disputations* 1.16.37; and Cicero, *On Divination* 1.68.132.

Nero often admitted that he was hounded by his mother's ghost and by the whips and blazing torches of the Furies; and he had rites performed by Persian magicians in order to summon her shade and entreat its forgiveness.

6.63 Cassius Dio 78.15. 3–4

History: late 2nd or 3rd c. AD. Events of early 2nd c. AD.

Caracalla was the eldest son of the emperor Septimius Severus. After his father's death Caracalla murdered his brother, Geta, to become sole emperor. Commodus was the predecessor of Septimus Severus and was famed for his dissolute ways.

See also Cassius Dio 79. 4–7 and Herodian 4. 12–14.

Caracalla was physically ill, from both apparent and non-apparent diseases, but he was also ill in his mind. He suffered from certain upsetting visions, and he often thought that he was being chased by his father and his brother, both armed with swords. Therefore he called up spirits, among them the spirit of his father and that of Commodus, to find some cure for these visions. But not one of the spirits spoke a word to him except Commodus. They say that Geta accompanied Severus, even though he had not been summoned. But even Commodus said nothing that would help him, indeed the opposite since he terrified him all the more.

APPENDIX

Sources

Authors

Ammianus Marcellinus (*c.* AD 330–95). Born in Antioch (Syria), Ammianus followed a military career before moving to Rome (mid 380s) and writing a 31-book history on the period AD 96–378. Books 15–31 have survived.

> *Histories* 31.13 (**1.32**).

Appian (2nd c. AD). Born in Alexandria, Appian became a Roman citizen and moved to Rome. Under the patronage of Fronto, Appian was honoured by the emperor Antoninus Pius and devoted his time to writing a Roman history (in Greek) from early times to Trajan. The work is only partially extant.

> *Civil Wars* (*Bella civilian*): 1.43 (**4.41**); 1.105–106 (**3.61**); 2.146–147 (**3.68**).

Apuleius (born *c.* AD 125). Apuleius was born in Madaurus (Mdaourouch, Algeria) into a prosperous family and was educated in Carthage, Athens and Rome. Apuleius was a public speaker and philosopher, and published speeches and a novel.

> *Metamorphoses* (*The Golden Ass*): 2.21 (**4.58**); 4.18 (**4.58**). [An epic, and often sensational, novel that tells of the adventures of Lucius, who is turned into an ass by witchcraft]

Ausonius (Decimus Magnus Ausonius) (4th c. AD). Ausonius was a statesman, teacher and writer from Bordeaux who rose from humble origins to become praetorian prefect and consul (AD 379). In his retirement Ausonius wrote poetry.

> *Parentalia*: 9 (**5.39**); 10 (**5.20**). [Commemorative poems dedicated to the deceased relatives of Ausonius]
> *Epitaphs*: 31 (**6.42**). [A series of poetic epitaphs]

Cassius Dio (Cassius Dio Cocceianus, *c.* AD 164–*c.* 230). A Greek senator from Nicaea (Bithynia) who held the consulship in AD 229, Dio wrote (in Greek) an 80-book history of Rome from its foundation to AD 229. The work is only partially extant.

> *Histories*: 68.24 (**1.20**); 68.8 (**4.47**); 67.9 (**3.59**); 69.11 (**6.22**); 78.15 (**6.63**).

Catullus (Gaius Valerius Catullus, *c.* 84 BC–*c.* 54 BC). Born in Verona to a distinguished family, Catullus spent most of his life in Rome pursuing a literary rather than a political career. Catullus wrote poetry (elegies and epigrams), including love poetry charting his relationship with Lesbia.

> *Poems*: 59 (**3.53**); 101 (**6.41**).

Cicero (Marcus Tullius Cicero, 106–43 BC). Born at Arpinum (Italy) to an equestrian family, Cicero pursued a distinguished public career, holding the consulship in 63 BC. He was exiled in 58 BC for his prosecution of the Catiline conspirators. Cicero returned to Rome in 57 BC where he observed the fall of the Republic, and became a victim to Antony in the proscriptions of 43 BC (see **2.62** and **4.50**). Cicero was a great orator and writer as well as statesman. Fifty-eight speeches of Cicero survive in whole or part, as well as significant works on rhetoric, philosophy and science. Cicero was also a frequent writer of letters, of which more than 900 survive.

In Defence of Cluentius (*Pro Cluentio*): 27 (**3.4**). [Defence speech in support of Cluentius delivered 66 BC]

Against Vatinius (*In Vatinium*): 30–2 (**3.30**). [An invective against Vatinius, 56 BC]

Philippics (*Orationes Philippicae*): 9.7 (**3.60**); 15.12 (**4.44**). [A series of speeches that expressed opposition to Marc Antony, delivered 44–3 BC]

On the Republic (*De republica*): 6.13 (**6.17**). [A dialogue on political philosophy, discussing the ideal state and the Roman constitution, published 51 BC]

On Divination (*De divinatione*): 1.27 (**6.50**). [A dialogue on religious philosophy, 45 BC]

Tusculan Disputations (*Tusculanae disputationes*): 1.5 (**6.28**); 1.9 (**6.1**); 1.11 (**6.7**); 1.14 (**2.46**); 1.16 (**6.21**); 1.30 (**1.43**); 1.35 (**1.16**); 1.39 (**5.15**); 1.45 (**3.36**); 2.17 (**1.34**); 3.27 (**5.10**); 3.28 (**5.4**); 3.32 (**5.52**); 5.41 (**5.50**). [A dialogue about death, grief, pain and fear and the essentials of happiness (influenced by Stoicism), published in 45 BC]

On Old Age (*De senectute*): 19 (**1.15**). [A philosophical dialogue purportedly between Cato and two younger men set in 150 BC, published in 44 BC]

On the Laws (*De legibus*): 2.22.55 (**3.37**); 2.22.58 (**4.2** and **4.10**); 2.23.59 (**3.67**). [A dialogue on law, *c.* 43 BC]

Letters to Atticus (*Epistulae ad Atticum*): 12.14 (**5.49**); 12.18 (**4.28**); 12.19 (**4.28**); 12.20 (**5.49**) 12.23 (**4.28**); 12.28 (**5.49**); 12.36 (**4.28**).

Letters to his Friends (*Epistulae ad familiares*): 4.6 (**5.47**); 4.7 (**5.48**); 5.12 (**2.47**); 5.14 (**5.46**); 5.16 (**5.45**).

Dionysius of Halicarnassus (1st c. BC). Dionysius taught rhetoric in Rome under Augustus, where he wrote his *Roman Antiquities*, a 20-book history of Rome (in Greek) down to the outbreak of the first Punic War. The work is only partially extant.

Roman Antiquities: 4.24 (**3.28**).

Epictetus (mid 1st to early 2nd c. AD). A slave from Hierapolis in Phrygia, Epictetus was freed by his master and taught Stoic philosophy in Rome and Nicopolis. His oral teachings (*Discourses*) were published by Arrian.

Discourses: 1.27.7 (**2.17**); 3.13 (**6.30**).

Fragment 26 (**6.5**).

Festus (Sextus Pompeius Festus, 2nd c. AD). A scholar who abridged an earlier work on words and their meanings, by Verrius Flaccus. The work of Festus was then epitomized by Paulus Dioconus in the 8th c. AD.

On the Meaning of Words 156 (**6.43**).

Fronto (Marcus Cornelius Fronto, *c.* AD 95–*c.* AD 166). Born at Cirta, Numidia (Constantine, Algeria) Fronto was appointed tutor by Antoninus Pius to Marcus Aurelius and Lucius Verus. He was suffect consul in AD 143. In his day, Fronto was famed for his oratory, but is best known now for his letters to members of the imperial family.

Letter to Antoninus Augustus.ii. 1–2 (**1.2**); 5 (**5.18**).

Horace (Horatius Flaccus Quintus, 65–8 BC). Born at Venusia (Venosa, Italy), Horace was the son of a wealthy freed slave who educated his son well. Horace fought with Brutus in the civil wars, which resulted in the loss of his family property. Horace was spared, then returned to Italy and focused on a literary career, entering the sphere of Maecenas.

> *Satires* (or *Sermones*): 1.8 (**4.8; 6.60**); 2.5 (**2.30**). [Satirical poems on private themes, published 30 BC]
>
> *Odes* (*Carmina*): 1.11 (**2.4**); 1.28 (**2.5; 3.39**); 3.30 (**2.49**). [A collection of lyric poems on a variety of themes, published 23–17 BC]
>
> *Epistles 1*: 1.7 (**3.7**). [A collection of poems written in letter form, published *c.* 21 BC]
>
> *The Art of Poetry* (*Ars poetica*): 429–33 (**3.32**). [On the composition of poetry, *c.* 18 BC]

Josephus (Flavius Josephus, AD 37–*c.* AD 100). Born in Jerusalem, Josephus was a Jewish priest who in the early years of the Jewish revolt (AD 66–70) was the military commander of Galilee. When captured by the Romans Josephus became sympathetic to the Roman cause, and moved to Rome where he took up a literary career. The best known work of Josephus is a history of the Jewish War composed in Greek.

> *Jewish War* (*Bellum Iudaicum*): 3.8 (**1.47**); 4.83 (**1.29**).

Juvenal (Decimus Iunius Iuvenalis, *c.* AD 65–*c.* AD 130). Little is known for certain of Juvenal's life. He wrote his *Satires*, a series of satirical poems, in the early decades of the 2nd c. AD, using an indignant *persona* to explore the decadence and immorality of life in Rome.

> *Satires*: 2, 149–52 (**6.31**); 3, 257–78 (**1.22**); 10, 198–204 and 241–5 (**1.12**); 15, 13–40 (**5.14**).

Livy (Titius Livius, 59 BC–AD 17). Born at Patavium (Padua, Italy), Livy came to Rome and won the interest of the emperor Augustus. His great work *Ab urbe condita libri* (Books from the foundation of the city) covered the history of Rome from the founding of the city to 9 BC. The work originally consisted of 142 books and is only partially extant.

> *Preface*: 10 (**2.48**).
>
> *Books*: 1.59 (**1.46**); 22.51 (**1.30**); 38.53 (**4.26**); 41.21 (**4.5**).
>
> *Summaries*: 48 (**3.5**).

Lucan (Marcus Annaeus Lucanus, AD 39–65). Born at Corduba (Córdoba, Spain) to an equestrian family (his uncle was Seneca the Younger), Lucan was educated in Rome and became part of Nero's circle. In AD 65 he was implicated in a conspiracy against the emperor and was forced to commit suicide. Lucan was a prolific writer, but his only well-preserved work is *The Civil War*.

> *Civil War* (*De bello civili*; or *Pharsalia*): 2, 21–8 (**3.16**); 3, 737–47 (**3.14**); 6, 667–717 (**6.61**); 7, 786–804 (**4.45**); 8, 729–58 (**3.42**). [A ten-book epic poem about the years 48–9 BC and the destruction of the Roman Republic]

Lucian (born *c.* AD 120). Lucian of Samosata was a prolific writer (in Greek) about whose life little is known, but he may have been an itinerant lecturer on philosophical themes. He wrote a variety of rhetorical works including dialogues which could fuse comedy and popular philosophy. Many of his works express a cynical or a satirical viewpoint.

Nigrinus: 30 (**2.20**). [A satirical dialogue in which a Platonic, and probably fictitious, philosopher critiques Roman life]

On Funerals: 2–9 (**6.12**); 11–15 (**3.20**). [A satirical essay on funeral customs]

True Story: 2.14–15 (**6.16**). [A parody of fantastic and mythical events and travels]

Charon: 22 (**6.47**). [A satirical dialogue on the mistaken beliefs of mankind]

Lover of Lies (*Philopseudes*): 27 (**6.51**). [A satire on superstition]

Lucretius (Titus Lucretius Carus, 1st c. BC). Almost nothing is known of the life of Lucretius, beyond speculation. He was a follower of Epicurean philosophy and is famed for his poem *On the Nature of Things* (*De rerum natura*). The poem is in six books and may be incomplete. It explores the nature of atomic phenomena, human beings and the world, while overall it tackles (and rationalizes) human fears about the gods and death.

On the Nature of Things: 2, 573–80 (**6.36**); 3, 323–26 (**6.2**); 3, 624–33 (**6.21**); 3, 870–93 (**3.35**); 3, 1087–94 (**2.16**).

Marcus Aurelius (Marcus Aurelius Verus Caesar, AD 121–80). Born into a senatorial family and related to the emperor Hadrian, Marcus Aurelius was adopted by Antoninus Pius in AD 138 and became emperor in AD 161. It seems probable that he wrote his *Meditations* during lengthy campaigns against the German tribes. The work is a Stoic-influenced but personal record (in Greek) of thoughts and reflections on human life.

Meditations: 4.21 (**6.6**); 4.48 (**2.6**); 9.33 (**2.6**).

Martial (Marcus Valerius Martialis, *c.* AD 40–*c.* AD 103). Born in Bilbilis (Spain), Martial came to Rome around AD 64. He became a celebrated poet upon whom Domitian conferred equestrian rank. He returned to Spain in AD 98. Martial is famed for his *Epigrams*, in 12 books, short poems on varied themes that often have satirical, polemical and sometimes a complimentary tone.

Epigrams: 1.47 (**3.8**); 2.26 (**2.32**); 2.81 (**3.26**); 4.73 (**2.1**); 4.70 (**2.25**); 5.34 (**5.19**); 5.64 (**2.11**); 8.75 (**3.26**); 9.1 (**6.23**); 10.5 (**4.6**); 10.97 (**3.46**); 11.54 (**3.46**).

Ovid (Publius Ovidius Naso, 43 BC–AD 17). Ovid was born at Sulmo (Sulmona, Italy) into an old equestrian family. He was educated at Rome, but abandoned a public career for poetry. He became a leading poet in Augustan Rome, but in AD 8 was banished to Tomis (Constantsa) on the Black Sea, where he remained until his death.

Amores: 2.6, 39–40 (**1.14**); 2.6, 51–62 (**5.63**); 3.9, 35–8 (**2.10**); 3.9, 41–54 (**5.62**). [Three books of elegies about the misadventures of a poet in love, published *c*. 15 BC]

Heroines (*Heroides*): 7, 183–196 (**5.33**). [A collection of poems, in letter form, from female figures to their absent husbands or lovers, published *c*. 5 BC]

The Art of Love (*Ars Amatoria*): 3, 429–32 (**3.56**). [Poems on the art of seduction, published *c*. 2 BC]

Metamorphoses (Transformations): 4, 430 (**6.11**); 15, 871–9 (**2.50**). [An epic in 15 books of a collection of tales from near eastern myth and legend, composed before AD 8]

Fasti (Calendar): 2, 533–70 (**6.44**); 5, 429–44 (**6.45**). [A poetical calendar of the Roman year, only the first six books (January–June) survive, published after AD 8]

Tristia (Sorrows): 3.3, 37–46 (**3.13**). [Poems from exile, composed after AD 8]

Consolation to Livia: 113–19 (**5.60**). [A poetic consolation to Livia on the death of her son Drusus; attributed to Ovid, but of uncertain authorship]

Petronius (Petronius Arbiter, 1st c. AD). The author Petronius may have been the politician and arbiter of elegance at the court of Nero who was forced to suicide in AD 66. The *Satyrica* (known as the *Satyricon*) is a satirical novel that tells of the adventures of Encolpius and his lover Giton. Much of the work is lost, the most complete section being the feast of Trimalchio (*cena Trimalchionis*).

    Satyricon: 34 (**2.12**); 65 (**3.55**); 71 (**2.56**); 77–8 (**3.58**); 94 (**1.48**); 111 (**5.44**); 116 (**2.28**).

Philostratus (Lucius Flavius Philostratus, late 2nd c. AD to early 3rd c. AD). From a distinguished family from the island of Lemnos, Philostratus was commissioned to write (in Greek) the life of Apollonius (a miracle worker of the 1st c. AD) by Iulia Domna the wife of the emperor Septimius Severus.

    Life of Apollonius: 3.38 (**6.56**).

Plautus (Titus Maccius Plautus, late 3rd c. BC to early 2nd c. BC). Comic playwright whose plays are the earliest Latin works to survive complete. Twenty-one plays, adaptations of Greek new comedy, survive.

    The Two Bacchises (*Bacchides*): 816–17 (**1.13**).
    The Swaggering Soldier (*Miles Gloriosus*): 705–9 (**2.27**).
    The Haunted House (*Mostellaria*): 496–505 (**5.57**).

Pliny the Elder (Gaius Plinius Secundus, AD 23/24–79). A Roman equestrian from Novum Comum (Como, Italy), Pliny the Elder followed a public career, becoming the commander of the Misenum fleet. He died in this role while attempting to rescue victims of the eruption of Vesuvius. Pliny's sole surviving work is the Natural History (*Naturalis Historia*), an encyclopaedic work that surveyed aspects of 'scientific' knowledge.

    Natural History: 7.54 (**3.40**); 7.55 (**6.37**); 7.139–40 (**3.33**); 11.55 (**3.43**); 12.41 (**3.44**); 16.60 (**3.52**); 25.7 (**1.17**); 28.2 (**4.59**); 28.11 (**4.59**).

Pliny the Younger (Gaius Plinius Caecilius Secundus, *c.* AD 61–*c.* 112). Born at Comum, Pliny the Younger was brought up and adopted by his uncle Pliny the Elder. He entered the Senate and pursued a distinguished career in the civil courts, holding the consulship in AD 100. He was sent, by the emperor Trajan, to govern Bithynia Pontus where he died. He is best known for his nine books of letters, which were carefully crafted for publication. A tenth book contains his correspondence with the emperor Trajan while he held office in Bithynia.

    Letters: 1.22 (**1.18**); 2.20 (**2.31**); 3.10 (**2.52**); 3.14 (**1.25**); 3.16 (**1.51**); 4.2 (**3.48**); 5.16 (**5.27**); 7.27 (**6.58**); 8.18 (**2.22**); 8.23 (**5.57**); 9.3 (**2.45**); 9.19 (**2.58**); 10.75 (**2.39**); 10.76 (**2.39**).

Plutarch (Lucius Mestrius Plutarchus, *c.* AD 50–*c.* AD 120). Plutarch was born at Charonea where he spent most of his life, although he did travel to Rome. He had influential friends and became a priest at Delphi. Plutarch wrote (in Greek) biography, rhetorical works and philosophy.

    The Parallel Lives: *Numa* 12 (**5.1**); *Cato* 9 (**2.19**); *Crassus* 19 (**3.54**); *Sulla* 31 (**1.27**); *Brutus* 36–7 (**6.55**), 52–3 (**1.54**); *Antony* 20 (**4.50**), 77 (**5.9**). [A collection of paired biographies of eminent Greeks and Romans]
    Consolation to his Wife: 11 (**5.13**); 3 (**5.56**). [A philosophical consolation to his wife on the death of their daughter]
    Divine Vengeance: 30 (**6.14**). [A vision of punishments inflicted after death]

Letter to Apollonius: 19 (**5.31**); 22 (**5.7**); 36 (**6.3**). [A philosophical consolation to Apollonius on the death of his son; attributed to Plutarch, but authorship is uncertain]

Polybius (*c.* 200–*c.* 118 BC). A Greek noble who was held hostage in Rome for many years, Polybius became a friend of Publius Cornelius Scipio Aemilianus and may have travelled with him to Spain and Africa. He wrote a history of the world (in Greek) in 40 books, covering the period from 266–144 BC; his aim was to tell the story of Rome's rise to world dominion. The work is only partially extant.

Histories: 6.53–54 (**3.65**); 10.15 (**1.28**); 15.14 (**1.31**).

Propertius (Sextus Propertius, *c.* 50 BC–15 BC). Born at Asisium (Assisi, Italy) into a noble family, whose property was diminished by the confiscations of Octavian (41–40 BC), Propertius became a distinguished poet in Rome under the patronage of Maecenas, writing elegies on a variety of themes. Propertius is best known for his love poems in which he celebrates his devotion to Cynthia.

Elegies: 1.19 (**5.40**); 2.1 (**1.50**); 2.8 (**1.50**); 2.13b (**3.6**); 3.18 (**2.9**); 4.7 (**6.52**); 4.11 (**5.61**).

Quintilian (Marcus Fabius Quintilianus, *c.* AD 35–*c.* AD 90). Born at Calagurris (Calahorra, Spain) to an orator father, Quintilian established a school of oratory in Rome and may have been the first rhetorician to receive a state salary. He taught for more than 20 years before retiring, with consular honours, to write his *Training in Oratory* (*Institutio Oratoria*).

Prologue to Book 6: 7–9 (**5.25**); 11–12 (**5.25**).

Sallust (Gaius Sallustius Crispus, 86–35 BC). Born at Amiternum (Italy) to an aristocratic family, Sallust pursued a public career and became a follower of Julius Caesar. He was charged with malpractice after being governor of Africa and withdrew from public life. He devoted himself to history, writing two monographs that emphasized moral decline. His other works do not survive substantially.

Conspiracy of Catiline (*Bellum Catilinae*): 51.20 (**6.9**). [An account of the Catiline conspiracy of 62 BC]

Scriptores Historiae Augustae (4th c. AD?). A collection of biographies of Roman emperors from AD 117 to AD 284, authorship and date are uncertain. The biographies are traditionally ascribed to six authors and may have been written in the late 4th c. AD.

Hadrian: 25 (**6.10**).

Marcus Aurelius: 13 (**3.3**); 21 (**5.3**).

Seneca (the Younger) (Lucius Annaeus Seneca, *c.* 4 BC–AD 65). Born at Corduba (Córdoba, Spain) into a wealthy equestrian family, Seneca became a distinguished statesman, writer, orator and Stoic philosopher. He was banished to Corsica in AD 41–9 by the emperor Claudius, but returned to Rome to become tutor to Nero; and he acted as minister and political adviser to the latter during the early years of his reign. Eventually Seneca fell from favour, retired from public life and was then forced to suicide by the emperor (**1.45**). Seneca's extant works include ethical treatises, moral letters, satires and tragic plays.

On the Shortness of Life (*De brevitate vitae*): 20.5 (**3.23**). [An ethical treatise on the brevity of life, written in AD 49]

On Benefits (*De beneficiis*): 4.11 (**2.21**); 4.20 (**2.29**). [An investigation of the Roman social code, AD 63]

Consolation to Marcia (*Ad Marciam de consolatione*): 3.2 (**5.5**); 19 (**6.29**). [A consolation addressed to the daughter of Aulus Cremutius Cordus, on the death of her son, written AD 39 or 40]

Consolation to Polybius (*Ad Polybium de consolatione*): 18.2 (**2.51**); 18.7 (**5.55**). [A consolation addressed to Claudius' freedman, Polybius; written *c.* AD 43]

Apocolocyntosis: 4 (**1.59**); 12 (**3.70**). [A satire on the deification of Claudius]

Moral Letters (*Epistulae morales*): 1 (**2.18**); 7 (**1.40**); 12 (**3.57**); 49 (**2.18**); 61 (**2.18**); 63 (**5.8**; **5.54**; **6.33**); 70 (**1.44**); 91 (**6.8**); 99 (**5.16**; **5.53**); 108 (**6.24**). [Addressed to Lucilius, the letters reflect philosophical discourse on Stoic doctrines rather than genuine correspondence and date to the final years of Seneca's life]

Servius (Marius/Maurus Servius Honoratus, 4th c. AD). A grammarian and commentator best known for his commentary on Virgil, which was based on an earlier work (now lost) by Aelius Donatus.

On Virgil's Aeneid: 11.143 (**3.22**); 11.201 (**3.47**).

Siculus Flaccus (date uncertain). A writer on surveying. *On the Conditions of Land* (*De condicionibus Agrorum*): 49 (**4.29**).

Sidonius Apollinaris (Gaius Sollius Modestus Apollinaris Sidonius, *c.* AD 430–*c.* AD 490). Born at Lugdunum (Lyons, France), Sidonius was well educated and held a prefecture in Rome in AD 468 and became bishop of Clermont in AD 470. Sidonius wrote panegyrics and letters.

Letters (*Epistulae*): 3.12 (**4.56**).

Statius (Publius Papinius Statius, 1st c. AD). Statius was born in the mid 1st c. AD at Naples. His father was a poet and teacher. Statius became a popular poet in Rome during the reign of the emperor Domitian.

Silvae: 2.1, 1–13 (**5.59**); 2.6, 84–93 (**3.45**); 5.1, 155–98 (**3.11**); 5.3, 264–5 (**5.28**); 5.5, 38–45 (**5.24**); 5.5, 56–64 (**5.11**). [Thirty-two poems, mostly in hexameters, take as their themes personal events of Statius' acquaintances, such as marriage and bereavement]

Thebaid: 3, 114–30 (**5.58**). [An epic poem about the mythical struggle for the Theban throne]

Strabo (64 BC–*c.* AD 21). Born at Amaseia (Amasya) in Pontus into a prominent family, Strabo travelled widely. He wrote (in Greek) a history (a continuation of Polybius) which is lost and the *Geography* (*Geographia*), an encyclopedia of geographic knowledge, in 17 books.

Geography: 5.3 (**4.20**); 6.2 (**1.38**).

Suetonius (Gaius Suetonius Tranquillus, *c.* AD 70–*c.* 140). Born into an equestrian family, Suetonius held posts in the imperial administration under Hadrian. Suetonius wrote biographies, the *De vita Caesarum*, twelve imperial biographies from Caesar to Domitian, being the best preserved and most famous.

Augustus: 18 (**4.60**); 66 (**2.23**); 99 (**1.55**); 100 (**3.69**).
Gaius: 7 (**1.1**); 15 (**2.63**); 59 (**6.53**).
Claudius: 27 (**1.8**).
Nero: 34 (**6.62**); 49 (**1.57**).
Galba: 20 (**4.51**).
Otho: 7 (**6.54**); 11–12 (**1.58**).
Domitian: 17 (**3.25**); 23 (**2.61**).
Vespasian: 19 (**3.66**).

Tacitus (Publius? Cornelius Tacitus, *c.* AD 56–*c.* 118). Little is known of the background of Tacitus. He was probably born in Narbonese or Cisalpine Gaul and pursued a distinguished career in Rome becoming suffect consul in AD 97. Tacitus wrote extensively: biography, an ethnography, dialogues and history. It is for his historical works that he is best known.

Agricola: 29 (**5.12**); 43 (**2.24**); 46 (**2.53**). [A biography of Tacitus' father-in-law Agricola, the governor of Britain, published AD 98]

Histories: 1.41 (**1.53**); 3.25 (**1.33**). [A history of the years AD 69–96, originally compromising of 12 or 14 books; only the first four and a quarter books survive; published early 2nd c. AD]

Annals (*Ab excessu divi Augusti*): 1.60 (**4.43**); 2.83 (**2.60**); 3.2 (**5.6**); 4.62 (**1.21**); 4.35 (**2.64**); 6.16 (**4.49**); 11.37–8 (**1.56**); 13.17 (**3.24**); 13.44 (**1.26**); 15.23 (**5.17**); 15.63–4 (**1.45**); 16.6 (**3.41**); 16.10 (**5.34**); 16.13 (**1.19**). [A year-by-year account of the reigns of the Julio-Claudian emperors beginning with the death of Augustus; it is only partially extant, published early 2nd c. AD]

Tertullian (Quintus Septimius Florens Tertullianus, *c.* AD 160–*c.* AD 240). Born in or near Carthage, the son of a centurion, Tertullian converted to Christianity and used his literary skills to defend the faith and explore ethical problems and Christian doctrine.

Apology (*Apologia*): 15 (**1.39**). [A defence of Christianity]

Tibullus (Albius Tibullus, 1st c. BC). Born in the mid 1st c. BC to an equestrian family, Tibullus made his name as a poet during the time of Augustus. He died in 19 BC. Tibullus wrote elegiac poetry, much of which takes love as its theme.

Elegies: 1.1, 59–68 (**5.32**); 1.3, 5–8 (**3.49**); 1.3, 57–66 (**5.43**).

Varro (Marcus Terentius Varro, 116–27 BC). Varro was born at Reate (Rieti, Italy) and studied in Rome and Athens before pursuing a public career which culminated in the holding of a praetorship. Varro supported Pompey in the civil war. Julius Caesar showed him clemency, although he would later be proscribed by Marc Antony. He escaped assassination and passed the remainder of his life in scholarly retirement. Varro wrote on a wide range of subjects including history, rhetoric, law, philosophy, medicine, architecture and language. Only two of his works survive substantially.

On the Latin Language (*De lingua Latina*): 5.23 (**3.38**); 5.25 (**4.7**); 6.49 (**2.44**); 7.70 (**3.31**). [A study on etymology and syntax. The work is partially extant]

Valerius Maximus (1st c. AD). Little is known of the life of Valerius Maximus, except that he was a contemporary of the emperor Tiberius and may have been a member of the élite. He composed a handbook, *Memorable deeds and sayings* (*Factorum ac dictorum memorabilium, libri IX*) of Romans and Greeks organized under moral or philosophical headings such as Chastity, Cruelty and Moderation.

Memorable deeds and sayings: 4.6 (**1.52**); 5.2 (**3.9**); 7.1 (**3.27**).

Velleius Paterculus (*c.* 20 BC–*c.* AD 31). Born into a distinguished family, Velleius followed the élite *cursus*, holding a praetorship in AD 15 after which nothing more is known of his public career. Velleius wrote a summary history in two books which began with Greek mythology and ended in the year AD 29. The work is only partially extant.

History: 2.66 (**2.62**).

Virgil (Publius Vergilius Maro, 70–19 BC). Born near Mantua (Mantova, Italy) to a family of uncertain status, in Rome Virgil became the poet of his age in the literary circle of Augustus and Maecenas. He wrote extensively, but it was his epic work the *Aeneid* that made him the Roman Homer.

Aeneid: 6, 218–20 (**3.17**); 6, 226–8 (**3.50**); 6, 434–40 (**1.41**); 6, 608–17 (**6.13**); 6, 640–92 (**6.15**); 6, 698–702 (**6.19**); 6, 743–51 (**6.25**); 9, 485–90 (**3.18**); 11, 184–202 (**4.42**); 12, 604–11 (**3.15**). [An epic poem about the flight of Aeneas from Troy and his battles in Italy to found Rome]

Legal texts

Digest. A collection of statements on Roman law by earlier jurists, compiled at the instigation of the emperor Justinian and completed in AD 533. One of the most frequently cited jurists is Ulpian (Domitius Ulpianus) who was a Praetorian Prefect AD 222–3. Others jurists include: Paulus (early 3rd c. AD – see below) and Pomponius (mid 2nd c. AD).

Digest: 3.2.11 (**1.42**); 11.7.6 (**4.30**); 11.7.10 (**4.18**); 11.7.12 (**3.1**); 11.7.14 (**3.1**); 11.8.3 (**4.19**); 35.1.27 (**2.33**); 47.12.3 (**4.57**).

Paulus (Iulius Paulus) (late 2nd c. AD to early 3rd c. AD). A lawyer of unknown origin who flourished under the emperor Septimius Severus and his immediate successors. He wrote extensively on legal matters.

Opinions (Responsa): 1.21.2 (**4.1**); 1.21.14 (**5.2**).

Inscriptions

The standard corpus of Latin inscriptions is the *Corpus Inscriptionum Latinarum* (*CIL*). For the most part this is arranged by geographic regions. Most volumes of *CIL* were published between 1870 and 1890, and have since been updated by supplements. *L'Année épigraphique* (*AE*) is an annual survey of epigraphic publications which collects and publishes new finds. Regional and site-specific volumes complement and supplement the standard publications (e.g. Thylander 1952; Vorbeck 1980; *Inscriptiones Aquileia* (*IA*)). Volumes of selected texts such as *Inscriptiones Latinae Selectae* (*ILS*) organize the inscriptions by themes, while verse inscriptions are found in *Carmina Latina Epigraphica* (*CLE*). The equivalents to *CIL* for Greek inscriptions are *Inscriptiones Graecae* (*IG*) and *Corpus Inscriptionum Graecorum* (*CIG*). It should be noted that many epigraphic volumes provide few details. Many inscriptions are now lost and others survive removed from their original context, but even for well-preserved examples it is often necessary to look in volumes on sculpture to find out on what type of monument an inscription was located and the nature of any accompanying décor. Note for example the volumes in the *Corpus Signorum Imperii Romani* series, such as Boppert 1992a and 1992b.

CIL I: 1219 (**2.3**); 6298 (**6.32**).

CIL III: 293 (**2.15**); 2875 (**5.26**); 3247 (**6.4**); 4471 (**1.6**); 11213 (**4.38**); 14214 (**4.46**).

CIL V: 952 (**4.53**); 1365 (**2.54**); 1419 (**4.17**); 5262 (**2.40**); 5933 (**1.36**).

CIL VI: 1319 (**4.34**); 1374 (**2.35**); 1527 (**3.34**); 2489 (**6.18**); 6221 (**3.29**); 7308 (**1.4**); 7470 (**4.31**); 10197 (**1.37**); 10230 (**2.26**); 11743 (**2.2**); 11602 (**5.36**); 13244/5 (**4.33**) 15258 (**2.13**); 15546 (**5.37**); 16740 (**1.23**); 18131 (**2.14**); 20569 (**5.41**); 24085 (**5.42**); 26003 (**6.40**); 29436 (**1.24**); 31615 (**4.4**); 31670 (**3.34**); 35050 (**5.38**); 36467 (**4.54**).

CIL VII: 66 (**4.39**).

CIL VIII: 212 (**6.49**); 1558 (**1.9**); 2815 (**2.36**); 2961 (**4.40**); 2985 (**1.10**); 3463 (**6.39**); 4387 (**2.55**); 11594 (**6.35**); 27279 (**6.34**).

CIL IX: 2128 (**2.7**); 3184 (**1.3**); 5407 (**5.30**).

CIL X: 484 (**5.29**); 1019 (**4.12**); 1024 (**3.62**); 1026 (**4.22**); 5056 (**2.42**).

CIL XI: 5745 (**2.41**); 6243 (**2.8**); 6528 (**4.15**).

CIL XII: 807 (**5.23**); 1657 (**4.35**); 3327 (**4.48**); 3329 (**4.48**); 3332 (**4.48**); 4015 (**6.26**); 5102 (**6.48**); 5193 (**6.27**); 7113 (**1.5**).

CIL XIII: 530 (**6.38**); 842 (**5.22**); 5708 (**2.37**); 6940 (**4.37**); 7070 (**1.49**); 7101 (**1.11**); 7123 (**5.21**).

CIL XIV: 321 (**3.64**); 2112 (**3.2**).

CIG 2942 (**1.35**).

AE 1945, 136 (**2.34**).

AE 1971, 88 (**3.10**).

AE 1986, 166a (**2.57**).

ILS 6468 (**2.43**).

IA 601 (**4.13**); 812 (**5.35**).

Thylander 1952: A25 (**4.32**); A96, A124, A251 (**4.14**).

Espérandieu 1929: 429 (**3.63**).

Papyrus

Papyrus was a writing material, produced in Egypt from the papyrus plant, that was used extensively throughout the Roman world. However, very few papyrus documents have survived, except from the dry areas of Egypt. There are many collections of papyri; the following have been used here:

Oxyrhynchus Papyri: 744 (**1.7**)

SB (Sammelbuch griechischer Urkunden aus Aegypten): XIV 11646 (**5.51**).

BIBLIOGRAPHY

Baldassere, I. (1996), *Necropoli di Porto: Isola Sacra*, Rome: Istituto Poligrafico e Zecca dello Stato.

Barber, B. and Bowsher, D. (2000), *The Eastern Cemetery of Roman London. Excavations 1983–90*, London: Museum of London Archaeological Service.

Bernstein, A. (1993), *The Formation of Hell: Death and Retribution in the Ancient and Early Christian Worlds*, London: University College of London Press.

Bettini, M. (2005), 'Death and its double. *Imagines, ridiculum* and *honos* in the Roman aristocratic funeral', in K. Mustakallio, J. Hanska, H.-L. Sainio and V. Vuolanto (eds.), *Hoping for Continuity. Childhood, Education and Death in Antiquity and the Middle Ages*, Rome: *Acta Insituti Romani Finlandiae* 33: 191–202.

Boatwright, M. (1985), 'The Ara Ditis-*ustrinum* of Hadrian in the western Campus Martius, and other problematic Roman *ustrina*', *American Journal of Archaeology* 89: 485–97.

Bodel, J. (1994) [1986], 'Graveyards and groves: A study of the *lex Lucerina*', *American Journal of Ancient History* 11.

—— (1995), 'Minicia Marcella: taken before her time', *American Journal of Philology* 116(3): 453–60.

—— (1997), 'Monumental villas and villa monuments', *Journal of Roman Archaeology* 10: 5–35.

—— (1999a), 'Punishing Piso', *American Journal of Philology* 120(1): 43–63.

—— (1999b), 'Death on display: looking at Roman funerals', in B. Bergmann and C. Kondoleon (eds.), *The Art of Ancient Spectacle*, New Haven and London: Yale University Press: 259–81.

—— (2000), 'Dealing with the dead. Undertakers, executioners and potter's fields in ancient Rome', in V. Hope and E. Marshall (eds.), *Death and Disease in the Ancient City*, London: Routledge: 128–51.

—— (2004), 'The organisation of the funerary trade at Puteoli and Cumae', in S. Panciera (ed.), *Libitina e Dintorni: Atti dell' XI Rencontre franco-italienne sur l'épigraphie (Libitina, 3)*, Rome: Quasar: 149–70.

Boppert, W. (1992a), *Militärische Grabdenkmäler aus Mainz und Umgebung. Corpus Signorum Imperii Romani Deutshland II.5*, Mainz: Römische-Germanischen Zentralmuseums.

—— (1992b), *Zivile Grabsteine aus Mainz und Umgebung. Corpus Signorum Imperii Romani. Deutshland II.6*, Mainz: Römische-Germanischen Zentralmuseums.

Bradley, K. (1991), *Discovering the Roman Family*, Oxford: Oxford University Press.

Bremmer, J. (2002), *The Rise and Fall of the Afterlife*, London and New York: Routledge.

Brusin, G. (1941), *Nuovi monumenti sepolcrali di Aquileia*, Venice: Le Tre Venezie.

—— (1991–3), *Inscriptiones Aquileiae*, Udine.

Calza, G. (1940), *La necropoli del Porto di Roma nell'Isola Sacra*, Rome: Libreria dello Stato.

Carp, T. (1980), '*Puer senex* in Roman and medieval thought', *Latomus* 39: 736–9.

Carroll, M. (2005), 'Portraying opulence at the table in Roman Gaul and Germany', in M. Carroll, D. Hadley and H. Wilmott (eds.), *Consuming Passions: Dining from Antiquity to the Eighteenth Century*, Stroud: Tempus: 23–38.

—— (2006), *Spirits of the Dead. Roman Funerary Commemoration in Western Europe*, Oxford: Oxford University Press.

Champlin, E. (1991), *Final Judgments. Duty and Emotion in Roman Wills, 200 BC–AD 250*, Berkeley: University of California Press.

Chapa, J. (1998), *Letters of Condolence in Greek Papyri. Papyrologica Florentina* 29.

Cokayne, K. (2003), *Experiencing Old Age in Ancient Rome*, London and New York: Routledge.

Coleman, K.M. (1990), 'Fatal charades: Roman executions staged as mythological enactments', *Journal of Roman Studies* 80: 44–73.

Collingwood, R. and Wright, R. (1995), *The Roman Inscriptions of Britain*, Volume I, Oxford: Oxford University Press. First published 1955.

Collis, J. (1977), 'Owlesbury (Hants) and the problem of burials on rural settlements', in R. Reece (ed.), *Burial in the Roman World, Council of British Archaeology Research Report* 22: 26–34.

Cooley, A. (2000), 'Inscribing history at Rome', in A. Cooley (ed.), *The Afterlife of Inscriptions. Reusing, Rediscovering and Revitalizing Ancient Inscriptions*, London: Institute of Classical Studies: 7–20.

—— (2007), 'Commemorating the war dead of the Roman world', in P. Low, G. Oliver and P. Rhodes (eds.), *Cultures of Commemoration*, Oxford: Oxford University Press/British Academy: forthcoming.

Corbier, M. (2001), 'Child exposure and abandonment', in S. Dixon (ed.), *Childhood, Class and Kin in the Roman World*, London and New York: Routledge: 52–73.

Cormack, S. (2004), *The Space of Death in Roman Asia Minor*, Vienna: Phoibos.

Corrigan, K. (1986), 'Body and soul in ancient religious experience', in A.H. Armstrong (ed.), *Classical Mediterranean Spirituality*, London: Routledge: 360–83.

Courtney, E. (1995), *Musa Lapidaria. A Selection of Latin Verse Inscriptions*, Oxford: Oxford University Press.

Crawford, M. (1996), *Roman Statutes*, Volumes I and II, London: Bulletin of the Institute of Classical Studies, Supplement 64.

Crook, J.A. (1970), *Law and Life of Rome*, London: Thames and Hudson.

Cumont, F. (1922), *After Life in Roman Paganism*, New Haven: Yale University Press.

Curchin, L.A. (1997), 'Funerary customs in central Spain: the transition from pre-Roman to Roman practice', *Hispania Antiqua* 21: 7–34.

Davies, J. (1999), *Death, Burial and Rebirth in the Religions of Antiquity*, London: Routledge.

Davies, P. (2000), *Death and the Emperor. Roman Imperial Funerary Monuments from Augustus to Marcus Aurelius*, Austin and Cambridge: University of Texas Press.

D'Ambrosio, A. and De Caro, S. (1983), *Un Impegno per Pompeii. Fotopiano e documentazione della Necropoli di Porta Nocera*, Milan: Touring Club Italiano.

D'Arms, J.H. (2000), 'Memory, money and status at Misenum. Three new inscriptions from the *collegium* of the *Augustales*', *Journal of Roman Studies* 90: 126–44.

Davis, H.H. (1958), 'Epitaphs and the memory', *Classical Journal* 53: 169–76.

Dixon, S. (1992a), *The Roman Family*, Baltimore: John Hopkins University Press.

—— (1992b), 'A woman of substance: Iunia Libertas of Ostia', *Helios* 19: 162–73.

Dragendorff, H. and Krüger, E. (1924), *Das Grabmal von Igel*, Trier: von Jacob Lintz.

Dorutiu, E. (1961), 'Some observations on the military funeral altar of Adamclisi', *Dacia. Revue D'Archéologie et D'Histoire Ancienne* 5: 345–63.

Dunbabin, K. (2003), *The Roman Banquet. Images of Conviviality*, Cambridge: Cambridge University Press.

Duncan-Jones, R. (1977), 'Age-rounding, illiteracy and social differentiation', *Chiron* 7: 333–53.

—— (1982), *The Economy of the Roman Empire: Quantitative Studies*, Cambridge: Cambridge University Press.

—— (1990), *Structure and Scale in the Roman Economy*, Cambridge: Cambridge University Press.

—— (1996), 'The impact of the Antonine plague', *Journal of Roman Archaeology* 9: 108–36.

Eck, W. (1987), 'Römische Grabinschriften. Aussageabsicht und Aussagefähigkeit im funerären Kontext', in H. Von Hesberg and P. Zanker (eds.), Römische Gräbertrassen: Selbstdarstellung, Status, Standard, Munich: C.H. Beck: 61–83.

Eck, W., Caballos, A. and Fernández, F. (1996), *Das Senatus Consultum de Cn. Pisone Patre*, Munich: C.H. Beck.

Edmondson, J. (1999), 'Epigraphy and history of Roman Hispania: the new edition of *CIL* II', *Journal of Roman Archaeology* 12: 649–66.

Edwards, C. (1996), *Writing Rome. Textual Approaches to the City*, Cambridge: Cambridge University Press.

Erskine, A. (1997), 'Cicero and the expression of grief', in S. Morton Braund and C. Gill (eds.), *The Passions in Roman Thought and Literature*, Cambridge: Cambridge University Press: 36–47.

Espérandieu, E. (1929), *Inscriptons Latines de Gaule Narbonnaise*, Paris: Leroux.

Fantham, E. (1999), 'The role of lament in the growth and eclipse of Roman epic', in M. Bessinger, J. Tylus and S. Wofford (eds.), *Epic Traditions in the Contemporary World: The Poetics of Community*, Berkeley: University of California Press: 221–35.

Favro, D. (1996), *The Urban Image of Augustan Rome*, Cambridge: Cambridge University Press.

Feldherr, A. (2000), '*Non inter nota sepulcra*: Catullus 101 and Roman funerary ritual', *Classical Antiquity* 19(2): 209–31.

Felton, D. (1999), *Haunted Greece and Rome. Ghost Stories from Classical Antiquity*, Austin: University of Texas Press.

Flower, H.I. (1996), *Ancestor Masks and Aristocratic Power in Roman Culture*, Oxford: Clarendon Press.

Fontana, S. (2001), 'Leptis Magna: The Romanization of a major African city through burial evidence', in S. Keay and N. Terrenato (eds.), *Italy and the West: Comparative Issues in Romanization*, Oxford: Oxbow: 161–72.

Fowler, D. (2000), *Roman Constructions: Readings in Postmodern Latin*, New York and Oxford: Oxford University Press.

Frier, B. (2000), 'Demography', *The Cambridge Ancient History* 11 (second edition), Cambridge: Cambridge University Press: 787–816.

Friggeri, R. (2001), *The Epigraphic Collection of the Museo Nazionale Romano at the Baths of Diocletian* (translated by E. De Sena), Rome: Electa.

Futrell, A. (2005), *The Roman Games. A Sourcebook*, Oxford: Blackwell.

Gager, J. (1992), *Curse Tablets and Binding Spells from the Ancient World*, Oxford and New York: Oxford University Press.

Galsterer, B. and Galsterer, H. (1975), *Die römischen Steininschriften aus Köln*, Römische-Germanischen Museums Köln: Cologne.

Gardner, J.F. and Wiedemann, T. (1991), *The Roman Household: A Sourcebook*, London: Routledge.

Garnsey, P. (1991), 'Child rearing in ancient Italy', in D. Kertzer and R. Saller (eds.), *The Family in Italy: From Antiquity to the Present*, New Haven and London: Yale University Press: 48–65.

Golden, M. (1988), 'Did the ancients care when their children died?', *Greece and Rome* 35(2): 152–63.

González, J. (1999), 'Tacitus, Germanicus, Piso and the *tabula Siarensis*', *American Journal of Philology* 120(1): 123–42.

Gowing, A. (2005), *Empire and Memory: The Representation of the Roman Republic in Imperial Culture*, Cambridge: Cambridge University Press.

Gowland, R. (2001), 'Playing dead: implications of mortuary evidence for the social construction of childhood in Roman Britain', in G. Davies, A. Garner and K. Lockyear (eds.), *Proceedings of the Theoretical Roman Archaeology Conference 2000*, Oxford: Oxbow: 152–67.

Graham, E.-J. (2005a), 'Dining al fresco with the living and the dead in Roman Italy', in M. Carroll, D. Hadley and H. Wilmott (eds.), *Consuming Passions. Dining from Antiquity to the Eighteenth Century*. Stroud: Tempus: 49–65.

—— (2005b), 'The quick and the dead in the extra-urban landscape: the Roman cemetery at Ostia/Portus as a lived environment', in J. Bruhn, B. Croxford and D. Grigoropoulos (eds.), *TRAC 2004. Proceedings of the Fourteenth Roman Archaeology Conference, Durham 2004*, Oxford: Oxbow Books: 133–43.

—— (2007), *Death, Disposal and the Destitute: The Burial of the Urban Poor in Italy in the Late Roman Republic and Early Empire*. British Archaeological Reports International Series 1565. Oxford: Archaeopress.

—— (forthcoming). 'From fragments to ancestors: re-defining *os resectum* and its role in rituals of purification and commemoration in Republican Rome', in M. Carroll and J. Rempel (eds.), *Living through the Dead: Burial and Commemoration in the Classical World*, Oxford: Oxbow.

Gregori, G. (1989), *Epigrafia anfiteattrale dell'occidente romano* II. *Regiones Italiae VI–XI*. Rome: Quasar.

Griffin, J. (1985), *Latin Poets and Roman Life*, London: Duckworth.

Griffin, M. (1997), 'The Senate's story', *Journal of Roman Studies* 87: 249–63.

Grottanelli, C. (1995), 'Wine and death – East and West', in O. Murray and M. Tecuşan (eds.), *In Vino Veritas*, Oxford: Alden Press: 62–87.

Grünewald, T. (2004), *Bandits in the Roman Empire. Myth and Reality*, London and New York: Routledge. First published in German in 1999.

Gunnella, A. (1995), 'Morti improvvise e violente nelle iscrizioni latine', in F. Hinard and M. Lambert (eds.), *La Mort au quotidien dans le monde Romain*, Paris: De Boccard: 9–22.

Hackworth Petersen, L. (2006), *The Freedman in Roman Art and Art History*, Cambridge and New York: Cambridge University Press.

Hales, S. (2003), *The Roman House and Social Identity*, Cambridge: Cambridge University Press.

Harlow, M. and Laurence, R. (2002), *Growing Up and Growing Old in Ancient Rome. A Life Course Approach*, London and New York: Routledge.

Harris, W.V. (1994), 'Child-exposure in the Roman Empire', *Journal of Roman Studies* 54: 1–22.

Hatt, J.J. (1951), *La Tombe Gallo-Romaine*, Paris: Picard.

Hedrick, C.W. (2000), *History and Silence: Purge and Rehabilitation of Memory in Late Antiquity*, Austin: University of Texas Press.

von Hesberg, H. (1992), *Römische Grabbauten*. Darmstadt: Wissenschaftliche Buchgesellschaft.

von Hesberg, H. and Zanker, P. (1987), *Römische Gräbertrassen: Selbstdarstellung, Status, Standard*. Munich: C.H. Beck.

Heskell, J. (1994), 'Cicero as evidence for attitudes to dress in the late Republic', in J. Sebesta and L. Bonfante (eds.), *The World of Roman Costume*, Wisconsin: University of Wisconsin Press: 133–45.

Heulsen, C. (1890), 'Piante iconografiche incise in marmo', *Mitteilungen des Deutschen Archäologischen Instituts: Römische Abteilung* 5: 46–63.

Hill, T.D. (2004), *Ambitiosa Mors. Suicide and Self in Roman Thought and Literature,* New York and London: Routledge.

Hinard, F. and J.C. Dumont (2003), *Libitina. Pompes funèbres et supplices en Campanie à l'époque d'Auguste*, Paris: De Boccard.

Hitchner, R.B. (1995), 'The culture of death and the invention of culture in Roman Africa', *Journal of Roman Archaeology* 8: 493–8.

Hockey, J. (2001), 'Changing death rituals', in J. Hockey, J. Katz and N. Small (eds.), *Grief, Mourning and Death Ritual*, Buckingham and Philadelphia: Open University Press: 185–211.

Hodder, I. (1982), *The Present Past: An Introduction to Anthropology for Archaeologists*. London: Batsford.

Hope, V.M. (1997a), 'Words and pictures: the interpretation of Romano-British tombstones', *Britannia* 28: 245–58.

—— (1997b), 'A roof over the dead: communal tombs and family structure', in R. Laurence and A. Wallace-Hadrill (eds.), *Domestic Space in the Roman World: Pompeii and Beyond, Journal of Roman Archaeology Supplementary Series*, 22: 69–88.

—— (1998), 'Negotiating identity and status: the gladiators of Roman Nîmes', in J. Berry and R. Laurence (eds.), *Cultural Identity in the Roman Empire*, London: Routledge: 179–95.

—— (2000a), 'Contempt and respect: the treatment of the corpse in ancient Rome', in V.M. Hope and E. Marshall (eds.), *Death and Disease in the Ancient City*, London: Routledge: 104–27.

—— (2000b), 'Fighting for identity: the funerary commemoration of Italian gladiators', in A. Cooley (ed.), *The Epigraphic Landscape of Roman Italy*, London: *Bulletin of the Institute of Classical Studies* 73: 93–114.

—— (2000c), 'Inscription and sculpture: the construction of identity in the military tombstones of Roman Mainz', in G. Oliver (ed.), *The Epigraphy of Death*, Liverpool: Liverpool University Press, 155–86.

—— (2001), *Constructing Identity: the Roman Funerary Monuments of Aquileia, Mainz and Nimes, British Archaeological Report. International Series* 960.

—— (2003), 'Trophies and tombstones: commemorating the Roman soldier', in R. Gilchrist (ed.), *The Social Commemoration of Warfare, World Archaeology* 35(1): 79–97.

Hopkins, K. (1966), 'On the probable age structure of the Roman population', *Population Studies* 20: 245–64.

—— (1983), *Death and Renewal*, Cambridge: Cambridge University Press.

—— (1987), 'Graveyards for historians', in F. Hinard (eds.), *La mort, les morts et l'au-delà dans le monde Romain.* Caen: University of Caen Press: 113–26.

Hunt, A.S. and Edgar, C.C. (1970), *Select Papyri I. Non Literary Papyri and Private Affairs*, London and Cambridge, Mass.: Harvard University Press, Loeb Classical Library. First published 1932.

Huskey, S.J. (2005), 'In memory of Tibullus: Ovid's remembrance of Tibullus 1.3 in *Amores* 3.9 and *Tristia* 3.3', *Arethusa* 38(3): 367–86.

Huskinson, J. (1996), *Roman Children's Sarcophagi. Their Decoration and its Social Significance*, Oxford: Oxford University Press.

Jaeger, M. (1997), *Livy's Written Rome*, Ann Arbor: University of Michigan Press.

James, P. (2006), 'Two poetic and parodic parrots in Latin literature', in J. Courtney and P. James (eds.), *The Role of the Parrot in Selected Texts from Ovid to Jean Rhys: Telling an Alternative Viewpoint*, Edwin Mellen: Lampeter, New York: Queenston: 1–32.

Jashemski, W.F. (1979), *The Gardens of Pompeii, Herculaneum and the Villas Destroyed by Vesuvius*, New Rochelle and New York: Caratzas Brothers.

Jones, R.F.J. (1984), 'The Roman cemeteries of Ampurias reconsidered', in T.F.C. Blagg, R.F.J. Jones and S.J. Keay (eds.), *Papers in Iberian Archaeology Part 1, British Archaeological Reports International Series* 193: 237–65.

—— (1993), 'Rules for the living and the dead: funerary practices and social organisation', in M. Struck (ed.), *Römerzeitliche Gräber als Quellen zu Religion. Bevölkerungsstruktur und Sozialgeschichte*, Mainz: Mainz University: 247–54.

Joshel, S.R. (1992), *Work, Identity and Legal Status at Rome*, Norman and London: University of Oklahoma Press.

Kassel, R. (1958), *Untersuchungen zur griechischen und römischen Konsolationsliteratur*, Munich: C.H. Beck.

Kierdorf, W. (1980), *Laudatio funebris: Interpretationem und untersuchungen zur entwicklung der Römischen Leichenrede*, Meisenheim am Glam: Anton Hain.

King, M. (2000), 'Commemoration of infants on Roman funerary inscriptions', in G. Oliver (ed.), *The Epigraphy of Death: Studies in the History and Society of Greece and Rome*, Liverpool: Liverpool University Press: 117–54.

Kleiner, D.E.E. (1977), *Roman Group Portraiture: The Funerary Reliefs of the Late Republic and Early Empire*, New York: Garland.

Knight, J.F. (1970), *Elysion: On Ancient Greek and Roman Beliefs Concerning Life After Death*, New York and London: Barnes and Noble.

Kockel, V. (1983), *Die Grabbauten vor dem Herkulaner Tor in Pompeji*, Mainz: Zabern.

—— (1993), *Porträtreliefs Stadtrömischer Grabbauten*, Mainz: Zabern.

Konstan, D. (2001), *Pity Transformed*, London: Duckworth.

Koortbojian, M. (1996), '*In commemorationem mortuorum*: text and image along the "street of tombs"', in J. Elsner (ed.), *Art and Text in Roman Culture*, Cambridge: Cambridge University Press: 210–33.

Kyle, D. (1998), *Spectacles of Death in Ancient Rome*, London and New York: Routledge.

Lanciani, R. (1888), *Ancient Rome in the Light of Recent Discoveries*, Urbana: University of Illinois.

Lassère, J.M. et al. (1993), *Les Flavii de Cillium: étude du Mausolée de Kasserine*, Paris: de Boccard.

Lattimore, R. (1962), *Themes in Greek and Latin Epitaphs*, Urbana: University of Illinois Press.

Le Bohec, Y. (1991), *Le Testament du Lingon. Actes de la journée d'études du 16 Mai 1990*, Lyon: de Boccard.

Levick, B. (1983), 'The Senatus Consultum from Larinum', *Journal of Roman Studies* 73: 97–115.

Lindsay, H. (1998), 'Eating with the dead: the Roman funerary banquet', in I. Nielsen and H. Sigismund Nielsen (eds.), *Meals in a Social Context*, Aarhus: University of Aarhus Press: 67–80.

—— (2000), 'Death-pollution and funerals in the city of Rome', in V.M. Hope and E. Marshall (eds.), *Death and Disease in the Ancient City*, London: Routledge: 152–73.

Macdonald, M. and Pinto, J. (1995), *Hadrian's Villa and Its Legacy*, New Haven and London: Yale University Press.

McKinley, J. (2000), 'Phoenix rising: aspects of cremation in Roman Britain', in J. Pearce, M. Millet and M. Struck (eds.), *Burial, Society and Context in the Roman World*, Oxford: Oxbow: 38–44.

MacMullen, R. (1981), *Paganism in the Roman Empire*, New Haven: Yale University Press.

—— (1982), 'The epigraphic habit in the Roman empire', *American Journal of Philology* 103: 234–46.

McWilliam, J. (2001), 'Children among the dead: the influence of urban life on the commemoration of children on tombstone inscriptions', in S. Dixon (ed.), *Childhood, Class and Kin in the Roman World*, London and New York: Routledge: 74–98.

Mann, J.C. (1985), 'Epigraphic consciousness', *Journal of Roman Studies* 75: 204–6.

Markus, D.D. (2004), 'Grim pleasures: Statius's Poetic *Consolationes*', *Arethusa* 37(1): 105–36.

Martin-Kilcher, S. (2000), '*Mors immatura* in the Roman world – a mirror of society and tradition', in J. Pearce, M. Millet, M. Struck (eds.), *Burial, Society and Context in the Roman World*, Oxford: Oxbow: 63–77.

Meiggs, R. (1973), *Roman Ostia*, Oxford: Clarendon Press.

Meyer, E. (1990), 'Explaining the epigraphic habit in the Roman empire: the evidence of epitaphs', *Journal of Roman Studies* 80: 74–96.

Miles, G. (1995), *Livy: Reconstructing Early Rome*, New York: Cornell University Press.

Molyviati-Toptsis, U. (1994), 'Vergil's Elysium and the Orphic-Pythagorean ideas of after-life', *Mnemosyne* 47(1): 33–46.

Morgan, M.G. (1992), 'The smell of victory: Vitellius at Bedriacum (Tac. *Hist.* 2.70), *Classical Philology* 85: 14–29.

Morris, I. (1992), *Death-Ritual and Social Structure in Classical Antiquity*, Cambridge: Cambridge University Press.

Mouritsen, H. (2005), 'Freedmen and Decurions: epitaphs and social history in Imperial Italy', *Journal of Roman Studies* 95: 38–63.

Mustakallio, K. (2005), 'Roman funerals: identity, gender and participation', in K. Mustakallio, J. Hansks, H.-L. Sanio, and V. Vuolanto (eds.), *Hoping for Continuity. Childhood, Education and Death in Antiquity and the Middle Ages*. Rome: *Acti Instituti Romani Findlandiae* 33: 179–90.

Nock, A.D. (1932), 'Cremation and burial in the Roman Empire', *Harvard Theological Review* 25: 321–59; reprinted in *Essays on Religion and the Ancient World* (1972: two volumes), Oxford: Clarendon Press.

Noelke, P. (1998), 'Grabreliefs mit Mahldarstellung in den germanisch-gallischen Provinzen – soziale und religiöse Aspekte', in P. Fasold, T. Fischer, H. von Hesberg and M. Witteyer (eds.), *Bestattungsitte und kulturelle Identität. Grabanlagen und Grabbeigaben der frühen römischen Kaiserzeit und den Nordwest Provinzen*, Cologne: 399–418.

Noy, D. (1998), 'Where were the Jews of the Diaspora buried?', in M. Goodman (ed.), *Jews in the Graeco-Roman World*, Oxford: Clarendon Press: 75–89.

—— (2000a), 'Building a Roman funeral pyre', *Antichthon* 34: 30–45.

—— (2000b), 'Half-burnt on an emergency pyre: Roman cremations which went wrong', *Greece & Rome* 47: 186–96.

—— (2000c), *Foreigners at Rome. Citizens and Strangers*, London: Duckworth.

Ogden, D. (2001), *Greek and Roman Necromancy*, Princeton and Oxford: Princeton University Press.

—— (2002), *Magic, Witchcraft and Ghosts in the Greek and Roman Worlds. A Sourcebook*, Oxford and New York: Oxford University Press.

Pagán, V. (2000), 'The mourning after: Statius Thebaid 12', *American Journal of Philology* 121(3): 423–52.

Parkin, T. (1992), *Demography and Roman Society*, Baltimore and London: Johns Hopkins University Press.

—— (2003), *Old Age in the Roman World*, Baltimore and London: Johns Hopkins University Press.

Patterson, J.R. (1992), 'Patronage, collegia and burial in imperial Rome', in S. Bassett (ed.), *Death in Towns*, Leicester: Leicester University Press: 15–27.

—— (2000a), 'Living and dying in the city of Rome: houses and tombs', in J. Coulston and H. Dodge (eds.), *Ancient Rome: The Archaeology of the Eternal City*, Oxford: Oxford University School of Archaeology Monograph 54: 259–89.

—— (2000b), 'On the margins of the city of Rome', in V.M. Hope and E. Marshall (eds.), *Death and Disease in the Ancient City*, London: Routledge: 85–103.

Pearce, J. (2000), 'Burial, society and context in the provincial Roman world', in J. Pearce, M. Millet and M. Struck (eds.), *Burial, Society and Context in the Roman World*, Oxford: Oxbow: 1–12.

Pearce, J. (2001), 'Infants, cemeteries and communities in the Roman provinces', in G. Davies, A. Garner and K. Lockyear (eds.), *Proceedings of the Theoretical Roman Archaeology Conference 2000*, Oxford: Oxbow: 125–42.

Pearce, J., Millet, M. and Struck, M. (2000), *Burial, Society and Context in the Roman World*, Oxford: Oxbow.

Phillips, O. (2002), 'The witches' Thessaly', in P. Mirecki and M. Meyer (eds.), *Magic and Ritual in the Ancient World*, Brill: Leiden: 378–86.

Plass, P. (1995), *The Game of Death in Ancient Rome: Arena Sport and Political Suicide*, Wisconsin: University of Wisconsin Press.

Polfer, M. (2000), 'Reconstructing funerary rituals: the evidence of *ustrina* and related archaeological structures', in J. Pearce, M. Millet and M. Struck (eds.), *Burial, Society and Context in the Roman World*, Oxford: Oxbow: 30–7.

Pomeroy, S. (ed.) (1999), *Plutarch's Advice to the Bride and Groom and a Consolation to his Wife: English Translations, Commentary, Interpretative Essays and Bibliography*, Oxford and New York: Oxford University Press.

Poortman, B. (1994), 'Death and immortality in Greek philosophy, from the Presocratics to the Hellenistic era', in J.M. Bremer, Th.P.J. van den Hout and R. Peters (eds.), *Hidden Futures. Death and Immortality in Ancient Egypt, Anatolia, the Classical, Biblical and Arabic-Islamic World*, Amsterdam: Amsterdam University Press: 197–220.

Potter, D.S. and Damon, C. (1999), 'The *Senatus consultum de Cn. Pisone Patre*', *American Journal of Philology* 120(1): 13–40.

Price, S. (1987), 'From noble funerals to divine cult: the consecration of Roman emperors', in D. Cannadine and S. Price (eds.), *Rituals of Royalty. Power and Ceremonial in Traditional Societies*, Cambridge: Cambridge University Press: 56–105.

Purcell, N. (1987), 'Tomb and suburb', in H. von Hesberg and P. Zanker (eds.), *Römische Gräbertrassen: Selbstdarstellung, Status, Standard*, Munich: C.H. Beck: 25–42.

Ramage, E.S. (1994), 'The so-called Laudatio Thuriae as Panegyric', *Athenaeum* 82: 341–70.

Rauh, N. (2003), *Merchants, Sailors and Pirates in the Roman World*, Stroud: Tempus.

Rawson, B. (2003), *Children and Childhood in Roman Italy,* Oxford: Oxford University Press.

Reusser, C. (1987), 'Gräberstrassen in Aquileia', in H. von Hesberg and P. Zanker (eds.), *Römische Gräbertrassen: Selbstdarstellung, Status, Standard*, Munich: C.H. Beck: 239–49.

Richlin, A. (1999), 'Cicero's head', in J. Porter (ed.), *Constructions of the Classical Body*, Ann Arbor: University of Michigan Press: 190–211.

Robert, L. (1971), *Les Gladiateurs dans l'Orient Grec*, Amsterdam: A.M. Hakkert. First published Limoges 1940.

Rose, H.J. (1923), 'Nocturnal funerals in Rome', *Classical Quarterly* 17: 191–4.

Sabbatini Tumolesi, P. (1988), *Epigrafia anfiteattrale dell'occidente romano I. Roma*, Rome: Quasar.

Saller, R. (1987), 'Men's age at marriage and its consequences in the Roman family', *Classical Philology* 82: 21–34.

—— (1994), *Patriarchy, Property and Death in the Roman Family*, Cambridge: Cambridge University Press.

Saller, R. and Shaw, B. (1984), 'Tombstones and Roman family relations in the Principate: civilians, soldiers and slaves', *Journal of Roman Studies* 74: 124–56.

Scheidel, W. (2001a), 'Roman age structure: evidence and models', *Journal of Roman Studies* 91: 1–26.

—— (2001b), 'Progress and problems in Roman demography', in W. Scheidel (ed.), *Debating Roman Demography*, Leiden, Boston, Cologne: Brill: 1–81.

Schoonhover, H. (1992), *The Pseudo-Ovidian Ad Liviam de Morte Drusi*, Groningen: E. Forsten.

Scobie, A. (1986), 'Slums, sanitation and mortality in the Roman world', *Klio* 68: 399–433.

Scott, E. (1990), 'A critical review of the interpretation of infant burials with a particular reference to Roman Britain', *Journal of Theoretical Archaeology* 1: 30–46.

—— (1999), *The Archaeology of Infancy and Infant Death, British Archaeological Reports, International Series* 819, Oxford: Archaeopress.

—— (2001), 'Unpicking a myth: the infanticide of female and disabled infants in antiquity', in G. Davies, A. Garner and K. Lockyear (eds.), *Proceedings of the Theoretical Roman Archaeology Conference 2000*, Oxford: Oxbow: 143–51.

Segal, C. (1990), *Lucretius on Death and Anxiety. Poetry and Philosophy in the de rerum natura*, Priceton: Princeton University Press.

Selzer, W. (1988), *Römische Steindenkmäler. Mainz in Römischer Zeit*, Mainz: Zabern.

Senatore, F. (1999), 'Necropoli e societa nell'antica Pompei: considerazioni su un sepolcreto di poveri', in W. Scheidel (ed.), *Pompei, il Vesuvio e la Penisola Sorrentina*, Rome: Bardi: 91–111.

Shaw, B. (1984), 'Latin funerary epigraphy and family life in the later Roman empire', *Historia* 33: 457–99.

—— (1991), 'The cultural meaning of death: age and gender in the Roman family', in D. Kertzer and R. Saller (eds.), *The Family in Italy. From Antiquity to Present*, London: Routledge: 66–90.

—— (1996), 'Seasons of death: aspects of mortality in Imperial Rome', *Journal of Roman Studies* 86: 100–38.

—— (2001), 'The seasonal birthing cycle of Roman women', in W. Scheidel (ed.), *Debating Roman Demography*, Leiden, Boston, Cologne: Brill: 82–103.

Sigismund Nielsen, H. (1996), 'The physical context of Roman epitaphs and the structure of the "Roman family"', *Analecta Romana Instituti Danici* 23: 35–60.

—— (1997), 'Interpreting epithets in Roman epitaphs', in B. Rawson and P. Weaver (eds.), *The Roman Family in Italy. Status, Sentiment, Space*, Oxford and Canberra: Clarendon Press: 169–204.

Sinn, F. and Freyberger, K. (1996), *Vatikanische Museen: Museo Gregorio Profano ex Lateranense: Die Grabdenkmäler 2: Die Ausstattung des Hateriergrabes*, Mainz: Zabern.

Small, J.P. (1997), *Wax Tablets of the Mind. Cognitive Studies of Memory and Literacy in Classical Antiquity*, London: Routledge.

Small, N. (2001), 'Theories of grief: a critical review', in J. Hockey, J. Katz and N. Small (eds.), *Grief, Mourning and Death Ritual*, Buckingham and Philadelphia: Open University Press: 19–48.

Steinby, E.M. (1987), 'La necropolis della Via Triumphalis. Pianificazione generale e tipologia dei monumenti funerari', in H. Von Hesberg and P. Zanker (eds.),

Römische Gräbertrassen: Selbstdarstellung, Status, Standard. Munich: C.H. Beck: 85–110.

Stevens, S. (1991), 'Charon's obol and other coins in Ancient funerary practice', *Phoenix* 45: 215–29.

Strubbe, J.H.M. (1991), 'Cursed be he that moves my bones', in C. Faraone and D. Obbink (eds.), *Magika Hiera*, New York: Oxford University Press: 33–59.

Struck, M. (1995), 'Integration and continuity in funerary ideology', in J. Metzler, M. Millett, N. Roymans and J. Slofstra (eds.), *Integration in the Early Roman West. The Role of Culture and Ideology*, Luxembourg: Musée Nationale d'Histoire et d'Art: 139–50.

Sumi, G.S. (1997), 'Power and ritual: the crowd at Clodius' funeral', *Historia* 46: 80–102.

—— (2002), 'Impersonating the dead: mimes at Roman funerals', *American Journal of Philology* 123: 559–85.

Thylander H. (1952), *Inscriptions du Port d'Ostie*, Lund: C.W.K. Gleerup.

Toynbee, J.M.C. (1971), *Death and Burial in the Roman World*, London: Thames & Hudson.

Tranoy, L. (2000), 'The living and the dead: approaches to landscape around Lyon', in J. Pearce, M. Millet and M. Struck (eds.), *Burial and Society in the Roman World*, Oxford: Oxbow Books: 162–8.

Treggiari, S. (1999), 'The upper-class house as a symbol and focus of emotion in Cicero', *Journal of Roman Archaeology* 12: 33–56.

Tupman, C. (2005), 'The *cupae* of Iberia in their monumental contexts: a study of the relationship between social status and commemoration with barrel-shaped and semi-cylindrical tombstones', in J. Bruhn, B. Croxford and D. Grigoropoulos (eds.), *TRAC 2004. Proceedings of the Fourteenth Roman Archaeology Conference, Durham 2004*, Oxford: Oxbow Books: 119–32.

Väänänen, V. (1973), 'Le iscrizioni della necropolis dell'autoparco Vaticano', *Acta Insituti Romani Finlandiae* 6.

Van Hoof, A.J.L. (1990), *From Autothanasia to Suicide. Self-killing in Classical Antiquity*, London: Routledge.

Varner, E.R. (2001a), 'Portraits, plots and politics: *Damnatio memoriae* and the images of imperial women', *Memoirs of the American Academy at Rome* 46: 4193.

—— (2001b), 'Punishment after death: mutilation of images and corpse abuse in ancient Rome', *Mortality* 6: 45–76.

—— (2004), *Mutilation and Transformation. Damnatio memoriae and Roman Imperial portraiture*, Leiden, Boston and Cologne: Brill.

Versnel, H.S. (1980), 'Destruction, devotio and despair in a situation of anomy: the mourning for Germanicus in triple perspective', in *Perennitas: studi in onore di Angelo Brelich*, Rome: Edizioni dell'Ateno: 541–618.

—— (1991), 'Beyond cursing: the appeal to justice in judicial prayers', in C.A. Faraone and D. Obbink (eds.), *Magika Hiera. Ancient Greek Magic and Religion*, Oxford: Oxford University Press: 60–106.

Voisin, J.L. (1984), 'Les Romains, chasseurs de têtes', in *Du Châtiment dans la Cité: Supplices Corporels et Peine de Mort dans le Monde Antique*, Collection de l'école Française de Rome 79: 241–93.

Vorbeck, E. (1980a), *Militärinschriften aus Carnuntum*, Vienna: G. Grasl.

—— (1980b), *Zivilinschriften aus Carnuntum*, Vienna: G. Grasl.

Walker, S. (1985), *Memorials to the Roman Dead*, London: British Museum.

—— (1990), *Catalogue of Roman Sarcophagi in the British Museum. Corpus Signorum Imperii Roman, Great Britain* II.2, British Museum: London.

Walter, T. (1999), *On Bereavement the Culture of Grief*, Buckingham: Open University Press.

Warren, J. (2004), *Facing Death. Epicurus and His Critics*, Oxford: Oxford University Press.

Webster, G. (1993), 'Military equestrian tombstones', in M. Henig (ed.), *Roman Sculpture from the Cotswold Region. Corpus Signorum Imperii Romani Great Britain* 1.7, Oxford: Oxford University Press: 45–8.

Weekes, J. (2005), 'Reconstructing syntheses in Romano-British cremation', in J. Bruhn, B. Croxford and D. Grigoropoulos (eds.), *TRAC 2004. Proceedings of the Fourteenth Roman Archaeology Conference, Durham 2004*, Oxford: Oxbow Books: 16–26.

Wenham, L.P. (1968), *The Romano-British Cemetery at Trentholme Drive, York.* London: Her Majesty's Stationery Office.

Wesch-Klein, G. (1993), *Funus publicum. Eine Studie zur öffentlichen Beisetzung und Gewährung von Ehrengräbern in Rom und den Westprovinzen*, Stuttgart: F.Steiner.

Whitehead, J. (1993), 'The "Cena Trimalchionis" and biographical narration in Roman middle-class art', in P. Holliday (ed.), *Narrative and Event in Ancient Art*, Cambridge: Cambridge University Press: 299–325.

Wiedemann, T. (1992), *Emperors and Gladiators*, London: Routledge.

Wilcox, A. (2005), 'Sympathetic rivals: consolation in Cicero's letters', *American Journal of Philology* 126(2): 237–55.

Williams, F. (2003), 'The hands of death: Ovid *Amores* 3.9.20', *American Journal of Philology* 124: 225–34.

Williams, J. (2001), *Beyond the Rubicon: Romans and Gauls in Republican Italy*, Oxford: Oxford University Press.

Wilson, M. (1997), 'The subjugation of grief in Seneca's *Epistles*', in S. Morton Braund and C. Gill (eds.), *The Passions in Roman Thought and Literature*, Cambridge: Cambridge University Press: 48–67.

Wistrand, E. (1976), *The So-called Laudatio Turiae: Introduction, Text, Translation, Commentary*, Lund: Acta Universitatis Gothoburgensia.

Woolf, G. (1996), 'Monumental writing and the expansion of Roman society in the early Roman empire', *Journal of Roman Studies* 86: 22–39.

Wrede, H. (1981), *Consecratio in formam deorum: vergöttlichte Privatpersonen in der Römischen Kaiserzeit*, Mainz: von Zabern.

Wright, R. and Richmond, I. (1956), *Catalogue of Roman Inscribed and Sculpted Stones in the Grosvenor Museum Chester*, Chester: Chester and North Wales Archaeological Society.

Zanker, P. (1975), 'Grabreliefs römischer Freigelassener', *Jahrbuch des Deutschen Archäologischen Instituts* 90: 267–315.

—— (1988), *The Power of Images in the Age of Augustus* (translated by A. Shapiro), Michigan: University of Michigan Press.

INDEX

Lightning Source UK Ltd.
Milton Keynes UK
UKHW022135051219
354839UK00008B/223/P